MORE TIME

MORE TIME

CONTEMPORARY SHORT
STORIES AND LATE STYLES

LEE CLARK MITCHELL

OXFORD
UNIVERSITY PRESS

OXFORD

UNIVERSITY PRESS

Great Clarendon Street, Oxford, OX2 6DP,
United Kingdom

Oxford University Press is a department of the University of Oxford.
It furthers the University's objective of excellence in research, scholarship,
and education by publishing worldwide. Oxford is a registered trade mark of
Oxford University Press in the UK and in certain other countries

© Lee Clark Mitchell 2019

The moral rights of the author have been asserted

First Edition published in 2019

Impression: 1

Published in the United States of America by Oxford University Press
198 Madison Avenue, New York, NY 10016, United States of America

British Library Cataloguing in Publication Data

Data available

Library of Congress Control Number: 2018958834

ISBN 978–0–19–883922–4

Printed and bound in Great Britain by
Clays Ltd, Elcograf S.p.A.

"For Cameron"

Acknowledgments

Critical books on short fiction need hardly be short themselves, nor need they rely any less on a wide circle of friends and colleagues for ideas and support. In this case, the list is not especially long, though I have benefitted immensely from those who are on it. Maria DiBattista has been there all along, helping me hone ideas and readings, and in this case is specifically responsible for alerting me to the delights of reading Joy Williams. Frank Bergon first pointed me in useful critical directions and latterly read the introduction, offering valuable suggestions for further fine-tuning. Brian Gingrich, my co-teacher of a course in short stories that inspired the idea for this book, broke into his own busy schedule to give the final draft a close reading that has improved the whole immensely; and his index is a model of how to outline a book from the back. My gratitude runs deep. Among students in that shared course, I would be remiss not to name those whose own ideas surface in the following pages, suitably altered to make them at least partly my own: Aranya Jain, You-You Ma, Zoë Perot, Cameron Platt, David Pugliese.

Among short story colleagues, Alfred Bendixen, Olivia Carr Edenfield, and James Nagel have each lent an ear (and a helping hand) at critical moments, as well as themselves offering models for ways to interpret the form. Anne Sobel was there early on, reading occasional rough drafts with deft and nuanced advice for reshaping; I hope the final version comes close to meeting her scrupulous standards. The three outside readers for Oxford University Press were each exemplary in their reports, with Kasia Boddy and Coral Anne Howells rightly reminding me to make the book longer ("more time!") by pursuing endnote discussions in the main text itself. I have willingly obliged. And Andrew Kahn laid into my flawed assumptions about "late style" as well as my equally faulty assumptions about Chekhov (among assorted other topics), spurring me on with good humor and better advice on ways to reconsider. I hope the revisions here go some way to satisfy each of their reservations. Lastly, my editor Jacqueline Norton was supportive of the idea from the beginning, and I am grateful to her for making the sometimes painful process of producing a book a thorough delight.

Table of Contents

The present letter is a very long one, simply because I had no leisure
to make it shorter.

Blaise Pascal, 4 December 1656 (571)

Tchehov made a mistake in thinking that if he had had more time
he would have written more fully, described the rain, and the mid-
wife and the doctor having tea. The truth is one can get only *so much*
into a story; there is always a sacrifice. One has to leave out what one
knows and longs to use. Why? I haven't an idea, but there it is. It's
always a kind of race to get in as much as one can before it *disappears*.
But time is not really in it. But wait.

Katherine Mansfield, journal entry, January 17, 1922 (251)

The perception that we are all, as Kafka's dog puts it, "bulwarks of
silence," informs much of the finest storytelling in all languages.…
The short story's success often lies in conveying a sense of unwritten,
or even unwriteable things: the storyteller accepts the limitations of
his art, and makes his freedom an aspect of those same restrictions.

Valerie Shaw (255)

Introduction

Bulwarks of Silence

G reat writers immediately grasp the hallmarks of their chosen mode, transforming constraints into opportunities, reshaping conventional forms and quirky materials into newly vested meanings. Lyric poets (Marianne Moore, Wallace Stevens) tease resonant meditations out of vivid scenes; realist novelists (George Eliot, Philip Roth) spin unsettling webs into sonorous revelations of our social construction; short story practitioners (Ernest Hemingway, Eudora Welty) keep it short, beguiling us with singular moments rather than the unfolding drama of tangled lives.[1] The imperative of that latter form in its miniaturizing gesture is to keep us reading all at one sitting by shearing away casual details and ancillary emotions, stepping clear of fleshed-out histories and complicating psychologies. Yet the fleeting nature of stories paradoxically injects life into our imaginations where moments continue to shimmer precisely by not being laid bare on the page. Like poems, their success depends on leaving things out, on the suggestible suasions of compression and elision.

---

1. Some prose authors are equally expert, though rarely at poetry and prose. But great novelists can be just as successful with the short form (William Faulkner and Willa Cather, Henry James and Guy de Maupassant), even as others (notably, Anton Chekhov and Katherine Mansfield, Mavis Gallant and Saki) realized their talent lay largely with stories. Notoriously, Faulkner claimed that "Maybe every novelist wants to write poetry first, finds he can't and then tries the short story which is the most demanding form after poetry. And failing at that, only then does he take up novel writing" (Stein 30). By contrast, Charles McGrath has claimed that most students in writing programs are aspiring novelists, "but novels don't lend themselves very readily to the workshop format, and so would-be novelists these days spend at least part of their apprenticeship working on stories. They're a little like those people who learn golf by never venturing onto a golf course but instead practicing at a driving range" (McGrath).

Of course, the decision of *what* to leave out or in defines a writer's vision, as Margaret Atwood wittily attests in her tightly focused miniature, "Happy Endings" (1983), adumbrating something like a narrative "garden of forking paths." The opening dispenses with formalities as slickly as any smiling game-show host: "John and Mary meet. What happens next? If you want a happy ending, try A" (Atwood, 22). And then follow six brief entries each a paragraph long marked A to F, each offering a variant couple's biography. A blithely proclaims that "John and Mary fall in love and get married," living a life of conventional aspirations, stultifying in its humdrum predictability. That allegedly "happy" account is followed by ever more slyly tormented versions that nonetheless end each much the same: "everything continues as in A, but under different names" (23). Finally, the narrator, grown a tad truculent, admits that despite apparent differences, "You'll have to face it, the endings are the same however you slice it" (24). Plots, as she concludes, "are just one thing after another, a what and a what and a what. Now try How and Why." Brief as it is, this compound "story" offers a deft progression, initially engaging readers as a review of love's possibilities, then beguiling them via an exploration of storytelling's defaults, with the closing "How and Why" meant to point us to what stories can so often more interestingly do. And that is to focus attention on explored narrative middles, on the psychological rationale for surprising plot turns or idiosyncratic details or even simply odd diction and equally unsettling syntax (as reflected in a progression among the versions stylistically).

In fact, Atwood's nimble version of "reader's choice" updates Vladimir Propp's ground-breaking treatise, *Morphology of the Folktale* (1928), which organized oral storytelling into thirty-one stable "functions" that frame any traditional tale. What contributes to the immense variety of tales across both centuries and continents is the ease with which narrative units can be substituted, since characters and events in what initially appear like different narratives reveal themselves as structurally similar, able in different settings to be easily replaced or exchanged. Propp's enduring influence on folklore studies owed to his powerful claim for the tale's generic shape. And that has paralleled sweeping assessments by scholars eager to categorize the modern short story, hoping to identify its own constituent patterns, its distinctive plot requirements and character types. Yet such investigations have seen little success, failing to agree on the short story as a recognizably coherent form—this in a period when its growing appeal has been matched, however ironically, by a general indifference to efforts at explaining why.

I. Story History and Requirements

More Time not only shares that indifference but in passing joins studies that argue against the premise of common structural underpinnings to the short story, any more than to the novel or to drama. The misconception is perhaps most starkly revealed at the willfully disparate margins of the field, where outliers illustrate how hard it is to draw them into the fold. And that is exemplified no better than in the four recent story collections that focus the following chapters: Alice Munro's *Dear Life* (2012); Andre Dubus's *Dancing After Hours* (1996); Joy Williams's *The Visiting Privilege* (2015); and Lydia Davis's *Can't and Won't* (2014). Each volume has appeared near the conclusion of a career devoted either exclusively or largely to short stories, with each refining a style carefully honed over a lifetime. As well, each diverges from others in ways that have profoundly shaped generic conceptions, and collectively they represent the four most innovative practitioners of the past half-century (with the arguable exception of Raymond Carver). Yet in an era when writing programs, *The New Yorker*, and distinguished journals have promulgated the short story, it remains under-examined as a major literary form, despite a modest upsurge of critical interest in the past few decades.

We continue to argue about what a story inherently is (other than reasonably "short"), ignoring how differences among brilliant practitioners enliven rather than diminish the field. My effort means to open up discussion not by looking to general principles, nor even focusing exclusively on individual accomplishments (though that is certainly central to this investigation) but by contrasting quite different stories and practitioners, shifting from close analysis into larger speculation about directions taken by the most innovative writers in their later work. Admittedly, the selection is fairly narrow and somewhat arbitrary, centered on four celebrated North American authors meant to be taken as exemplary of possibilities rather than as exhaustive of the field.[2]

2. For recent surveys and histories of the (particularly American) short story, see Bendixen, Boddy, Lohafer, May, Reid, Scofield, Shaw, and Silber.

Munro, Dubus, Williams, and Davis each elude critical efforts to pinpoint any presumed underlying constitution of the short story, marked by a supposedly special configuration or requisite length or distinct narrative trajectory. The very contrast among their efforts reveals its shape-shifting expansiveness, even though few have taken such a cross-glancing interpretive approach. Most critics, in fact, divide between those inclined to construct fixed general models and those eager instead to simply delight in the accomplishment of individual authors. Yet both approaches tend to miss what is most exciting about contemporary examples, either by relying on template abstractions that fail to embrace many brilliant outliers, or by focusing so specifically on individual instances as to obscure larger strategies transforming the field.

Edgar Allan Poe has much to answer for, starting us off misguidedly with his customary aplomb by affirming that any story's success depends on producing a "preconceived effect," achieved exclusively through a "pre-established design" (647). Granted, he was first to enter the fray of those eager to sort out this new literary form, two decades after Washington Irving had inaugurated a series of casual "sketches" that all but invited imitation. And Poe's stories along with Hawthorne's and Melville's met that invitation triumphantly, even if his theoretical argument serves to describe only his own efforts, with even the "pre-"s in his description already registering a process that seems disconnected from the prose that produces it. Despite this, however, admirers persuaded by his confident claims have continued the misdirection. A half-century later, the Columbia University professor Brander Matthews endorsed Poe's implicit contrast of short story and novel by arguing for "a difference of kind. A true Short-story is something other and something more than a mere story which is short. A true Short-story differs from the Novel chiefly in its essential unity of impression" (Matthews 73). Much like Poe's tightly bound "pre"s, Matthews's reiterated "true"s declare a *cordon sanitaire* around the form, without attempting to define what constitutes a so-called "unity of impression" or otherwise distinguishes it from a "preconceived effect."

At roughly the same time, halfway around the globe, Anton Chekhov powerfully shifted the terms of discussion, if only via the palpable success of his stories themselves. In hundreds of narratives, he variously dismantled the assurances of Poe and Matthews by avoiding obvious summary claims, and instead defining characters fleetingly, in passing, often ambiguously, then bringing things to a close that rarely settles accounts.

As he observed of his expressive technique, if apocryphally: "Don't tell me the moon is shining; show me the glint of light on broken glass."[3] And contrary to Matthews's demand for "unity of impression," Chekhov seizes on irrelevant petty frustrations and minor foibles.

What perhaps most impressed readers of his stories were their defiance of interpretive effort, their challenge to confident assumptions about what has actually ensued, and what will likely continue to unfold. Instead of a single clear effect, his stories present us with ambiguous possibilities, with characters as mixed personalities, with readers often left hanging by narratives that seem unresolved, barely holding together. Famously, this affront to conventional expectations prompted Virginia Woolf's musical analogy: "it is as if a tune had stopped short without the expected chords to close it. These stories are inconclusive, we say, and proceed to frame a criticism based upon the assumption that stories ought to conclude in a way that we recognise" (176). As she then unerringly added: "In so doing, we raise the question of our own fitness as readers." Ever since, stories have chipped away at the mold established via so many plot-driven narratives of the late nineteenth century.

Of course, Chekhov was hardly alone in this, and his actual effect on Anglo-American writers in the teens is unclear, when Constance Garnett's translations of him became well known (her first collection appeared in 1912). Katherine Mansfield was dramatically impressed by such efforts, but James Joyce claimed not to have read him until after writing his own stories, and while Hemingway certainly did read Chekhov early, it is hard to know how familiar Sherwood Anderson

---

3. Chekhov's actual comment was less brief: "Descriptions of Nature must above all be pictorial, so that the reader, reading and closing his eyes, can at once imagine the landscape depicted; but the aggregation of such images as the twilight, the sombre light, the pool, the dampness, the silver poplars, the clouded horizon, the sparrows, the distant meadow,—that is not a picture, for, however much I try, I can in no way imagine this as a harmonious whole" (To A. V. Zhirkevich, February 2, 1895, 74). In an earlier letter, he affirmed that "in short stories it is better to say not enough than to say too much, because,—because—I don't know why!" (To I. L. Shcheglov, January 22, 1888, 106). A year and a half later, he continued: "The short story, like the stage, has its conventions. My instinct tells me that at the end of a novel or a story I must artfully concentrate for the reader an impression of the entire work, and therefore must casually mention something about those whom I have already presented. Perhaps I am in error" (To A. N. Pleshcheyev, September 30, 1889, 17). Both admissions, of course, confirm his flexibility, his nuance, if only in the tentativeness of his assumptions about the form he masters. For good analyses, see Chudakov, Hunter (39), Loehlin (34, 75).

was with him.[4] Independently, Joyce devised a similarly distinctive impressionist palette and matched Chekhov's indeterminate endings via moments of apparent revelation, though epiphanies that occur in the final paragraphs of *Dubliners* (1918), for all their influence on the form, are hardly systematic in effect.[5] Few are favorable or otherwise unambiguous, any more than Chekhov's closing insights, which share at times an ironic edge or even a cruel unmasking of pretension.

More generally, each of these successors to Chekhov creates characters likewise elusive, with psychologies revealed via narratives that worked as much by indirection as not. Anderson's innovative *Winesburg, Ohio* (1919) had prominently explored how stories might be linked in a cycle, borrowing something of the effect of a novel's capaciousness in punctuated narratives that stand alone. And Hemingway learned from that with *In Our Time* (1925), likewise threading together a medley of episodes about tormented characters that offers a fictional biography of Nick Adams's experiences circa World War I. Perhaps as relevant, Hemingway's vignettes and minimalist conceptions seem influenced by Chekhov in leaving important facts unclear, expressing personality through elusive dialogue and descriptions more evocative than declarative.

In the post-war period, the popularity of the form grew substantially, with practitioners creating widely varied versions of short fiction. By the 1930s and '40s, perhaps no one was so closely identified with the short story as John O'Hara, who still holds the record for contributions to *The New Yorker*. His recognizable technique proved exceedingly spare and plotless, so much so as to seem in Morris Dickstein's analogy "more a finely limned snapshot than an unfolding narrative" (Dickstein). O'Hara extended Hemingway's penchant for abbreviated sketches in which dramatic events are avoided (indeed, in which nothing seems to happen at all), with neither author nor character offering expansive gestures or much more than fleeting implication. These camera portraits

4. Richard Ellmann confirms that "Joyce said he had not read Chekhov when he wrote" his own stories (166). There is no available evidence among biographies of Sherwood Anderson for his own reading, though reviews of *Winesburg, Ohio* do make comparisons with Chekhov. Carlos Baker's biography of Hemingway fails to mention any influence, though his earlier critical study claims that in 1923 "he gave himself an intensive course of reading in certain of the prose masters," including Chekhov (27). Robert Paul Lamb more confidently states (if without corroborating evidence) that Hemingway "learned a great deal from" Chekhov, as well as from Anderson and Joyce (15).

5. Already in 1941, Harry Levin proclaimed of Joyce's epiphanies: "It is hard to appreciate the originality of Joyce's technique, twenty-five years after the appearance of *Dubliners*, because it has been standardized into an industry" (31–2).

came to be identified with *The New Yorker*, establishing the "style" of the most influential weekly short story publication over the next eight decades. The form, it need hardly be added, has progressively become less distinct, more diverse, more conceptually sweeping than earlier authors could ever have anticipated.

Given this range of experimentation, it may be understandable why prescriptive judgments of the short story in the half-century following Matthews were rarely convincing, when ventured at all. The most forceful critic was the Russian Formalist Boris Eichenbaum, who argued in apparent response to Chekhov's indeterminate conclusions for the requirement of firm dramatic closure (even if bolstering the principle with a dismaying bow toward O. Henry's broadly melodramatic formulations). Only belatedly would Anglo-American scholars emerge to argue broader principles, though in the meantime such eminent academics as Sean O'Faolain (1948), Frank O'Connor (1963), and Wallace Stegner (1965) did try to rank the field with book-length studies that avoided larger, theoretical appraisals. Tending toward the descriptive, given to paraphrasing stories they admired, usually organized as separate chapters on individual authors, they seemed to share a view that it was "an essentially minor form" (Stegner 3). Yet even so, as Stegner judiciously added: "I don't think we should define or prescribe" any larger principles that position the field (11).

Not until recently have younger critics entered the lists, rejecting dismissive claims about the form, though often in an effort to draw connections and posit principles about the kind of "continuity, coherence, or development for a narrative to be read as a story" (Ferguson, "Sequences" 8). Some have turned to questioning the absolute minimum required for a story's construction, captured in Susan Lohafer's notable reason for becoming intrigued (nicely defined as at once local, syntactical, and periodic): "What appealed to me was the idea of the sentence offering a kind of temporary resistance to the impetus to closure. I wanted to find a way of describing what it is like to enter, move through, and get out of a sentence" (Lohafer, *Coming*, 5). Others have pointed to historical continuities binding together stories written in similar periods. As Valerie Shaw observes, "I have tended to substitute for the question 'what ought a short story to be?', the question 'what can a short story do particularly well *because* it is short?'" (Shaw 21). That seems an appropriate resolution, though it persists even so in tilting towards large theoretical justifications for the form, drawn to the appeal of knotting an analytic net capacious enough to hold an impossibly diverse group together.

Still, Shaw puts her finger on a fallback position based on cumulative pages, repeated well before Frank O'Connor dismissively invoked the form's pivotal contrast with the novel: "At its crudest you can express the difference merely by saying that the short story is short" (21). Flannery O'Connor (no relation) offered no better wisdom in her uncertain agreement: "Perhaps the central question to be considered in any discussion of the short story is what do we mean by short" (O'Connor, "Writing," 94). Little could she have anticipated how fully flash fiction would later come to test the limits of such a question. Not until a quarter century after did Norman Friedman hint at a more incisive direction when he suggested (with wry simplicity) that the common assumption is probably wrong: "'A short story is a story that is short' is not so circular as it first appears" (Friedman 15). In a pointed rebuke to those eager to move beyond this logic to "a deductive, single-term, and mixed-category definition" (20), he revealed the lack of any "inherent relationship between a characteristic structure and a characteristic theme" (22). As he argued, no convincing rationale explains the short story being short "because it deals with a special, brief sort of experience and that this experience is most suited to the short story" (22).

There are no techniques, no sets of actions, no end effects that automatically qualify for short story status. An entire line of thought is dismissed in the shrewd reminder that we need always to return to "analyses of particular cases" instead of reverting to supposed "genre principles" (Friedman 23). Suzanne Ferguson joins arms with Friedman, defying those inclined nonetheless to firmer prescriptions, rightly choosing to reframe the issue:

"What is a short story?"... is probably not as important a question in the long run as other, specific questions we might ask about the relations of long and short stories, popular and high-brow stories, hypothetical and actual plots, or stories and reality. The object of such criticism is not, finally, to find generic or modal boxes to put stories into, but to open the boxes and let stories out for more illumination.   ("Defining" 229)

This calm effort to quietly ignore the requirements reflexively advanced for the short story will have little effect on those eager to hew to sharp distinctions, or who are inclined to dictate a configuration threading through or otherwise patterned in all story efforts. As Atwood's anonymous narrator affirms, it is less the "what" then the "How and Why" that compels continuing interest in the shapes and forms taken by short stories, in all their similarities but just as well in their differences. Moreover, a large part of their allure lies in "conveying a sense of unwritten, or even unwriteable things," as Valerie Shaw observes, invoking Kafka's wise dog who reaches across languages and species to assure us how evocative canine "bulwarks of silence" can be (Shaw 255). Stories likewise "survive all questions," offering up omission, elision, even silence itself as the sometimes constitutive aspects (but only sometimes) of a form that need not be saddled with "constitutive" principles to be enjoyed.[6]

II. Richard Ford and Memory

It is worth reminding ourselves how disarming stories can be on similar subjects by different authors. What is it that holds them together when strategies diverge so pointedly yet with equal success—whether for rendering temporality and memory, or for imagining dialogue and description, or even narrative voice? Richard Ford and Jhumpa Lahiri are among the more distinguished of contemporary practitioners, and might well have had a larger presence in this book had they altered the landscape of structural possibilities dramatically enough to warrant a full-scale review. But their very mastery of conventional strategies and subjects itself warrants consideration, if only to confirm that every accomplished writer challenges neat assumptions about what makes a story magical. The rationale for choosing them, instead of Ann Beattie or Deborah Eisenberg or some other equally distinguished author, lies in a pairing of stories in which memory looms large and problematic, and in which silence forms a crucial thematic consideration. This is not, of course, to suggest that those features form a distinguishing condition of short stories, even as the separate treatments offer a testament

---

6. The full citation from Kafka's "Investigations of a Dog," narrated by a dog, is: "I shall very likely die in silence and surrounded by silence, indeed almost peacefully, and I look forward to that with composure. An admirably strong heart, lungs that it is impossible to use up before their time, have been given to us dogs as if in malice; we survive all questions, even our own, bulwarks of silence that we are" (323).

to the ever-present potential of the form (as Valerie Shaw observes in this book's epigraph).

Ford's collection *Rock Springs* (1987) focuses largely on parents and children, arguably the best story of which is "Great Falls." In it, an adult narrator recalls the end of his parents' marriage one night when he was fourteen, when "the unhappy things came about" (32). Jackie's father precipitates the breakup by confronting his mother with her youthful lover, then forcing her to leave. The narrative's power resides less in its actions, however, than in Jackie's passive response to them, and in the sharply bi-focal, split temporal perspective he offers as an adult: "My father looked back at me where I was standing in the gravel, as if he expected to see me go with my mother toward Woody's car. But I hadn't thought about that—though later I would. Later I would think I should have gone with her, and that things between them might've been different. But that isn't how it happened" (42). The prose rhythm itself activates an alternation between present and past, adolescent and adult perspectives ("as if he . . . But I hadn't . . . though later . . . Later I . . . But that isn't"), confronting syntactically his earlier passivity with his present impotence. That disjunction continues to torment him, in the recognition of what he was unable to recognize at the time.

Only in retrospect does Jackie consider alternative actions he might have taken, though no other choice had readily been apparent, locked as he was in an adolescent frame of mind. Instead of interpreting the past from his present sensibility, Jackie recovers the ways in which he had then comprehended nothing of what Woody might have known. As Elinor Walker observes:

> The verb "to know" dominates many of Jackie's sentences. Woody "*knew* nothing about anything that was here" (38; italics mine). While talking to Woody, Jackie finds himself wondering "what Woody *knew* that I didn't. Not about my mother—I didn't *know* anything about that and didn't want to—but about a lot of things, about the life out in the dark, about coming out here, about airports, even about me. He and I were not so far apart in age, I *knew* that. But Woody was one thing, and I was another" (39; italics mine). Jackie appears certain of what he does know, and he knows enough to realize just how much is left unknown.   (105)

The strange tightrope of consciousness on which Jackie fitfully balances links him to an adolescent empathy with Woody, though he realizes his younger self could not (and his older self cannot) comprehend what might have taken place between Woody and his mother: "These are not the kinds of things you can know if you were not there. And I was not there and did not want to be. It did not seem like I should be there" (44). Again, the prose adroitly registers a recovered immaturity, capturing as if under glass the way he actually felt. In its awkward repetitions and unnecessary reiterations, it suggests an adult Jackie trying to inhabit the consciousness of his earlier self, uninformed and hence hardly in command. Jackie in the present appears like a ghost in an adult drama he is otherwise not part of, unaware of the emotions attached to events that recur from long-distant memory—a past that seems somehow ineluctable, and yet inevitable via its narrative strategy, compelling the reader likewise into a distancing mode.

Part of this effect accrues through Ford's mimicking an adolescent's voice, at times simply with a fevered excess of words and information that seems unrelated to the events reviewed. The contrast between states of consciousness—one present and mature; the other naive, distant, and wide-eyed—sets up a tension that makes us wonder at the transforming powers of recollection. After all, the ability to keep those no longer in our lives somehow still intelligibly there in our pasts seems undone by their having had minds of their own, as if resisting our present importunings in the desire to speak from a sovereign perspective. And if not accessible now, in the twenty-twenty accuracy of hindsight, could they have been even less so in our mutually ignorant shared pasts? Elinor Walker concurs, in comparing the story to Ford's novel *Wildlife* (1990), which appeared immediately after *Rock Springs*: "Told in the past tense, each text is narrated by an adult speaker who structures his story carefully, editorializing and revising the incidents that changed the course of his teenage years and shaped his attitudes toward others. Significantly, this mature perspective confirms each speaker's ability to recast an emotionally volatile time as an open-ended story" (Wachtel 100). Yet far from representing for Ford an aspect of "language's failure," as Wachtel concludes, it points instead to the very capacity of narrative to recover a paradoxical feature of psychology (Wachtel 104). One might more appropriately claim that the story successfully embodies the experience of childhood as so often a solitary one, even when one is not alone, in our separate efforts to *gain* a self, to achieve an individualized, private understanding of others, walled off imperiously from adult judgments and interpretive suasions. Memory serves not to restore a fleshed-out past but stands instead as testament to how little can actually be recovered.

That isolation—or rather, the balanced, fine-tuned evocation of it—helps to define Ford's mastery of the short story. Even in what may seem a more conventional guise, he offers a contrast with the common understanding of childhood as a state often brokered through memory. That necessarily, inevitably means that the past is reshaped according to current rather than initial demands. Memories, after all, notoriously plunder and select, making it hard to recover the narrative of an experience that actually restores the childlike perspective we endured at the time. Once we float into the calmer, less buffeted harbors of adulthood, the intense, seemingly unmoored incidents of childhood are recovered as mistakenly coherent, misshapen through a mature frame that distorts what we recall. In fact, one might almost claim that "discovery" doesn't seem like something that actually happens *in* childhood, at least as Ford imagines it (and Freud would concur) but only long after the fact, when the distortions of memory disappear *as* distortions. The disruptive contrast is heightened in the evocative transition between the story's bluntly mature, declarative opening sentences— "This is not a happy story. I warn you." (29)—and the tentatively expressed, unstable narrative that follows before the whole turns back to serene retrospection. We tilt between adolescent incomprehension and ruminative speculation, of irrelevant details that seem to confirm a childish inability to prioritize and the confident concluding questions and broad assertions that define a mature perspective.

The title itself reinforces this sense of division, perhaps especially given the strange blankness of landscape and utter lack of local details. The opening paragraphs briefly describe "the flat, treeless benchland" (29), with the rental house Jackie grew up in now long gone; soon after, he recalls his father shooting ducks, "thirty ducks in twenty seconds' time" (31). Otherwise, "Great Falls" becomes an odd, even self-consciously ironic topographical title, if only because the narrative has been all but stripped of any geographic allusions to instead explore a more telling figurative expression for tumbling into adulthood.[7] Moreover, the story ends as it begins, with bookends of adult consciousness encapsulating

7. Interestingly, Ford admitted in an interview: "I have loved writing about Great Falls...because of where it is in the world and on the map, and also because it has that wonderful name. The name was just magic in my ears. I like the way it has a long 'a' and short 'a.' I like the way it makes a kind of iamb in your mind's ear—*Great Falls, Great Falls.* I like the idea of things going downhill. I like the idea that 'falls' has a huge force in it. A regenerative force" (Paul 87).

a narrative that simply happened to form an adult we have not actually met, do not know, and who in the present does not seem otherwise worth any further description. The reductive warning that opens the story may sum it up entirely, though no sense is given thereafter of what has driven his parents apart. The narrator himself (as well as the reader) is left with a series of silent questions registered in Ford's signature, appositional style that nicely places "answers" as provisional, if cumulative:

I have never known the answer to these questions, have never asked anyone their answers. Though possibly it—the answer—is simple: it is just low-life, some coldness in us all, some helplessness that causes us to misunderstand life when it is pure and plain, makes our existence seem like a border between two nothings, and makes us no more or less than animals who meet on the road— watchful, unforgiving, without patience or desire.   (49)

The marvel of the story lies in exactly how little a mature perspective casts a net of understanding around the past it recovers. That past survives as something not quite flattened, remaining approximate, open, unconfirmed. It simply cannot be fleshed out with the presumed emotional preciseness we once felt. To provide answers for an adolescent consciousness that never at the time considered asking those questions would be to belie the experience that rivets a grown-up Jackie in retrospect. The story, in short, attests to its own profound impossibility as either account or revelation.

III. Jhumpa Lahiri and Revelation

If the distorting revelations of memory rest at the heart of narrative itself, they are configured quite differently in Lahiri's "A Temporary Matter," the opening story of her breakthrough 1998 collection, *Interpreter of Maladies*.[8] The plot in this case pivots not on the displaced, filtered recollection of a life-changing turn in a narrator's youth, but in the suppressed revelation of a stillborn birth that has evoked the parents' tormented response to their loss. Knowledge, instead of being somehow

8. Since this becomes a major consideration with Alice Munro, it is worth noting that there are two distinct versions of "A Temporary Matter": the first, published in *The New Yorker* (20 April 1998: 80–5); and the second, notably longer, describing the couple's earlier life together, shopping, cooking, holding hands, in *Interpreter of Maladies*.

sequestered off, or partially foreclosed, is regained in a narrative no
more straightforward than Ford's, even as emotional crevices are gradually, harrowingly revealed. And it is the husband's point of view we
share in free indirect discourse, as Shukumar wanders their apartment
six months after the infant's death, wondering at how assiduously "he
and Shoba had become experts at avoiding each other" (4). Partly, that
avoidance is conveyed physically, metonymically, through the stockpiling
of irrelevant details in the apartment, though in contrast again to Ford's
story, here the accumulation of things reveals an emotional disturbance.

Earlier, Shukumar has wondered at the exuberance of Shoba's purchases, her "endless boxes of pasta" (6), her stocked larder, her frozen
bags of meat, cooked chutneys and "labeled mason jars [that] lined the
shelves of the kitchen" (7). But following the baby's death, these things
become oppressive, a baleful reminder of feelings that no amount of
abundance can assuage.

Shukumar returned to the kitchen and began to open drawers. He tried to
locate a candle among the scissors, the eggbeaters and whisks, the mortar and
pestle she'd bought in a bazaar in Calcutta and used to pound garlic cloves and
cardamom pods, back when she used to cook. He found a flashlight, but no
batteries, and a half-empty box of birthday candles. Shoba had thrown him a
surprise birthday party last May.   (8–9)

And suddenly, his thoughts revert to the party, as remembrance flood-
ing in registers a distant country of lost possibilities. Where Ford invoked
a memory of the past that might have dictated a more hopeful present,
Lahiri allows a memory of hope distantly recalled of this very present,
though a memory since long gone up in flames. The mere detritus of
a promise once certified by purchases so eagerly made can only now
be summoned grudgingly, in painstaking, agonizing detail.

The paradox is that loss is now measured by accumulation, the
wealth of physical objects that link the couple's pasts together. Their
apparent lack of mutual affection is reflected in the larger and smaller
spaces that alternate through the story, of moments of amplitude and
flatness, of pregnancy and barrenness, even in ostensibly unconnected
ways. As Shukumar recalls, in a characteristic allusion to the capaciousness he covertly fears:

the last moment he saw Shoba pregnant, it was the cab he remembered most,
a station wagon, ... cavernous compared with their own car. ... [H]e imagined a
day when he and Shoba might need a station wagon of their own ... He imagined

himself gripping the wheel, as Shoba turned around to hand the children juice boxes. Once, these images had troubled Shukumar...But that early-autumn morning, he welcomed the image for the first time.   (3)

In unanticipated ways, the alternation between profusion and privation becomes a running theme throughout. Possibilities represented by material abundance and the vision of a conventional family outing are denied by the very gossamer quality of fleeting images themselves.

But Lahiri also evokes the death of the couple's relationship syntactically, notably via the only person (other than the couple) whose presence has registered over six months: Shoba's mother, whose effect on Shukumar emerges in the plain, dulling anaphora of her demeanor, the simple cumulative addition of details: "She cooked...She was...She set up...She was..." (9). Amid mundane objects and tedious people, Shukumar sets the table before serving dinner just as the electric company cuts power for the evening in order to make its repairs. Then he lights left-over birthday candles, before Shoba suggests they confess in the dark to "something we've never told before" (13). Intriguingly, we are misled in hoping this will bind them more closely together, since she has (unknown to us and Shukumar) already signed a lease elsewhere, confirming her plans to move out.

Each night, the two continue to exchange secrets in the hour when repairmen have shut the electricity off, with the dark seeming to release them from their lingering emotional paralysis: "Something happened when the house was dark. They were able to talk to each other again" (19). Once again, possibility and denial alternate in our reading of the couple and their relationship, as they become physically closer, even going to bed together, though their new ease is belied by a notable shift in the story's syntax that is obviously unapparent to Shukumar but is clear to the reader. For when the power company at last completes its repairs, with electricity finally restored and lights turned on, the whole becomes more mechanical and abridged, disconnected and hypotactic:

When she came downstairs they ate together. She didn't thank him or compliment him. They simply ate in a darkened room, in the glow of a beeswax candle. They had survived a difficult time. They finished off the shrimp. They finished off the first bottle of wine and moved on to the second. They sat together until the candle had nearly burned away. She shifted in her chair, and Shukumar thought that she was about to say something. But instead she blew out the candle, stood up, turned on the light switch, and sat down again.   (20)

It is as if the prose itself were announcing in its broken rhythms the dissolution of all that had brought them momentarily together.

As well, Lahiri offers in her title (much as Ford had done) a punning description of the whole, in the duplicate meanings that emerge from the story. For the magical moment of Shukumar's emotional transformation becomes itself "a temporary matter," as provisional as the electric company's promise in the narrative's opening sentence. The confessions they exchange, which once again open them up to each other, may free them from their paralysis but only insufficiently so. Shoba finally announces her firm decision, sickening Shukumar as he realizes that this was the actual point of her wanting to play the confession "game." And out of spite, he reveals what Shoba never wanted to hear, "the sex of their child" (21). So far, their stillborn baby has been a disfiguring absence, converted by Shukumar's admission into a remembered presence that the two must now confront before they can move on.

Lahiri has nicely adapted strains first perfected by Chekhov, in offering a delayed revelation that is once indeterminate and somehow prolonged—perfectly done as a culmination of the story. Given their mutual anger, nothing seems capable of saving the marriage, though that conviction is never quite expressed:

[Shukumar] carried the plates to the sink, but instead of running the tap he looked out the window. Outside the evening was still warm, and the Bradfords were walking arm in arm. As he watched the couple the room went dark, and he spun around. Shoba had turned the lights off. She came back to the table and sat down, and after a moment Shukumar joined her. They wept together, for the things they now knew. (22)

Oddly, perhaps predictably, interpretations of their mutual cruelty tend to split along gendered lines whenever I teach the story, as women align with Shoba and men with Shukumar, though all agree to the ambivalence of the whole, and the way in which it keeps slipping back and forth between viewpoints. Alternating mercurially among filled and emptied spaces, harsh light and shimmering darkness, obscured sight and impaired hearing, it culminates in support of the couple's efforts to come to a resolution, whether in clarity or at least some sort of partial reconstruction of the past and what has been left behind. The house's objects continue to speak, however ignored, laden with memories of a marriage that is now in the process of falling apart. Loss is irreparable, again because of things abandoned, reminding us that feelings have also been ignored, and that the process of letting go can never be neat or straightforward. In that regard, the very labor of recovery becomes a labor of love.

Lahiri's conclusion seems poignant because at once hopeless and calm, with knowledge itself become a balm that is nonetheless insufficient to the moment. Again, where Ford offers a character looking retrospectively, disappointed at not knowing, Lahiri has hers look with unalloyed disappointment at prospective certainties. Both offer deft investigations of memory and its sway, in stories that reveal how fully any simple narrative sequence necessarily misrepresents. And if little connects their stories, it is the unwillingness to move into a longer, larger narrative of lives unfolding, of characters met and parted, that finally compels us into a fuller imagining. That in itself is salutary, reminding us of what stories are and do, summarily and so often without further explanation. The very silence that persists behind the bulwarks Lahiri has established is at once an enticement to further reflection and a caution against what we can never know. Different as that conclusion is from Ford's silent admonition against adult assumptions involving the presumed wisdom of age, both authors adroitly use the short story form to warn against what novels too often presume to know. Silence, in other words, offers a tantalizing gesture of alternative possibilities in imaginative worlds where we regularly presume to know what will happen. The paradox of the short form is to encourage us to believe what we cannot otherwise quite rest assured in, and in that teetering between conviction and misgiving, to learn to value a generative indeterminacy.

IV. Raymond Carver: Whose Style?

Perhaps the most significant near-contemporary in expanding our notion of the short story (and equally in raising questions about it) is Raymond Carver, who by the 1980s seemed to have capped a shift toward an extreme minimalist aesthetic. Relying on Hemingway's "iceberg principle" of omitting large parts of a narrative that supposedly are felt by readers nonetheless, Carver as writer came to stand for the quandary of more or less, long or short, and the perpetually unresolved question of how to tell the difference in effect that a story should produce. Moreover, critics post-Carver began to wonder in a mood of deepening uncertainty about what effectively happens when too many lines are excised. Granted, since Hemingway we have come to admire the intriguing emotional effects of brevity, accompanied by an interpretive uncertainty that keeps speculation alive. But can something valuable conversely be lost in making a short story shorter, indeed finally too short for its own best effect?

The reason Carver looms so large is because he himself never resolved those questions, or negotiated a single theoretical stance. Indeed, his very career unsettles the customary judgments between early and later styles to be more fully explored momentarily. His stylistic biography, that is, dramatically anticipates questions yet to be raised about "late style" as a categorical judgment, if only because Carver himself seems more victim than instrument of the directions his career would take. Before plunging into an investigation of questions about altering styles, or about tendencies that mark artists' later years, we might well pause over this celebrated minimalist writer as a figure anguished by stylistic demands. For in the evolutions and jump starts his career represents, in the reconnoiterings and reconsiderations he experienced so painfully, we can recognize a deep insecurity about the very directions he felt his wayward style was pressuring him. That alone proves salutary in understanding how complicated the question of late style can be.

Consider that his second collection, *What We Talk About When We Talk About Love* (1981), lit up the literary firmament, though the book was *not* what Carver had intended to write or even the book he *actually* did write. His editor, Gordon Lish, had earlier been hired at *Esquire* to reinvigorate the magazine and bring it "the new fiction" (Sklenicka 188). Lish succeeded in the 1970s with an array of writers, confidently editing their prose, rewriting Richard Ford, Don DeLillo, T. Coraghessan Boyle, David Leavitt, and Amy Hempel, each of whom felt deeply indebted to him for his efforts. Admiring what he called "a peculiar bleakness" in Carver's early writing (2009, 991), Lish overhauled the stories Carver gathered together for his first collection, *Will You Please Be Quiet, Please* (1976), eliciting initial appreciation from Carver for "the fine eye you turned on" the first, heavily revised story. He felt the changes lent the story a "cooler, more frightening tone" (Sklenicka 185). Yet when Carver then read an edited version of the second story, "Neighbors," he grew wary, feeling that Lish's cuts had "downplayed sexual motives. He added lines that suggest a philosophical bleakness that supersedes the mundane horniness of the story," and Carver worried that the story "feels a little thin now" (Sklenicka 186). The disheartened author sent an anguished letter, though he finally came around, and a week after wrote once again with enthusiasm: "I'm thrilled about the book and its impending publication. I'm stoked about it." Later, when Lish moved to Knopf, he took Carver with him and encouraged the writer to submit his second collection in 1980, only then ruthlessly to cut the whole by more than half, with close line editing and the titles of stories, endings, even characters changed. Not until 2007 would the original, unedited version of Carver's manuscript be published as *Beginners*, the name of the title story ("What We Talk About…") before Lish got hold of it.

This charged account raises difficult questions about both authorial intention and execution, and not so much because of editorial high-handedness; American literary history is chock-full of such examples, after all, ranging from Theodore Dreiser and Stephen Crane to T. S. Eliot and Thomas Wolfe, all of whom had their work revised brutally, if arguably for the better. What makes Carver's case particularly interesting as a short story writer and notable stylist, however, is that his reputation as a radical and influential "minimalist" rests so largely on Gordon Lish's severe cuts, frequently more than Carver himself had wanted or first appreciated (and in fact, Carver always disliked the description of himself as a "minimalist"). Consider "So Much Water So Close to Home," about a wife realizing her husband Stuart has committed an unforgivable if undisclosed act on a three-day fishing trip with friends. As Claire Kane admits in the initial manuscript's opening, "Something has come between us" (Carver, 864). Only gradually do we learn that the body of a woman raped and murdered, discovered by her husband's friends, had been tied up to prevent it floating away so they might continue unabated with fishing. Claire is horrified and feels violated herself, identifying with the dead woman, reminding her of a girl in high school murdered by brothers, who like Stuart maintained their innocence. She sleeps separately from Stuart, drives out to the Naches River to see the site (explaining the story's title), and later goes to the dead woman's funeral. The story as Carver initially conceived it concludes with Stuart and Claire thoroughly, perhaps permanently unreconciled, Stuart angrily leaving the house.

That original story, however, inspired a completely different version nearly half the length and published (decades before Carver's manuscript version would appear) in *What We Talk About*. Notably, that is widely considered the best-known title of a story collection over the past half-century and representative of a deeply influential new aesthetic.

Embodying that aesthetic impeccably, Lish's revisions break the whole into brief paragraphs, strip out modifiers, offer faster pacing with more jagged locutions, and completely alter the ending, with Claire agreeing to quick, furtive sex as a resolution to their altercation, putting it behind them. Moreover, the uncanny quality of Carver's longer original version lies in knowing that Claire had shown signs of potential delusion prior to this episode, having been sent away to a clinic, helping explain her over-identification with the victim. Lish simply excises six straight pages midway through that lend a haunting sense of Claire's chronic hysteria, as she speaks of herself in the third person, her life thoroughly alienated from her, now "slipping away" (Carver, 872).

It becomes hard to know where to place our sympathies in the longer version, which is at once more detailed and even in some ways more evocative (though we usually understand *less* as being inherently suggestive). Moreover, the added length allows an obsession to be detailed that would itself ironically become Carver's recurrent theme. Stuart remains unchanged here, unaffected by his grotesque behavior, while Claire is transformed into something like a victim herself. Consider her confession to Stuart of the girl murdered long before at her high school—a confession cut by Lish though it succinctly explains how Claire has been altered: "I look at the creek.... until I am carried into the lake where I am pushed by the breeze. Nothing will be any different. We will go on and on and on and on. We will go on even now, as if nothing had happened. I look at him across the picnic table with such intensity that his face drains" (Carver, 870). The rest of this section is likewise cut, revealing Claire's defiance, her violence, slapping Stuart: "There is nothing I can say to him now.... He knows. I could laugh in his face. I could weep" (Carver, 870–71). The larger question prompted by the story's twin versions is whether Hemingway's iceberg principle actually works in every case. Is less really more in this story? Alternatively, does Carver's initial version haunt us with greater success than Lish's severe minimalism? Or are they finally just two different stories? Answers to these questions resonate in our readings, leaving us with no genuine standard for judging a story's effectiveness. Perhaps all we can concede is that what works for one reader fails for another.

While this may invariably be true for different versions of the same story (as seen with writers below), Carver presents a special case, since we cannot avoid addressing his resounding reputation as a master of minimalism, a style defined as "equanimity of surface, 'ordinary' subjects, recalcitrant narrators and deadpan narratives, slightness of story, and characters who don't think out loud" (Herzingen 11). That early 1985 description, weak as it is, seems nonetheless to apply more to Lish than to Carver, whose writing teacher, John Gardner, purportedly advised him whenever possible to reduce fifty words to twenty-five, while Lish then notoriously reduced those twenty-five to five. As words are excised, however, we wonder whether a story is empowered or simply disappears; did Carver initially weigh things down with detail inessential to the looming menace that otherwise drives his stories?

Compare once again the versions of "So Much Water," as Stuart and Claire confront each other over his troubling fishing expedition, with his simple repetition of "You're going to get me riled" (Carver, 870) coming to sound as threatening as Lish had desired, simply stripping away verbiage to leave a mere eerie repetition. Other similar turns have the same effect, lending a unified shape to the story less clear in Carver's longer version, leaving Claire finally neither defiant nor principled but rather somehow pathetically submissive: "I can't hear a thing with so much water going" (Carver, 279). In the end, of course, such judgments again become a matter of literary taste, demanding we as readers choose between what a story *is* doing and what it supposedly *should* be doing. Carver himself teetered between enthusiasms, for his initial lengthier stories and for Lish's diminished renditions, anguished by what he could not quite admit was a vision competing with and compounding his own. After his own untimely death, at the height of his popularity, his wife and supporters fought fiercely to suppress Lish's versions, and succeeded in persuading the Library of America to include unedited early stories. Yet Carver's letters reveal an author more deeply divided than they were, joining readers and critics just as divided. And it is worth keeping in mind that though Carver sometimes protested on behalf of his own initial versions, he readily included Lish's revisions in subsequent collections.

Given a study of selected authors' later styles and the gradual transitions they would make, Carver's uncertainties about directions he had taken and would in turn take after leaving Lish become of some importance. If nothing else, they remind us of how unsettled a writer can be and how divided one may remain *between* styles until the end. Carver's own post-Lish creations illustrate dimensions of this tension, written when he returned shell-shocked and beaten down to a narrative mode that seems distant from the minimalism for which he became well known.[9] Consider his most celebrated late story, "Cathedral" (1983), in which the first-person narrator Bub describes his wife's invitation to her blind employer for dinner. Bub begins with his wife's recollected account of the man asking to touch her face, having a transforming effect on her. Through the course of the evening, over drinks and dinner, Bub agrees to keep his eyes closed in sympathy with his blind guest, finally coming to feel an imagined cathedral materialize before his inner eye. His prejudices against the blind, laid out in the opening paragraphs, become by the closing a series of revelations about seeing anew, though he cannot explain what has happened to himself (as often occurs with Carver).

Physically touching Robert's face has apparently erased his knee-jerk bigotry, even as it brings him emotionally closer to his wife. Importantly, the style itself here becomes once again Carveresque, in the starkly simple syntax, the obviously repetitive diction and descriptions that move beyond marital familiarity to something like a new vision. Yet the story more generally is far from minimalist, and achieves an epiphany that seems unusual for Carver, whose early efforts point to Chekhov in refusing to end in resolution rather than indeterminately. They tend not to break off but to gradually invoke moments rendered mostly in dialogue. The stress in "Cathedral" as well seems to fall on statements that come to seem more meaningful than they initially sound, reminding us as well of earlier Carver in a less abrupt, more languorous style. It is almost as if the very style Carver had deliberately forsaken came back ineluctably, resurrected by apparent narrative demands for an expression more abrupt, more abbreviated and elusive.

Whether Carver's well-known minimalism was instrumental in a larger, recent turn to such preferences, or less a matter of causation than correlation, his popularity has accompanied less lingering narrative gestures, embodied in stories collectively known as flash fiction,

9. Carver admitted in a 1983 interview: "When I wrote 'Cathedral' I experienced this rush and I felt, 'This is what it's all about, this is the reason we do this.' It was different than the stories that had come before. There was an opening up when I wrote the story. I knew I'd gone as far the other way as I could or wanted to go, cutting everything down to the marrow, not just to the bone. Any farther in that direction and I'd be at a dead end—writing stuff and publishing stuff I wouldn't want to read myself, and that's the truth. In a review of the last book, somebody called me a 'minimalist' writer. The reviewer meant it as a compliment. But I didn't like it. There's something about 'minimalist' that smacks of smallness of vision and execution that I don't like. But all of the stories in the new book, the one coming out next fall, were written within an eighteen-month period; and in every one of them I feel this difference" (Simpson 210).

narratives of a thousand words or less that compress considerations of form. That his late efforts moved in the opposite direction, toward a more expansive, less precipitous mode, makes us once again wonder at how much (and of course how little) stories need to tell. Whether Carver would have freely chosen his own early published style, in contrast to the more leisurely, less minatory rhythm of his unedited stories, is a question still contested. His tormented example, however, certainly offers a striking contrast to writers who evolved independently, far less contentiously and with considerably less anguish, into their own late styles.

V. Genre and Late Style

Despite this review, the following assessments ignore speculation on any personal reasons for stylistic developments. They make no effort to be comprehensive or prescriptive, partly in protest against those twin interpretive gestures when applied to short stories, but partly out of general principle. Instead, something like the opposite premise informs the selection of four practitioners, each of whom takes the so-called genre in a new direction, in one case dramatically, in the others more gradually and incrementally. All four together offer a distinct array of possibilities for the short story as it tests different assumptions, different expectations, different stylistic suasions. And though others have written prize-winning stories, most have not as persistently strayed from patterns recognized as tried-and-true, or staked out so deliberately new narrative "How"s and "Why"s. Ford and Lahiri are examples of this, but other reasons preclude their presence here, including the fact that a youthful Lahiri has hardly reached a "late stage" of anything, while Ford is perhaps more distinguished as novelist than as occasional story-teller. Munro, Dubus, Williams, and Davis are each in their seventies or dead, and not only were they all but exclusively writers of stories but as well they define thoroughly idiosyncratic personal visions that warrant further investigation, veering consistently in unexpected directions, upending in the process our expectations for what a story can do.

Before turning to them more fully, we need to address two "problems" silently threading through the following pages, the first, of why the short story should ever have seemed to require a particular shape. And my answer is that it does not, as dramatized by the authors here, whose diversity tests the limits of any claim for generic sanctions (or even supposed general solutions). Their salient differences from each other (and from anyone else) defy conventional patterns, and put into question what is meant by "genre," a term frequently invoked but rarely examined with regard to the short story. The second "problem" hinges on their notable differences not from others but from their earlier selves, which requires a fuller investigation of what is meant by "late style" and why that phrase demands some review.

To take the first problem first: why is the short story referred to as a genre? In fact, the standard forms of the drama, poetry, and the novel are not customarily referred to this way, but rather as modes or kinds of literature, constrained by audience expectations for a certain variety of performance (dialogue on-stage; lyricism expressed in lines; large baggy monsters of sheer narrative). Genres certainly likewise are constrained by expectations, but those tend to be identified with a particular set of syntactic and semantic earmarks.[10] Revenge tragedies, say, or epic poems, spy novels, and Western films: these distinctive genres define themselves all but immediately through setting, characteristic expression, recognizable costumes, and central plot tensions, among other considerations. Instead of a short story "genre," then, it is more accurate to talk about "kind" or "form." Having established that distinction, however, it is worth acknowledging that even so the invocation of "genre" has become so commonplace when talking about short stories that one needs occasionally to bow to common usage.

The second problem concerns the identification of artistic "late style," popularized through Edward Said's posthumous *On Late Style: Music and Literature Against the Grain* (2006). Said resurrected and expanded Theodor Adorno's notion of a transcultural, transhistorical condition in which artists nearing death were presumed to defy earlier accommodations to the social order, freed at last to express themselves not in decorous commonplaces associated with old age but in often contentious, sometimes irascible, even anguished artistic gestures. Said's (and Adorno's) model was Beethoven, though even so it is not clear that his musical style can be read so transparently. More generally, it is certainly not the case that artists in radically different cultures, at

---

10. For an excellent introduction to questions raised by genre analysis, see Rick Altman ("American" and "Film/Genre"). And for an intriguing distinction between story and novel, see Jameson (138). For somewhat weaker discussions, see May ("Introduction," "Nature") and Pratt.

various stages of "old" age, accomplished in separate arts, respond the same way in their creativity.

To take some obvious contradictory notions of age, it is clear that the coupling of serenity and withdrawal, of rage and resistance, of innovation and experimentation differs in almost every individual case. As astute commentators have argued—Linda and Michael Hutcheon; Gerald McMullan—it is impossible to generalize about so many figures in such different artistic enterprises. The Hutcheons rightly point out that "old," "late," and "style" are all separately problematic concepts, not reducible to common understanding and all leading to a series of confused contradictions. In fact, they caution, "What is clear is that it is the aesthetic values of the critic that in the end determine what is deemed positive or negative in the last works of an artist" (Hutcheon 5). Turning away from such loose generalizations, the Hutcheons point to the need for close individual studies, declaiming: "of what use is a single discourse of late style, whether used to celebrate or to dismiss final works?" (11). Or as they peremptorily conclude: "There are as many late styles as there are late artists" (11). Gordon McMullan reinforces that claim in his study of critics' creation of a period defined as Shakespeare's "late writing," offering in turn a comprehensive scholarly overview of other figures in distinctly varied fields. As he admits, while artists may "develop a new and striking style in their latter years, lateness as a critical category is a construct, not a given" (16). In short, Said's melodramatically singular view is deeply flawed, requiring a more attentive notion of possible (though not invariable) plural "late styles."

Still, the power of stylistic evolution and transformation does remain a tantalizing mystery for artists who persist over long careers. My own use of the term strips it of assumptions gathered together by Said: that it forms a response to the imminence of death, say, or that it transcends the individual markers that identify a particular established career. Late style exists not as a general condition, then, but as a specific possibility only sometimes registered by an artist, and in turn only occasionally forming a dramatic (at others, a subdued) response to questions and engagements often engaged for a lifetime. My interest lies in how each of four select writers crafts a later evolution, explaining the following focus on transitions from their early writing. In fact, none of the four made a radical transformation in style (condensation, fragmentation, technical development) or philosophy, but each did develop more focused techniques. Even when they may seem to maintain a certain continuity, they rarely persist as static or unchanging, though what we observe in late efforts often illustrates what has been latent all along.

In fact, our larger quartet of authors can be seen instead as a smaller if shifting set of couples, each of a different sort. Dubus and Williams made a relatively severe break with their earlier choices, and share as well a tendency to revelation, even epiphany in their narratives. Munro and Davis have seemed to mature more moderately over the course of various collections, developing late styles that seem an extension of strains there all along. As well, they both share a conjoint resistance to resolving tensions developed through the course of their narratives (forming in that regard a more direct tribute to Chekhov). Yet as if to challenge these couplings, however partially, Munro and Dubus both acknowledge (in some surprise) that their fictional characters seem entirely independent of them as authors (Dubus admitting that his efforts to change his character's minds regularly prove in vain; Munro referring repeatedly to her belief that her stories occur somehow outside of her, and that her revisions are intended to make those independent accounts more accurate).[11]

In all four cases, keep in mind that earlier strategies and themes are not abandoned, even as later works reflect a more self-confident willingness to leave contradictions and uncertainties in play. That explains why any understanding of an individual late style requires reviewing the whole career, which clarifies the shape of the following chapters: shifting from a focus on the salient features of an artist's later stories, then to a review of earlier accomplishments, before offering a broad overview of the forms taken by tightening technique and more mature themes, by confident and abrupt abridgements that define in each case a "late style." The argument is meant to provoke a reassessment of story practitioners whose late works offer a backwards introduction to their own early successes.

Curiously, the enigmatic titles of the collections reviewed here nicely anticipate larger late perspectives: Munro's *Dear Life*, then Dubus's *Dancing After Hours*, followed by Williams's *The Visiting Privilege* (2015),

---

11. In 2001, Munro admitted that "I'm never absolutely sure of anything, and that's probably why I write stories, because every story is an investigation for me. And sometimes I'm a little surprised by what I'm thinking about it, and I see how it's going to turn out and I think, 'Oh, is that what happens?'" As she added, "I do think of the story as happening, not of me making up the story. The story is happening, and I'm finding out about it. . . . It's as if I'm doing justice to something somewhere" (Gzowsky).

and finally Davis's *Can't and Won't* (2014). Each author's focus is reflected forthrightly, beginning with Munro's admission of the undercurrents screened by her favored expression:

Those words are very wonderful to me because I heard them when I was a child, and they had all kinds of meaning. "Oh, for dear life!" would just mean that you were kind of overwhelmed with all that had been required of you. I liked the contrast between that and the words "dear life," which are maybe a joyful resignation, but when you say "dear"—the word—it doesn't bring up sadness. It brings up something precious. (Awano 180)

The ambivalences tucked away in the familiar phrase capture the balance in all that occurs, with urgency and boredom linked in a kind of "joyful resignation." And this suggests something of her strategy, even her style, in late stories that one can take up at almost any point and leave off at any other (or so she would say, and has indeed argued). This becomes in fact a more pronounced dislocation, of *szujet* and *fabula* wrenched even further apart than we normally expect, certainly in earlier stories. But it also registers what seems like a less pronounced need to control characters authorially, to organize scenes chronologically, to end with some greater cumulative understanding.

More circumspectly, Dubus's titular phrase suggests a lingering sense of belatedness that so often recurs in his stories, in their persistent effort to register the sonorities and grasp the implications of something crucial that has already taken place, "after hours." As well, the title vaguely implies a special quality to the moment recalled—of intimacy secured, of emotion somehow heightened, outside the normal or expected run of events. The strain of regret and powerlessness that so often weaves through these stories may not itself emerge from the title's resonance, though we are reminded in its temporal gesture how much more than in his earlier work Dubus does seem concerned with time's irrevocable nature. "After hours" by definition points to the present as well as the past, if only by contrast. Whatever backward look is encouraged registers an ongoing sense of connection to a time now foreclosed, where freedoms once possible are possible no more, with new restrictions on what is no longer feasible. The past looms as possibility but also as memory of life now sequestered.

Williams, like the other two, takes a similar familiar phrase, though instead of teasing out its common meanings curiously skews them by altering it from a plural to singular mode. Hospital visiting privileges have been oddly expressed as an isolated entitlement, a singular advantage, offering a beguiling entry into her efforts. We are forcefully reminded of the exceptional "privilege" conferred on readers as they enter a set of other lives lived so often on the margins, of recognizable psychologies pressed against imagined possibilities that seem bizarre, estranged, even otherworldly. In that sense, the conversion of a well-known phrase by dropping the plural offers a weird indication that things will be off-balance, askew, with an atypical perspective on normal patterns. We suspect our focus is being interestingly narrowed even as we abruptly shift from customary ideas of banal access to "patients" to something more idiosyncratic and possibly bizarre.

Finally, Davis's "can't and won't" resembles nothing so much as Munro's own ambivalent outburst expressed more straightforwardly in the title story's anecdote of firm editorial resistance to social and lexical contractions (in her publishing house's effort to restore appropriate diction and good form). Yet the phrase resonates once again, as Davis (much like the other three) offers a larger contrarian defiance of conventional ideas about what short stories more generally might be considered to be. She, like them, resists having her efforts measured and parsed against misplaced expectations for a narrative curve ("can't and won't"), or of plot and character dictated according to what has long been practiced and regularly expected. Like the others, she defies our understanding of what constitutes "story," even as she and they delight in expanding the terrain, inventing ever new possibilities that redefine what "short" can do. In that regard, her title might well have been adopted by any of the other three as well.

VI. Chapter by Chapter

The following chapters each consider the customary strategies an author either grew into or let go, each serving as introductions as well as exploring new terrain. Early and late stories are compared in order to identify earlier and later styles, in the process revealing the persistent vision of the writer. As well, however, an effort has been made to clarify how each of the quartet differs from the others: Munro, with her early incisive vision of what she only achieves consistently later; Dubus, who makes a more dramatic transition in his stories toward a violent premise, possibly due to effects of his own debilitating accident; Williams, as conceivably "late" all along, with early stories anticipating in their mildly grotesque imaginings a vision she would perfect; and Davis, driven to explore a series of other narrative options, as if led to them by her own initial play with nonfictional elements that expanded exponentially.

This book's opening chapter focuses on Alice Munro's late quotidian rhythms, which avoid even the emotional disruptions that fluster her earlier characters' lives. As her affable title suggests, she embraces a certain meandering, itinerant, even Whitmanesque mode of curious delight mixed with mild bafflement. Indeed, the central feature of her later stories may well be bewilderment itself, with endings promising little more reassurance than beginnings have done. Life forms a simple continuation of crisscrossing patterns and diverse desires, which resist progressive understanding and in which narrative sequence tends to reveal little by way of conventional development.

By contrast with a certain dominant strain of story-telling, her endeavors are pitched to derail the very possibility of epiphany. Instead of the promise that characters will somehow grow or a changed perspective will transform one's life, her stories variously reveal how fully we live in the here and now, sometimes mired in fixed patterns, sometimes simply persistent and engaged by the moment. But experience is rarely conceived as "educational" or "progressive," with knowledge seldom upending our perspectives and the future playing out much as the past has done. In contrast to Atwood's promise in "Happy Endings" that narratives can be inventively rejiggered, Munro creates a set of moments that exist simply as moments, each separately transfixing, each part of a life's hopes and uncertainties, while forming no particularly inherent sequence of promising beginnings nor culminating in predictably profitable ends.

That may help explain why she so often returns to earlier stories to make additional revisions, from publication to re-publication, altering narratives that never quite feel completed in her own head, and that may well bend anew as she reconsiders. The appropriate balances and pleasurable pressures that lead to a successful story are never, in Munro, to be confused with a successful or good life; aesthetics and ethics seem for her only loosely conjoined. It also clarifies Munro's revelatory late habit of beginning randomly in stories she enjoys, not necessarily at the beginning, confirming her presumed belief in a certain dazzling circularity at the heart of experience. And this importance of perspective—of who is seeing what, from whatever blinkered angle—helps explain not only her stories' crucial malleability but her need to adjust them in published reincarnations. Contrary to conventional notions of "reading for the plot," Munro celebrates a non-teleological process of reading for an enjoyment of episodes and occasions, which rarely leads to some encompassing wisdom. "Dear life" (presumably expressed with a sigh) simply continues, high and low, up and down.

The effect of this, however, is to infuse her stories with a poetic intensity that focuses the reader's attention not on before and after but through a psychological lens that in disrupting plot, perhaps even character, concentrates instead on the disorientations of consciousness in its alternating rhythms of fervor and indifference. Munro inspires confusion as itself basic to the process of story-telling, with an exhilaration that results from singular events failing to align according to customary impressions of sequence. Instead, they may correspond to the way we more immediately experience them, in the midst of dramatic acts, ghostly remembrances, vague affections, mild obsessions, always amid other moods and demands. Lock-step sequence is simply the retrospective narrative act we impose on the disarray of our lives, though in performing it we misrepresent experiences we otherwise want to memorialize. In fact, Munro's late stories repeatedly conclude with characters having failed to understand their past, sometimes affected by a sense of loss but no better able to fathom its implications or to grasp its import.

Turning from Munro's calmly intense but mostly benign vision, the second chapter investigates the violence (psychological as well as physical) that lies at the heart of Dubus's late work. While that pattern forms a central strain of stories by countless other practitioners, Dubus's distinction lies in revamping the effect of violence, refocusing the unusual transformations achieved by more than a century of fictional trauma. Poe, after all, established a pattern followed ever since in stories that celebrate physical brutality and psychological mayhem, with writers emulating him in registering the *after effects* of violation, the consequences as well as the reparative gestures we make towards an initiating ordeal. By contrast, Dubus resists shifting our attention to one side, refusing to avoid the reverberations of a body blow, facing head-on the impact yet to come, felt as it occurs. Seizing on such startling, eviscerating moments as themselves powerfully vivid, and therefore inspirational, he reconfigures what had otherwise seemed worth instantly forgetting into moments having an immediate capacity for transfiguration. The experience victims so often want to repress becomes for Dubus paradoxically a moment to embrace.

The very brevity of story form is thereby central to Dubus's vision, ever focused on a quicksilver narrative arc, as he deliberately suppresses information that might occlude the life-altering aura introduced by such violence. Ironically, devastating moments become Emersonian, not Poesque, defying anguish and refusing to close down possibility in favor instead of bringing characters surprisingly back to life and full expectation. In this, his deeply felt Catholicism forms a compelling strain throughout his career, of Christ's apostolic injunctions to focus on what is important in our lives, encouraging us to pay heed to central tenets of observation and renewal. Yet part of Dubus's transition into a later style accompanies his shift from an earlier fascination with liturgical commandments as narrative pivots to his increasing concentration on the enduring effect of spiritual and salvational experiences. He turns from questions of conventional performance to scenes of violent disruption where one is no longer insulated by habit or rule. Instead, characters are regularly exposed to a Melvillean universe in which we become aware of the emotional abyss over which we hang every moment, in contrast to the stultifying routines that succeed in burying us alive. Rather than being distracted by a laundry list of compulsory activities, by customary rituals and onerous daily rounds, these traumatic moments suddenly allow characters to realize the miracle of being, coming as a revelation in the midst of calmly structured experiences.

Compounding the effects of this vision is late Dubus's characteristic opening strategy, in which he introduces central characters in an all but formulaic fashion. It is as if, in marking the sameness of our individual identities, he lends a more intense weight to events that remake us anew. Violence may be transformative, but it is invariably for figures who otherwise seem initially more or less the same, given how they are equivalently named and identified. Extending that odd opening gesture, moreover, he regularly offers narratives in which anticipation and retrospection confer importance on inadvertent moments. In the stories that comprise *Dancing After Hours*, he defies far more than his earlier works the notional patterns we tend to devise for ourselves— either in the brutality that topples banal conceptions, or the impossibility of resurrecting former routines of acquiescence. Repeatedly, he places us in the recognizable world limned above—of keeping house, attending school, pursuing predictable careers, making a life with another—and just as regularly reveals how often we lose sight of the wonder of simply (or rather, miraculously) living through the moment.

Williams shares with Dubus a deep religious faith, if Protestant rather than Catholic, and is drawn as well to the transformative effects of violence. But her take on their intersection is pitched less towards revelatory insights, or the mystery of life's precariousness, than to a certain otherworldliness, even mysticism, that has always lain at the heart of religion. Just as much an outlier among recent practitioners, Williams has clearly been influenced by Flannery O'Connor in her Southern Gothic mode—particularly in self-consciously weird, fractured descriptions of character. She too steps on the traces of short story conventions, deliberately defying a sustained concern with character or sequence but doing so differently from Munro and Dubus in her abrupt conflations of death and comedy. Disarming the reader through a strangely wrenching, dissociative style, Williams offers her vision at a slant, where the familiar, settled quality of life becomes instantly strange. In that regard again she seems akin to Dubus, though taking a more distanced, even intellectual perspective rather than immersing the reader emotionally. More strangely hallucinatory rather than fearful, consciousness is presented as at once banal and bizarre through common patterns of speech blurted out of context, with customary assumptions exposed as invariably failing to apply. Eroding the border between danger and security, her depictions cast a shadow of mild mysteriousness in stories that themselves come to seem escapes, with reading reconfigured as a process that magically takes us to a realm outside the commonplace or habitual.

Williams's late stories, moreover, defy even more intently a sense of chronological sequence. Unlike Dubus, whose continuities are dismantled through violence, or Munro, who unsettles us through arbitrary selection, Williams's narratives devolve into a series of details whose cumulative importance fails to quite add up. It is as if we were immured in a Kafkaesque world where all is familiar yet somehow nonetheless strange. Continuously, we are reminded how far her scenarios are from our daily lives, however constructed according to common patterns that largely resemble our own. For what tirelessly recurs in Williams is the notion that the straightforward, realist fabric of our experience—the events, characters, patterns of behavior, expectations, and so on—can suddenly shift, revealing a landscape awry, a universe alternative to the one we share, operating just as effectively through transgressive similes, odd punctuation, weird events weirdly described that converge despite our understanding.

This signature effect becomes stranger and more surreal later on, as realistic details are massaged into resonances that seem at first impossible yet nonetheless emotionally valid. Can one actually speak with the dead? Might inanimate objects possess consciousness? What is a weekly group meeting of serial killer moms really like? Joining together the mystical and the mundane, Williams's wrenched style reveals characters unable to understand what is going on, reduced to seeing things from a woefully obstructed perspective, which likewise becomes our own abiding experience.

Lydia Davis turns her back on all this, though her own innovations may seem something of a reversion to earlier premises, silently adopting Poe's notion of "unified effect" but without any of the apparatus he presumed essential to its achievement. For her, an effect is neither instrumental nor functional, something which contributes to further plot development or somehow helps resolve all that has gone before; instead it is simply an end in itself. Or rather, Davis has (unlike the rest of the quartet, plus most other contemporary writers) no particular end in mind, since her extremely short performances are meant to arouse curiosity and provoke expectations without at the same time doing anything to shape or extend possibilities. Far more than Munro, who questions in celebratory tones where we begin and end, Davis turns to a species of non-narrative, focusing on strategies that actually seem to stop temporal progress or otherwise appear urgent simply for their own sake, offering a series of *amuse-bouches* in her single, bite-sized stories.

As well, she orients narrative invention toward nonfictional situations, whether philosophical inquiries or biographical conundrums. What increasingly intrigues her are not decisive imagined episodes (as in Dubus), or ruptured, even random sequences (as in Munro), or a dreamlike clash of consciousness and event (as in Williams), but more elementary interstices among unhinged moments of abrupt observation and fleeting impressions. Davis's stories explore the spaces *among* narrative conventions we think of as obvious or unquestioned, helping explain her sustained focus on "short short" stories (now regularly known as "flash fiction") rather than the more elaborate subjects that engross other writers.[12]

At the same time, she more interestingly raises the stakes and adjusts the baseline of what any story involves—of how we might turn a skeptical eye on not simply elliptical narratives but the briefest of situations, the most momentary of questions, emotions so evanescent that they pass before we have the wherewithal to consider them. In fact, she extends Munro's focus on the routine, everyday aspect of life, as Larry McCaffery observes: "At first glance what is likely to strike most readers about her writing is not its innovative features but the ordinariness of its characters and situations (mainly women undergoing experiences that hardly seem extraordinary or even dramatic by most standards) and its matter-of-fact delivery" (McCaffery 60). Or as Davis herself boldly concedes: "Confusing the distinctions seems like a very healthy thing" (McCaffery 76). Contrary to contemporaries, she wants to muddy the literary waters, collapsing categories and bringing together the philosophical and nonfictional, public announcements and private letters, banal expressions and lyrical insights.

Admittedly, Davis is a contrarian fiercer than anyone else in the quartet, evident to those who most enjoy her solitary strain of fiction. McCaffery thinks her so *sui generis* that he questions the presumed nationality of her imagination:

Davis seems somehow not distinctly American: Her works are nearly devoid of the particularizing details routinely used by most writers as a kind of shorthand method for introducing specific resonances that encourage the reader's empathy and understanding. In Davis's fiction surface details are emptied of such ready-made associations and instead are used as indicators of primal fears, undercurrents of dread and existential nausea, a pervasive sense of betrayal, worthlessness, and loss evoked in Kafka or Beckett rather than the highly particularized anomie or bored-but-hyper attitudes found in most examples of American minimalism.   (McCaffery 62)

---

12. It is likely that neither author actually influenced Davis, but both anticipated her condensed narrative mode. The apocryphal six-word "novel" composed by Hemingway is: "For sale: baby shoes, never worn" (Hemingway). And Nabokov has Humbert Humbert admit in *Lolita*, "My very photogenic mother died in a freak accident (picnic, lightning) when I was three" (Nabokov 10). For other such examples, consider the online series of "six-word quotes": Margaret Atwood's "Longed for him. Got him. Shit"; Alistair Daniel's "Without thinking, I made two cups"; and Joyce Carol Oates's "Revenge is living well, without you."

This observation on her style is acute, though Davis rarely elicits a distinctive literary enthusiasm among her critics, and this despite her own nuanced attention to others' play of syntax and diction. This chapter therefore concentrates again on craft, in stories so abbreviated they sometimes seem to test some unstated limit of how short short stories can be. The point is that her single sentences, conjoined with a distinct notion of witnessing—treating even mild dissatisfactions as worthy of attention—lends a renewed dignity to the everyday experiences celebrated by all four writers. Yet in her case, that interest extends to her own scattered dreams, to Flaubert's offhand comments, to surreal everyday encounters, to found objects and simple grammatical problems: all encapsulated in Davis's own transforming verbal style. Like no other writer, Davis offers a bouillabaisse of subjects and characters that disrupt thought itself.

VII. Conclusion, Disruptions

This gathering together of four such different figures is intended to be disruptive, revealing the disparate ways in which writers continue to alter, develop, and finally unravel the conventional definition of what a short story can be. There may seem something unusual in the constellation—three women and one man, three Americans and one Canadian—though that seems finally insignificant. More distinctive are considerations that involve narrative structure, characterization, and verbal delight, all arrayed in dramatically varied form, ranging from the immediacy of vignettes and flash fiction (Davis) to the ever-impinging pressure of long story cycles (Munro, Dubus).

Cycles of stories, it should be added, are nearly always possible to connect, depending on the inventive interpretations of critics able to identify repeated and parallel motifs in separate collections. As Suzanne Ferguson has written:

Before we get into mis-categorizing works containing short stories, I would like to see *more* attention rather than less to the special aspects of the short stories as stories, respecting the intentions of the authors (where evident), and helping readers rather than getting in their way. What does it take to have enough continuity, coherence, or development for a narrative to be read as a story or novel, and what differences in reading experience or interpretation do we register with sequences or cycles? Why do some writers avoid sequencing

their related stories, and why do readers apparently like to make them into
sequences regardless? These and other related questions need to be addressed
as we pursue the elusive issues of genre in books of short stories, not because
we need convenient pigeonholes but because we need to understand how
formal concerns influence interpretation.   (Ferguson, "Sequences")

The questions persist, as they must, though it helps to have such innovative
writers as Dubus, Munro, Williams, and Davis to press readers in different directions, and to press writers as well. One might take Ferguson up
on her challenge even more broadly, turning not only to cycles but to the
entire array of story possibilities that have recently enriched the form.

If the short story seems to have released itself over time from earlier
constrictions, it still engages theorists unable to escape the hold of formal dictates. Should we need further encouragement to do so, it may
be salutary to consider a writer as traditional as Henry James, authoring
long stories that are often classed as novellas and otherwise seem novelistic, who evoked a promising assessment of one of his early stories
from his older brother. As William, ever impatient and judgmental,
conceded at last:

It makes me think I may have partly misunderstood your aim heretofore, and
that one of the objects you have had in view has been to give an impression
like that we often get of people in life: Their orbits come out of space and lay
themselves for a short time along of ours, and then off they whirl again into
the unknown, leaving us with little more than an impression of their reality
and a feeling of baffled curiosity as to the mystery of the beginning and end
of their being, and of the intimate character of that segment of it wh. we have
seen.   (James 29)

That response should strike us today as fully engaging so much of what
Henry wrote, in all its fulsome detail, as well as so much of more recent
flash fiction, otherwise known as "Skinny Fiction, or Mini-Fiction:
a single-episode narrative with a single setting, a brief time span, and
a limited number of speaking characters (three or four at the most); a
revelation-epiphany: the click of a camera, the opening or closing of
a window, a moment of insight" (Peden 233). For all their differences,
the quartet gathered here have seized on aspects of this description, varied and contradictory as they are, in an effort to sharpen visions hewn
out of a lifetime's effort. It might be said that their late styles represent
an increasing commitment to the vision of Kafka's dog, at once terse
expressions of narrative possibility and yet wondrous testaments to a

certain final inscrutability: "we survive all questions, even our own, bulwarks of silence that we are." We recall that storied dog for "leaving us with little more than an impression...and a feeling of baffled curiosity," though unfortunately not all stories bless us with such an afterlife. The late stories of Munro, Dubus, Williams, and Davis do, most of them, and now it is worth turning our gaze more intently upon them.

I

Bewilderment in *Dear Life*

What can one make of a Nobel Prize winner, the first ever for short stories, who over a sixty-year career has shifted gradually away from the customary pressures of stories themselves? How might we understand her loosening of narrative sequence, her easing of temporal pressure, her avoidance of templates that make happenstance seem somehow fated or that otherwise shape idiosyncratic moments into plot? Alice Munro has long honed a distinctive vision of narrative sequence that paradoxically undercuts expectations for sequence itself. As well, she has revealed a fictional landscape where people seem enigmatic, as much to themselves as to one another, effectively freeing characters from a narrator's (and a reader's) imperious gaze. That crafted practice, long celebrated, has become clearest in her latest (rumored "final") collection, *Dear Life*, where scenes register as solitary moments that fail to lead to resolution, or to sometimes even add up at all. The effect, however, is to infuse these stories with a poetic intensity as fervid as her earlier collections, achieved even more effortlessly by focusing the reader's attention less on before and after than through a psychological lens that defies plot, perhaps even character, in preference for the bewilderments of consciousness in all its contradictory demands. As Isla Duncan has recently asserted, "This image of an intense experience isolated, shut off, and untainted so that it retains its distinct intensity is not new in Munro's fiction, but is especially prevalent in her later work, when her older characters are wont to reflect on their days of youth" (113–14). And yet, Helen Hoy reminds us, the image owes as much to deft narrative strategies as to aging characters reminiscing: "Not only the themes of her fiction but the structures as well increasingly reflect her sense of reality's multiplicity, indeterminacy, flux" (17).

That defiance of predictability weaves thematically through Munro's stories, which are intended to surprise not only readers but herself as writer, and to do so through formal strategies as unanticipated as the lives they represent. "What I want now in a story is an admission of chaos" (Hoy 17), Munro declared in 1991, speaking not only of reading pleasures forty years after her first story, but writing ones as well that would continue more intently over the next two decades. The confession may seem odd initially, until we realize how fully she conceives of life mercurially, indeterminate, always in the process of being interpreted anew, qualities that make her stories ever less open to paraphrase. For what distinguishes Munro's later style is how much more fully she continues to relax into possibilities already explored, if tentatively, in earlier stories. Progressively, she lets go of recognizable strategies for distinguishing characters, abandoning the scaffolding on which her narratives had long relied. That willingness to commit unconditionally to a vision only evident provisionally before in her work, relinquishing the typical means by which authors treat characters and characters treat themselves, becomes a sign of her late achievement.

Few would argue that *Dear Life* is any more accomplished than earlier work, story by story, but her later style more starkly achieves thematic goals suggested by earlier examples, simply by progressively casting off narrative ploys that no longer serve her purpose. Her willingness to revise assumptions of authorial control first questioned by Henry James—which have nonetheless endured—involved adjusting techniques of story-telling that subject characters to strict imaginative oversight, instead extending more autonomy to them.[1] Munro's early collections reveal a habit of summing up and narratively anticipating events, in what becomes a means of controlling the flow of her story more fully as events are linked into a self-conscious pattern. She seems, in short, still bound by an omniscient impulse, either via an impersonal narrator or by adopting a first-person perspective. *Dear Life*, by contrast (along with a handful of stories in decades preceding), openly embraces sheer narrative uncertainty, often leaving the reader (and characters) in mild suspense or utter confusion, adrift in a less judgmental, more tentative state. Munro more self-confidently encourages readers to exist

---

1. I have argued elsewhere that *The Portrait of a Lady* (1881) forms James's "first great investigation of the way in which selfhood is produced as a mutual process of cross readings" (108). And then added: "Indeed, one way to think of the end of the novel is of Isabel finally escaping the frame, evading those of us who ask what she will do. It almost seems that she has decided to abandon the novel itself, as if she saw us watching her and refused any more to submit to our plots. That, of course, is the one way to ensure we persist in making them up" (109).

in half-knowledge, in the "chaos" of characters' (and readers') own lives. It is that shift to calmly accepted uncertainty accompanied by a nimble narrative tentativeness that forms a gift Munro gives herself near the end of a preeminent career. Shedding the last sign of techniques she had been relinquishing for decades, she at last defers to a more accommodating style, simply (or rather, not so simply) committed to letting go.

The following discussion traces that process of letting go as the means to greater bewilderment, which Munro has repeatedly expressed in later years as her prime fictional goal. In order to defy expectations, to avoid a comforting predictability, her stories increasingly veer from a straightforward temporal organization, becoming relatively fluid and engagingly unsettled by the 1990s in an effort to achieve a certain narrative even-handedness. In the process, she mixes anticipation with recollection, history with fantasy, becoming more and more fragmentary in her presentation as a means of compelling the reader to reconsider the psychological patterns forged by events. Endings are less resolved, omniscient narrators less frequent, and a carefully calibrated, even somewhat mannered style is surrendered to one more interrogative, less direct, even expressionist.[2] Facts of biography, sometimes chronology, along with other explanatory details, tend to be neglected, as she embraces a more confident perspective on the confusion we inhabit in living our lives as well as in imagining others'. The unexpected not only characterizes her later style, then, but becomes the very point of it, with explanation or ready logic often suppressed. Of course, in a career that comprises fourteen impressive story collections, the unexpected emerges occasionally even in Munro's early efforts. And where to draw the line of "late" for an artist still productive in her eighties is hardly a clear-cut judgment, certainly not restricted to stories of only one final collection. As well, the argument for Munro's "late style" is defiantly not Said's sharp conversion to "intransigence, difficulty, and unresolved contradiction." Precisely because she represents instead his less notable but certainly less vexed possibility of "mature subjectivity," this chapter traces an overall continuity to her career. Earlier efforts are gradually modified and transformed in ways she had anticipated, in the process marking out newly accomplished, newly inventive narrative possibilities.

2. Virginia Woolf registered a similar effect in Chekhov: "Our first impressions of Chekhov are not of simplicity but of bewilderment. What is the point of it, and why does he make a story out of this? we ask as we read story after story" (Woolf 175).

I. Displacements and Architectonics

An intriguing place to begin is "Amundsen" (2012), the second story in *Dear Life*, if only because it unfurls a prosaic sequence of events that seems conventional, with chronology laid out straightforwardly (as if in exception to what I have claimed of Munro's late style): from Vivien Hyde's arrival at Amundsen as a new teacher to her secret engagement to the town's doctor, then to his unexpected abandonment of her. Automatically, the first-person account makes her experience central, but through the story's early sections it remains unclear how important others are, whether the headstrong student Mary or the narcissistic Dr. Alister Fox. The simple syntax fosters even more uncertainty about when the whole is being told: most likely as recollection, though shifts in tense throughout are puzzling. Increasingly, Munro has delighted in this bafflement, this disabling of determinate meaning, anticipated as early as 1987 when she admitted: "What I like is not to really know what the story is all about. And for me to keep trying to find out" (Hancock 196). Alternatively, she confessed at the same time: "it's torture to look at one of my books because I just want to pick up a pencil and change things. And take out things, usually. I feel awful because I can't do it. When I read aloud at readings I do. I change as I go along" (Hancock 194). Yet as Ajay Heble later observed: "the central drama of her stories is often precisely that which cannot be recuperated" (18).

Stripped-down descriptions in "Amundsen" also prove enigmatic, and although dialogue reveals something of Fox's small-town pretensions, the basis of his change of heart remains suitably obscure. We learn something about him in the cruel act of discarding Mary's cookies on the snow just after first making love with Vivien, a gesture that dismays Vivien. But the insight seems woefully meager, as is any corresponding appreciation of her presumed affection for him. She painfully resurrects her story, barely revealing her feelings, as it becomes increasingly clear how little she actually understands: "Every turn is like a shearing-off of what's left of my life" (63). That simile for her confusion, and ours, might equally well apply to other late stories, where events accrue but knowledge likewise seems to change very little. Seducing her, proposing, then driving to their wedding, Alister abruptly changes course before dropping her off at the train with the briefest pat assurance. Yet we are no closer to fathoming what has drawn her to him, him to her, especially given his insolent self-absorption and her artless generosity.

The story seems constructed all but deliberately to leave questions provoked by kaleidoscopic perspectives, compelling readers to wander among projected possibilities rather than in some clearly defined space. Part of the brilliance of that narrative strategy involves how things are revealed unexpectedly.[3] The signal experience in "Amundsen"—of Vivien's unaccountable, perhaps merely naive attraction to Alister— seems to disappear, or register only through its echoes, its shimmering impact on the moments that surround it. And that central transformation occurs in concert with his own sudden change of mind, revealed belatedly in shocked recollection as they silently drive to drop her at the train station: "I can't do it, he has said. He has said that he can't go through with this. He can't explain it. Only that it's a mistake" (62). The very lack of clarification may astonish us as well as Vivien, though Munro feels no need to fill us in—quite the contrary, the power of the experience is registered as one that happens often in "dear life."

To reiterate, nothing narratively explains what might have prompted his reversal, or even when he actually utters these shocking words, with the first indication only disclosed in his abrupt declaration after lunch, at the end of some paragraphs of simple, stunned description as they rest in a parked car: " 'Just leaving,' says Alister, the man sitting beside me who was going to marry me but now is not going to marry me. We were just leaving" (61). Left without explanation, Vivien can only attribute his change of heart to some unrevealed conversation: "what he was saying before... What he was saying then had been terrible" (61), as if reminding herself retrospectively of what will happen prior to the event that has led to his abandonment of her. Moreover, her anticipatory excitement in driving towards the wedding in Huntsville— "Now that we are away... I turn my mind to the future... I expect... I have known all my life. I recall times... " (59)—is matched by her retrospective anguish—"And a moment later I would be glad even to go back to that time" (62). The narrative strangely moves both ways,

---

3. In "Haven," a similar leap of narrative occurs midway through, in the young narrator's remarkable anticipation of information: "given my uncle's soon-to-be-revealed opinions on the... " (122). Munro's *New Yorker* editor observed in 2012: "Often when I'm editing a story of yours I'll try to cut something that seems completely extraneous on page 3, and then when I get to page 24 I suddenly realize how essential that passage was. The stories read as though you had written them in one long breath, but I'm betting that you spend a lot of time thinking about how and where to reveal what." Munro responded that "I do a lot of fooling around with stories, putting things here and there. It's conscious in that I suddenly think, Oh, that's all wrong" (Treisman).

forward and backward, even as the central black hole of Alister's change of heart remains unseen, unheard, unexplained. Vivien's feeling at the end years later, after accidentally encountering Alister, of being "still dazed and full of disbelief" (66), is strangely enough the feeling she has had throughout at nearly every moment, with no sense of resolution and even less of epiphany—as if the story were constructed precisely to induce this pattern (so unlike Joyce or Chekhov, Faulkner or Hemingway).

Asked to pick her favorite story in *Dear Life*, Munro admitted "I'm partial to 'Amundsen,'" adding as explanation that "it gave me so much trouble" (Treisman). And the changes she made in the initial *New Yorker* version were substantial, indicating how much craft goes into creating Munro's signature bewilderment, shifting among perspectives and defying predictability. After the pre-wedding description that "We are going to Huntsville," for instance, she added the ironic sentence, "We have begun the day that I am sure I will remember all my life" (59), a sentence that first reads expectantly, and on rereading flickers with irony. Earlier, describing Vivien's response to arriving in town, Munro added: "So still, so immense an enchantment" (33), making even more explicit Vivien's state of consciousness. Moreover, a long italicized list of classroom reminders that Vivien declares are "out of place here" (39) is postponed two pages later than the *New Yorker* version, where it anticipated not only her teaching but her experience of the school building itself. The *Dear Life* version informs us immediately following her deflowering—which she found unexpectedly passionate (as if, ironically, experienced instead as its opposite, a more natural flowering)—that "Imagination, as it turned out, might be as good a preparation as experience" (56). None of these separate textual changes decisively alters our view of Vivien, though their very creation suggests how fully Munro assumed her final stories remained far from final, essentially unfinished, always in progress.[4]

Importantly, these inventive series of displacements are assumed to form as much a syntactical as a thematic strategy. Isla Duncan has recently argued that "ellipsis is a distinctive and pervasive feature of Munro's narrative art" (153), pointing to "the frequency of parenthetical structures that disrupt its fluency. These are indicated by correlative

4. Though not invariably. "Haven," for instance, is the same in both its *New Yorker* iteration and in *Dear Life*. "To Reach Japan," moreover, has only minor emendations from its *Narrative* version. "Train" alters little in terms of edited prose, though curiously Munro transposes the white spacing among sections to break up the narrative differently.

punctuation marks—pairs of brackets or dashes" (154). Mark Levene
ups the ante by claiming that "in Munro's world, where categories never
hold—happiness and unhappiness, accident and purpose, fact and
fiction—parentheses may be anything but conventionally parenthetical,
something explanatory, an afterthought. Often Munro makes parentheses work in their ordinary, subordinate way; even more often she
does not" ("Alice" 157). Both critics address Munro's entire career, and
may actually be registering not syntax but semantics in dwelling on
general gaps in a story's time line. But in fact, parentheses are as rare in
her work as ellipses (and non-existent in *Dear Life*), though dashes
do proliferate in earlier stories, serving a similar purpose. For Judith
Miller, perhaps surprisingly, Munro can best be seen as a "mystery
writer... Where shades of meaning are multiple, where language rarely
means what it seems to mean. Where conclusions are suspect and
motives well hidden" (44). As she adds parenthetically: "all those commas make me think there is something even more sinister going on"
(49). It is as if Munro were self-consciously offering an authorial nod
to all that remains untold through the screen of presumably odd punctuation, making the reader aware of a persistent need for inference in
response to the pauses and hesitations that often mark her stories.

We look for clarity at moments when suggestion is all that suffices.
Meanwhile, the prospect of a clear, uninterrupted view of events or
feelings or relationships is deferred if not quite disrupted in the very
process of reading, reminding us of what we do not, cannot, and probably never will know. In this, her vision accords more sympathetically
with our conventional perception of life as we live it than with the
presumed understandings that inform so much of our literature, where
authors inhabit their characters' consciousnesses or provide overviews
of how relations supposedly function. Granted, this has all formed a
hallmark of Munro's lifelong style, though her later vision confirms
increasingly how little we can learn from what we do, even as delight
emerges in possibilities quietly lived through.

Examples from *Dear Life* reveal an almost self-conscious pleasure in
the indirection that has long marked her stories, arousing expectation in
their very denial of anything like full comprehension. One way to assess
Munro's continuing angle of vision is to take her provisionally at her
word, teasing out the implications in a provocative 1982 description of
her preferred approach to others' work. For in doing so, she describes

a prospective ambition not quite realized, at least as deftly as she would over the next three decades:

I can start reading them anywhere; from beginning to end, from end to beginning, from any point in between in either direction. So obviously I don't take up a story and follow it as if it were a road, taking me somewhere, with views and neat diversions along the way. I go into it, and move back and forth and settle here and there, and stay in it for a while. It's more like a house. Everybody knows what a house does, how it encloses space and makes connections between one enclosed space and another and presents what is outside in a new way. This is the nearest I can come to explaining what a story does for me, and what I want my stories to do for other people.

So when I write a story I want to make a certain kind of structure, and I know the feeling I want to get from being inside that structure.   ("What" 332)

Munro plays out this analogy in an ebullient, run-on sentence whose rhythm expresses her own enthusiasm: building up "a house, a story, to fit around the indescribable 'feeling' this is like the soul of the story, and which I must insist upon in a dogged, embarrassed way, as being no more definable than that. And I don't know where it comes from. It seems to be already there" ("What" 332). A preference for beginning anywhere in a story has become the very premise of the story's apparent revelation, with what we might have presumed as essential material left out or delayed or otherwise bracketed. That preference has become a technique.

Thinking back on "Amundsen," we realize the narrative could function just as well by opening at a different place, certainly given Munro's architectural delight: "Once in a while I skipped lunch, even though it was part of my salary. I went in to Amundsen, where I ate in a coffee shop" (43). Or later, as Vivien figures out where Alister resides: "I was right about the house in Amundsen being where the doctor lived. He took me there for supper" (48). This leads just as unerringly to scenes capable of being read in either direction. Then again, the actual opening has its own spatial coordinate that offers a suitable entry for a story about the narrator's own lingering expectation: "On the bench outside the station I sat and waited" (31). The point is that we almost always know where we are architecturally in a Munro story, though in the midst of it, having started anywhere, we are in no better or worse position to grasp a narrative trajectory. As Michael Gorra observes of Munro's architectural analogy: "She has no peer in the pellucid ease with which she shifts back and forth in time, or changes one point of view for another. You will always know what room you're in, though maybe not how you got there. And sometimes in her pages we'll find a door that looks for a moment to swing open onto a dark receding hall—only to discover that it is almost immediately nailed shut before us" (Gorra). The idea of narrative as architecture is itself at once provocative and disarming, with temporal spaces presented as somehow magically physical.

Perhaps more astonishing than the unusual architectural analogy for narrative sequence is that Henry James initiated a similar idea more than a century before. At first, it seems that Munro inverts James's meaning when he declares that "The house of fiction has in short not one window, but a million . . . every one of which has been pierced . . . by the need of the individual vision" (james 7). Yet on reflection, a sly kinship emerges in his claim for an "individual vision," revealed as he describes having placed his main character as a "precious object . . . in the imagination that detains it, preserves, protects, enjoys it, conscious of its presence in the dusky, crowded, heterogeneous back-shop of the mind very much as a wary dealer in precious odds and ends, . . . is conscious of the rare little 'piece' left in deposit" (james 9). Munro's notion of walking randomly through a house, room by room, expands inventively on James by dealing with his analogy literally and then effectively translating its terms. Instead of an imagined character, invented by an author and treasured in turn by the responsive reader, Munro seizes on the imagined reader as a figure whose inventive choices of where to begin and end free the narrative from authorial control. For both, however, an architectural analogy reveals how fully character and narrative sequence depend as much on readers as on writers, or as James elsewhere said, "the reader does quite half the labour" (james, *Theory* 321).

If the architectonics of narrative have rarely been defined so literally, Munro intriguingly expanded on her "surprise" claim fifteen years later:

You go inside and stay there for a while, wandering back and forth and settling where you like and discovering how the room and corridors relate to each other, how the world outside is altered by being viewed from these windows. And you, the visitor, the reader, are altered as well by being in this enclosed space, whether it is ample and easy or full of crooked turns, or sparsely or opulently furnished. You can go back again and again, and the house, the story, always contains more than you saw the last time. It has also a sturdy sense of itself, of being built out of its own necessity, not just to shelter or beguile you.

To deliver a story like that, durable and freestanding, is what I'm always hoping for. (Munro, "Introduction" 34–5)[5]

The point seems to be that spatial imagination informs a temporal sequence, and that the revelatory independence of her reading experience depends on the freedom of physical indirection, with nothing constrained or entrenched by sequence.[6] Her architectural analogy suggests stories could conceivably start anywhere, then be read by either continuing onward or (as she suggests, if whimsically) going backwards (say, section by section). The exhilaration we feel in such narrative situations would seem to lie in finding that singular events do not align with conventional premises of incremental progression, but correspond instead to the idiosyncratic ways we more generally experience them. Sequence in reading, as in life, is simply the narrative act we perform on the disarray of our experiences, and Munro's "architecture" invites multiple perspectives and alternative insights. As architect of the stories she authors, those perspectives are carefully planned; but as readers, we are free to traverse her stories in different ways at different times. As Coral Howells has observed of this analogy, "a methodology might be developed for reading Munro's later stories where instability and irresolution characterise her narratives of human behaviour alone and in relationships" (86). The effect of walking erratically, in suspense, from room to room, shifts as we go, often taking future knowledge for something already known or experiencing an event yet to occur as (in Freudian terms) something secretly desired, otherwise avoided, merely indeterminate.

Few have taken Munro up on this analogy, though W. H. New is among them, offering an incisive reading based on starting smack in the middle of a collection, on p. 117 of a 233-page book, and grasping

---

5. Importantly, Munro's architectural analogy differs from Joseph Frank's discussion of "spatial form" among high modernists, who "ideally intend the reader to apprehend their work spatially, in a moment of time, rather than as a sequence" (9). Their effort was to create a "spatialization of form in a novel" or poem during which "the time-flow of the narrative is halted" (15).

6. Still, it is intriguing that given Munro's premise of starting anywhere, she revises and alters sequence so intensely. As Coral Howells states of multiple versions: "The drafts show Munro experimenting with the different kinds of significance that events may assume when they are put together in different orders, as if events in themselves have undecodable meanings and can only be taken account of by being fitted into a narrative framework constructed by the storytellers (who include, of course, Munro herself)" (99–100).

what ensues and what it means through that erratic technique. As he argues, by "reading backwards and forwards" from the middle of a story collection, he is able to recover Munro's recognition of "not just the potential arbitrariness of meaning, but also the possibility that when conventions are ignored, a surprise can startle one into insight" (127). That approach leads to a "dance with words" (128), in New's apt description, underlining an oddly compelling lack of narrative necessity even in middle-period stories. That strategy might well be extended further, from stories to story collections, engaging the question of their sequential ordering, since the same structural logic that normally dictates a narrative sequence of scenes in a story would seem as well to govern the sequence of entire stories in a published collection.[7] More often than not, critics read stories individually rather than inquiring how they work together in sequence, influencing each other. Rarely do we wonder about advantages of beginning anywhere in a story, or in a sequence of stories, to savor how fully our reading experience might be altered or enhanced.

Not only does that indeterminacy among readerly choices match Munro's habit of creating different versions of stories, the approach implicitly precludes the possibility of epiphany, or some larger convergence of consciousness and insight.[8] Robert McGill goes even further in arguing, "Alice Munro's fiction challenges any inclination her readers may have to attribute development to individuals, regions, or humanity as a whole. Repeatedly, her stories question the notion that a person who grows older necessarily grows wiser or more mature" (McGill 136). Munro herself would seem to agree: "I don't see that people develop and arrive somewhere. I just see people living in flashes" (McGill 136). Instead of gaining knowledge or developing psychologically or maturing

7. Certainly, this authorial ordering informs our conventional understanding of books of poetry (Yeats most prominently, but also Frost and Stevens). Yet students often admit to reading story collections out of sequence, in a pattern anticipated by Munro's claim for reading individual stories, and greater attention might be paid to the semantic consequences of that practice. Consider as well David Lynch's response to his new production of *Twin Peaks*: "in these days of binging and streaming, he is O.K. with however you want to watch it. He even suggests, with a smile, that the best approach may be to view the parts out of order. 'You know, the projectionist once in awhile would make a mistake and put reel four before reel two or something,' he says. 'People still made sense of it.'" (Bhattacharji).

8. For others who deny Munro offers epiphanies, see Crouse (57–9), Howells (94), and McIntyre (65–6). For two who somehow see epiphanies in Munro's stories, see Franzen (291) and Crouse (53).

emotionally, her characters remain largely untransformed, unimproved, more or less the same. They live largely in the moment, intensely responsive to their experience but rarely presuming much can be learned from it. And the "flashes" that constitute their hours and days are heightened incandescently by the discontinuities of a narrative strategy that Munro has honed for decades, though making it progressively less obvious.

Even a late story like "Amundsen," which seems to hew to chronology (or as Russian Formalists termed it, *fabula*), might well be read beginning at any point (in a new narrative configuration, termed *syuzhet*), helping to explain the reader's ever uncertain sense of narrative control. Of course, different meanings ensue from different entrance points absent the knowledge gained from earlier segments, which seems part of Munro's intent in making her segments *not* build on one another. Consider opening six pages in, with "I had not been there a week before all the events of the first day seemed unique and unlikely" (37); or five pages further along, with "He evidently thought me a bother and a fool. I discovered at lunch, from the aides, that somebody had not survived an operation that morning" (42). Or even consider Vivien's eagerness in early April as our introduction: "We are going to Huntsville. Going to Huntsville—our code for getting married" (58). Each of these works to explain an emotional response that then, as we read further (or even backwards in sequence), is reversed or reinforced in creating an equally compelling narrative arc.

Other dramatic entry points would work as well, including Vivien's "I could wish now to go back to what he was saying before" (61), when she first realizes she is being jilted. Or perhaps simply the closing scene, bordered by white space, when she admits, "For years I thought I might run into him. I lived, and still live, in Toronto" (65). That reversal of sequence, opening with the closing, may diminish suspense but once again offers another intriguing perspective. In short, this experiment in rearranging one's approach does more than confirm how much sequence matters in altering our reading (the typical point argued by Russian Formalists). On the contrary, Munro would seem to say, sequence finally does not matter as much as one would like it to, since moments become simply that, moments, with disappointment or remorse or development and revenge remaining beside the point for her. The marvel of the story and its dis- or un-organization is how it maps a relationship that turns out not to be one—leaving Vivien simply and utterly bewildered.

II. Earlier Patterns

Rather than accepting slicing and dicing as a serious critical blueprint, we might welcome the analogy as a reminder of Munro's evolving narrative imperative, which grows more obvious in the second half of her career. Beginning in the 1980s, coincident with interviews that announce her preferences, stories distinctively alter so as to resist predictable sequence, to flout closure and resolution, to embrace a certain serendipitous rhythm. Seizing on a less regulated, more free-flowing narrative schemata that spills among "connections between one enclosed space and another," her narratives more self-consciously seem to resist the change she earlier celebrated, as if "dear life" were now understood as unending, dramatically reduced to mild waves. If that strategy is disconcerting, it should also induce caution among critics disposed to settle interpretations before the fact. For by smoothing out unstable assumptions and prematurely aligning expectations otherwise left for pages in uncertainty, they ignore the state of uncertainty we so often feel even after having finished reading, much less before. And because Munro profoundly shapes her strategy of indirection well prior to *Dear Life*, earlier stories help us to see it as it emerges and develops.

In her first four collections, her stories tend to offer a predictably straightforward chronological sequence, forming at once part of their power but also registering a mildly more controlled perspective than she later found effective. As well, they move towards concluding insights, sometimes emerging from contradictory moments, that sum up or otherwise conclude what has transpired: "There is nothing you can do at present but put your hands in your pockets and keep a disaffected heart" (*Dance* 29); or "I am a grown-up woman now; let him unbury his own catastrophes" (*Dance* 88); or "because I like for people to think what pleases them and makes them happy" (*Something* 66). Yet this convergence of narratives tightly focused and richly detailed into assured revelations came to seem less "chaotic" than Munro found warranted her interest, and with *The Moons of Jupiter* (1983) she moves in a newly experimental direction, threading multiple accounts together, moving forward and backward in time. "Turkey Season" takes memory itself as its subject, with a narrator thinking back to her first job in the opening sentence: "When I was fourteen I got a job at the Turkey Barn for the Christmas season" (*Moons* 60). Thereafter, the narrative weaves in and out of that seasonal occupation, as she reviews relationships only clear to her retrospectively, including a worker's sexual orientation: "I think that probably he was, but maybe he was not. (Even considering what happened later, I think that.) He is not a puzzle so arbitrarily solved" (65). As she admits, "All this was what I wondered at the time. Later, when I knew more, at least about sex . . ." (74). And "Later still, I backed off from this explanation" (74). Critics have often reviewed this as a story about perceptions of sexual orientation, though it might more accurately be described as a story about narrative reconstruction itself, with the narrator continuously correcting herself. What seems new here is not so much her willingness to suspend judgment or mull over the past, but the way in which her prose itself embodies that wavering perspective.

In the same collection, "Accident" turns likewise from straightforward chronology to the dramatic intersection of past and present, depicting an affair between high school teachers punctuated by his son's fatal car accident. The unfolding tragedy is obviously the death of a child, but the looming presence haunting the whole is curiously the omniscient narrator, who stands aside from the woman's perspective: "It is in imagining her affair to be a secret that Frances shows, most clearly, a lack of small-town instincts, a trust and recklessness she is unaware of; this is what people mean when they say of her that it sure shows that she has been away" (*Moons* 80). Later, the narrator declares assuredly of the adulterers and their friends: "They were all in their early thirties. An age at which it is sometimes hard to admit that what you are living is your life" (82). Coalescing around an accident that has bound the adulterers together forever, leading to their marriage, what seems striking is not only the shifts in time and perspective (past and present, Frances and Ted), but the shifting alignment of the narrator with Frances's point of view, at times sympathetic, at others judgmental: "If he had not gone out in the snow that day to take a baby carriage across town, Frances would not live in Ottawa now, she would not have her two children, she would not have her life, not the same life. That is true. She is sure of it, but it is too ugly to think about" (109). It is as if the very linkages welded by accident had, through the oscillating narrative sequence and the narrator's dissociated perspective, been transformed into a weirdly self-confirming logic that sees their relationship as sheer fate.

A decade later Munro, well over sixty, confidently revealed how fully she had mastered the "chaos" first aspired to in *Open Secrets* (1994), perfecting the mercurial, indeterminate state that struck her as a desirable end in itself. "Carried Away" leaves the reader in a state of complete (and delightfully divided) uncertainty about its central characters, questioning whether the narrator's epistolary romance with Jack Agnew is resolved by death or not. When she later meets with him, is he a hallucination or a ghost? The narrative traces an evocation of love lost, somehow misplaced, but does so through a life laid out sequentially from 1917 to the 1950s, in something like a temporal lockstep that introduces information belatedly. Munro masters this trajectory over Louisa's life, focusing on her consciousness of what seems lapsed even as it is casually recollected. At the end, she presumes she must be talking with the ghost of Jack Dowd dead: "Oh, what kind of a trick was being played on her, or what kind of trick was she playing on herself! She would not have it" (49). Munro's triumph lies in evoking so compellingly Louisa's stupefied consciousness in the face of such confusion, despite her clear memory of what must have happened. It was like "going under a wave. She had gone under and through it and was left with a cold sheen on her skin, a beating in her ears, a cavity in her chest, and revolt in her stomach. It was anarchy she was up against—a devouring muddle. Sudden holes and impromptu tricks and radiant vanishing consolations" (50). The story's closing paragraphs now disclose Louisa's fading recollection of securing a job at the local library when only in her teens, as if time itself could rope in all the memories that intervened between early and late. Importantly, once again, this sweeping analeptic leap reminds us how easily it would be to read the whole in any direction, returning her to her still untrammeled youth at the end.

That reliance on chronology even as the narrative seems to interrupt itself characterizes the collection, most dramatically in the title story, which opens with Heather Bell mysteriously drowned on a hike (the result already anticipated!). The story then unfolds as a series of hiccups, with Maureen thinking back, recollecting, persistently resisting the account of her friend's untimely death, refusing to discuss it with her other friend Frances, who accompanied them on the hike. Still, a flashback to the event obtrudes, as do other recollections and news reports: "She was thinking now of the way the night's long adventure began, at camp" (138), when playing Truth and Dare she recalls "*I dare you to run away.* Was it possible?" (139). Heather's body is never found, the possibility that she escaped alive is regularly returned to, and Maureen realizes in closing that "she has life ahead of her" (160) despite the open secret of what we presume is Heather's uncertain status.

Throughout the stories of *Open Secrets* (1994), nearly all set in Carstairs, we wonder at not only the order in which they are presented, but as well at the regularly ordering principle behind each of the stories' relatively straightforward narrative organization, moving chronologically forward even while we are alerted to subjects ignored (as in "A Wilderness Station"): "I have left out something about how I was feeling but will leave it out no longer, due to the effects of a martini I am drinking now, my late-afternoon pleasure" (224). In "Vandals," we are informed that "She looked back on this moment as their real beginning. They both seemed uneasy and subdued, not reluctant so much as troubled, even sorry for each other" (274). The incremental accumulation of experiences that pivot on earlier incidents—whether Louisa's job at the library where Jack Agnew burst into her life, or Maureen's early disastrous hike with Heather—all seem to hold the lives together, bound like beads on a string.

Munro continues this way in her next collection, *Runaway* (2004), perhaps most obviously in "Chance," whose opening paragraphs are tightly cross-woven with temporal markers: "Halfway through June, in 1965 . . . About a month ago . . . Then . . . And shortly after that," as Juliet Henderson prepares to travel to Whale Bay to visit an older man who had briefly attracted her interest (48–9). Suddenly, a flashback occurs to a train trip "six months ago" (51), as she recalls abruptly withdrawing from a stranger next to her, who kept peppering her with questions, only later to learn he jumped from the train after she stood up and left him. Of course, whether that sequence proved mere correlation or was causation instead is all part of the unanswered narrative question, though she is left nonetheless convulsed by self-lacerating regret. The unfolding of memory in ripples of pain is part of Munro's achievement here, as if she were exploring the disruptions in our sense of the present and of the past, both intermingling. That mixture begins ever fortuitously, as the story's title declares, though the fallout occurs in a cycle of stories about Juliet whose titles are likewise revealing: first "Soon," then "Silence" all in chronological sequence more characteristic of her early efforts (and unlike Dubus, as we will see, presented one immediately right after the other).

Still, even chronology is never merely straightforward in Munro, at least as experienced in the moment, reflected in the regimentation of temporal adverbs that continues even here, as Juliet considers her own uncontrollable visceral response to the stranger: "She would not have said, afterwards, that he was remarkably ugly" (55), with that sequestered adverb "afterwards" offering once again a curious prolepsis. Later, the corrective gesture is repeated, in the narrator's reflection on Juliet's consciousness: "Never tell that to anybody. (Actually she did tell it, a few years later...)" (64). It is as if the narrative all but obsessively needs to keep straight the thoughts provoked by narrative itself, in Juliet's confession to the next man she meets of this strange chance figure who has galvanized the rest of her life. In the process, she repeats in detail the encounter already given, as the narrative circles back on itself. Now, on a similar train west to meet that "next man" Eric six months later, she recalls their evening when he calmed her down, returning to her present reason for wanting to see him again before offering once more a flashback to her initial attraction to him. The tight circle of accident and fate, of sympathy expressed and withheld, of a past unrepaired and still reparable, occurs in Munro's narrative waverings themselves.

Finally, Juliet arrives at Whale Bay as a surprise for Eric, doing so once again in a pattern that self-consciously foregrounds the story's construction, reining in thoughts, regrets, expectancies, all according to the mixed aspirations and lingering remorse that Juliet continues to feel. No one does this better than Munro, though even she at this point in her writing resists giving over narrative control. Instead of simply allowing the story to unwind according to its own architectural dictates, she enforces a certain oriented perspective on the facts she divulges simply by drawing so much adverbial attention to the switchbacks and detours of recollection. Reverting to an earlier pattern in collections devoted to a single figure, Munro's two subsequent accounts of Juliet form a linked circle tracing her life with Eric, their child Penelope, her career as a radio interviewer, and Penelope's escape to a Christian cult. Yet throughout, "Soon" and "Silence" are traversed by similar prolepses, sudden flashbacks, regretted betrayals recalled and then mulled over endlessly.

In "Passion," Munro tracks a temporal trail with another character in giving her narrative over once more to the very weight of narrative self-consciousness: "Describing this passage, this change in her life, later on, Grace might say—she did say—that it was as if a gate had clanged shut behind her. But at the time there was no clang—acquiescence simply rippled through her, the rights of those left behind were smoothly cancelled" (182). As so often in her stories, much to the delight of readers, Munro once again focuses more attention on the process of recollection than the bleak facts recalled, with sudden leaps back to the present, long after, that often seem at the same time like mere dreams or vivid hallucinations. Openings are offered (in "Trespasses") that remain unexplained, reverting to her earliest stories in which we do not know for pages who the figures are (gender invariably kept a secret). And in *The View from Castle Rock* (2006), a series of stories emerge about figures long dead, involving scattered fragments of lives intersecting, moving generation by generation.

Munro clearly excites attention through narrative strategies meant to disarm, to inveigle, to confuse, with her concentration on ways in which we actively create meaning through temporal shifts, juxtaposing scenes, inhabiting the contradictions of consciousness, placing the reader (like the narrator) in actual encounters that seem much like those merely imagined. Still, one of the startling insights offered by her later stylistic adaptations is the way in which control so often is better left behind, with less need expressed to carefully outline when and where things happen, and more attention paid simply to states of unhinged consciousness themselves. In the following, I want to pursue the beguiling bewilderment that often accompanies Munro's late stories, bewilderment too often ignored by interpreters. For the persistent effect of her fiction has been to alter our state of readerly consciousness *as we read*, an effect that has grown even more pronounced in later work.

III. Bewilderment and Sequence

Munro has repeatedly exclaimed how boring she finds predictability, and how the customary narrative ploys do no more than reinforce expectations rather than inspire the "completely unexpected" she prefers (Wachtel 208). Over the years, that preference for a mildly perplexing narrative style has drawn on juxtaposition, temporal dislocation, and structural switches among centers of consciousness as a way of inducing a kind of disequilibrium. Her stories are "constantly shifting ground," Helen Hoy observes, in part due to Munro's "repeated conviction that 'Life is little jumps' rather than an orderly development, that people's characters and experiences lack continuity over time (and have different realities from their viewpoints than from observers'), that a belief in progress is unfounded" (17). This mildly cautionary view has become ever more pronounced in recent stories, in Munro's more loosened control of narrative sequence. The disruptive temporal configurations described above have become, in Joan Silber's description, "switchback time...a zigzag movement back and forth...that doesn't give dominance to a particular time" (Silber 45). By resisting sequence, Munro effectively destabilizes expected roles and presumed plans in stories that increasingly seek to explode conventional presumptions.

In a 2004 interview, questioned why women run from marriage, Munro responded in a fashion more telling about her own narrative vision than about marriage itself:

> I think they run away from a life...they look ahead and they can see what their whole life is going to be. You wouldn't call that a prison exactly; they run away from some kind of predictability, not just about things that will happen in their lives but things that happen in themselves. Though, I don't think most of my characters plan to do this...They just demand more of life than what is happening at the moment.   (Wachtel 206–7)

Of course, men differ little in this regard, as Munro would surely acknowledge in expressing her fascination with the enlivening value of capriciousness. "I like the change not to be the change that you thought you were getting into," she added, "and for something to come that is completely unexpected, as if life had a mind of its own and would take hold of you and present you with something you hadn't anticipated." (208). The allure of "chaos" as a driving narrative force continues, with Munro as fully devoted as a decade before to the appeal of fiction that engages readers through its bewildering enchantments, drawing us in only to stymy interpretation. Douglas Glover has extended this view: "Munro forges her style in the furnace of opposition. She plays with expectation and denial of expectation; she insists upon difference.... The truth is never the truth but a truth with codicils, conditions, caveats, perorations, and contradictions" (45). If that "unexpected" quality has been a signal feature of Munro's work from the beginning, her later stories offer a fuller swerve into suppressed possibilities, in the sudden shifts and bewildering sequences that occur more abruptly, apparent already with the opening story of *Dear Life*.

"To Reach Japan" lets us know immediately that we are smack in the midst of things, informing us of characters we have yet to meet, alluding to events not at all clear, deliberately refusing explanation for a narrative well underway. The story progresses by fluctuating temporally much like earlier stories, but with the effect of keeping the reader ever more off balance, in free indirect discourse that suggests the main character knows well what we have yet to learn. Still, discussions of the story tend to erase this initial confusion, simply filling in details whose absence initially bewilders the reader: "Once Peter had brought her suitcase on board the train he seemed eager to get himself out of the way. But not to leave. He explained to her that he was just uneasy that the train should start to move" (3). It is hardly apparent who Peter is; or whether "waving" Katy (invoked three sentences later) is the "her" of the story's opening focalization; or what links Katy to Greta, introduced three sentences later in turn. The confusion is intentional, leading readers into a quagmire that refuses to provide firm footing. The paragraph ends with Greta realizing "it was unnatural for people who saw each other daily, constantly, to have to go through explanations of any kind" (3), all but proffering an ironic gesture to the reader in need of such explanation, having been barely introduced to these characters. That opening confusion lasts some paragraphs, as Peter's Czech mother is recalled, her immigration to Canada described, when it slowly becomes clear that the whole review is undertaken from Greta's older perspective as she sits on a train with her daughter, considering her husband, mulling over larger feminist possibilities and her own diminished past.

The narrative, well before we realize it, is conspiring to keep us uninformed, meaning that not until the next section, marked off by a border of white space, do we realize the train is headed to Toronto where mother and daughter plan to house-sit: "That was why they were now waving and waving" (7). And then, a third segregated section inexplicably whisks us back nine months, as Greta recalls a tipsy Vancouver party from which she was driven home by a stranger visiting from Toronto. Yet Harris Bennett pointedly announces he will not kiss her goodbye, leaving her in cheerless longing for him nearly every day thereafter, in just the way that memory drives desire. When months later she accepts an anonymous offer to house-sit in Toronto, she writes him a brief but buoyant letter, "like putting a note in a bottle—and hoping it will reach Japan" (14). She then belatedly adds "only the day of her arrival and the time of the train, after the bit about the bottle" (15). Still, the title's evocation remains enigmatic, at once underlining the importance of her crush on Bennett even as it otherwise evokes an unassuaged yearning rather than some desire for an exclusive relation

with him. That conclusion seems confirmed by ensuing events on the
train that constitute most of the narrative, similarly disconnected
from her final meeting with him. The story clearly resembles "Chance"
in its theme, its central relationship and the transcontinental train trip,
though the careful adverbial structure of that earlier narrative, sorting
out for the reader the chronology of events, has been largely abandoned. We are left with a lingering sense that Munro has moved even
further along in the desire for undirected narrative possibilities.

In fact, "To Reach Japan" seems even more deftly attuned than earlier
work to Munro's belief in stories that can be entered anywhere, continuing sequentially or just as readily unspooling backwards. Each moment
seems simply a part of Greta's consciousness, linked to another, as the
story moves with no particular order nor necessary progression. In some
ways, this is akin to Munro's favorite motif of train travel, with narrative sections coupled together in what might be seen as a narrative
modeled on railways themselves. Robert McGill has argued for this
analogy between her stories and trains: "a site for similarly fleeting,
desire-laden encounters between readers and authors. Moreover, a
train's cars, separate yet joined, resonate in terms of the short-story
collection with its separate texts bound in one volume" (McGill 137).
Sequences segregated by white space reveal moments that self-declaredly
decline to build on one another, as we are shuffled from Katy's local
incomprehension to the larger "decade that they had already entered"
(20). The pattern is conveyed arbitrarily, all but unpredictably, both
temporally and as a state of consciousness. Displaced as we are from
Greta's frame of reference to Peter's, then to their daughter, then to the
actor on the train to whom Greta is inexplicably attracted, the narrative
catches us up in the sexual frenzy that so compels her, as she loses
awareness of where her daughter has wandered off. The mood turns to
momentary panic before the whole ends with their arrival at Toronto,
even as the historical "story" might just as readily have been tran-
scribed, with an entirely different effect, by a different narrative "plot."

The relief Greta feels seems to emerge from being thrust nearly out
of narrative itself, directly back into straightforward chronology: "now
that they were off the train. Then up some steps, or maybe there would
be an escalator, and then they would be in a big building and then outside, where they would get a taxi. A taxi was a car, that was all, and it
would take them to their house" (29). A simple syntactical rhythm
reveals her own psychological disconnect, right before Harris greets

them at the station as Katy pulls away: "She didn't try to escape. She just stood waiting for whatever had to come next" (30). And even these brief final sentences close on the bracing indeterminacy of the repeated pronoun, since at first the "she" seems to refer to Katy—though then we realize it could also be Greta, now needing to escape. Clearly, Munro here achieves an admirable obscurity that unsettles our understanding of what Greta happens to be feeling. The revision of the story confirms that indeterminacy by simply dropping the descriptor "Downcast," an adjective that otherwise makes the final sentence more obviously refer to Katy alone. It is as if Munro were perfecting a mode that, instead of clarifying events and perceptions, deliberately sought to make them mildly obscure, in need of further reflection.

To reiterate: the story offers a house one can enter variously, rendering vivid states of mind in the interval between leaving Peter at the Vancouver station and arriving in Toronto. Of course, the memory of the former need not precede the latter, but the point is that as syntax varies, as moments alter, memory keeps intruding, with the lived or recollected drama of the train ride punctuating the whole. Nine blocks of paragraphs are separated once again by white space, much as occurs in earlier stories, though here the effect is to emphasize how easily uncoupled these units seem, ready to be rearranged for a slightly different effect. As Ailsa Cox has observed, "these intricate elliptical patterns disrupt chronological succession. We read across the text, relating individual sections to one another, as if they were pictures at an exhibition; or, to use Munro's analogy, as if we were roaming back and forth between the rooms of a house" (Cox 58). Again, this narrative roundelay keeps the reader in a vertiginous state, even as nothing finally changes, with Greta coming to no particular insight or revelation. In short, reading the story in conventional fashion is no more (nor less) bewildering than reading it according to Munro's preferred anarchic practice. Or it may be more accurate to say that she deliberately fosters in her writing itself a certain narrative even-handedness, and in resisting the idea that stories should have a distinct beginning, middle, and end, inspires in us an invigorating disorientation.

A similar structure occurs in "Leaving Maverley," likewise segregated by white space with characters unconnected to each other. The opening section concerns Leah, finding work at the local cinema; the next introduces Ray Elliott, the married policeman who meets her; the following sections track Leah's elopement, her work for a local minister, and her later return to town with her two children in tow; in the sixth section, the health of Ray's wife Isabel fails; in the seventh Leah's children are taken away; and finally the story ends with Isabel's death. Yet clearly, one might easily begin at any point to work forward or back, an effect that embodies Munro's increasing ease with her later style and growing confidence in unstable sequences. The exhilaration we feel in such situations lies in discovering how little singular events align with conventional notions of progression, corresponding instead to the way we more generally experience our lives in the midst of dramatic acts, ghostly remembrances, vague affections, mild obsessions, always amid other moods and demands. As W. H. New has aptly observed of characters themselves: "Revelation reads as a *process* here rather than as a *moment*, for insight seldom appears as an epiphany, a flash of total comprehension, but more often as a slow recognition that knowledge is ambiguous, certainty an illusion, and fixity a false goal. 'Story' unfolds cumulatively, from wherever it 'begins'—the structural arrangement directing the narrative effect" (116). His point is that where we end depends on where we start, which is often as much a matter of chance as of choice.

IV. Mysteries of Character

Munro's belief in life's "little jumps"—with individuals rarely defined by integrated gestures or glimpsed other than sketchily—even seems evoked by her titles, which beginning with *Runaway* become more cryptic, notably allusive, reduced to individual resonant words. It is as if such solitary inscriptions were intended to point the reader in divergent directions based on how one chooses to read. As James Grainger has observed of *Dear Life*, "Even the story titles—'Amundsen,' 'Pride,' 'Haven'—have a fragmentary quality, sliding past the reader's peripheral attention like road signs on a dreary country highway" (25). Those vague introductory tokens contribute to the enigmatic aura Munro creates not only within but between stories, which differ in psychologies and actions but which share a disorienting narrative strategy. Consider the transition from "Gravel" to "Haven," both narrated by women about events in their adolescence, self-conscious about their accounts but blinkered by youth or ignorance as each looks backward. "Gravel" presents an unnamed child unable to fathom her sister's drowning death in a flooded gravel pit, living now as an adult teacher with the uncertain consequences, "routing out my demons" (106). And though the title clearly refers to the place where Caro jumped, it also alludes to the lies Caro had the narrator tell their mother: "I believe I still put up some argument, along the lines of she hasn't, you haven't, it could happen but it hasn't" (102). It is as if tangential considerations and adjoining questions lingered to one side during her entire life, leaving the narrator "still caught, waiting for her to explain to me, waiting for the splash" (109). Nothing at the end is divulged or explained, leaving only indiscriminate "gravel."

"Haven" (2012) doubles down on the confusion of an anonymous teenager's perspective, compelled to live with her doctor uncle and stay-at-home aunt. At first resisting Jasper's sexist regime, she is gradually won over. And the narrative modulates along with her own animated sensibility as an older woman recollecting her uninformed youthful perspective. In such a despotic household, it seems sensible that attention should be focused on the overbearing Jasper, then on his scorned sister Mona, while the narrator's preternaturally silent Aunt Dawn disappears into inexplicable gestures. Yet after Mona's untimely death, the narrative focus mutely shifts to the oppressed aunt, whose inscrutable presence is revealed as more compelling than Jasper's narcissistic efforts to vex her. The story's revelation lies in the gradual emergence of an adolescent's consciousness, aware of unfair gender dynamics in the midst of filial strife. And with Mona's funeral, her sister-in-law is liberated from Jasper's expectations: "perhaps she realized that, for the first time, she didn't care. For the life of her, couldn't care. 'Let us pray,' says the minister" (132). The ending draws us back to the story's beginnings, reminding us of Munro's architectural premise, to register what we have missed and how central has been Dawn's oppression, her vitality and silent resistance, more so than Jasper's smug misogyny and parallel to the narrator's self-conscious coming of age. Dawn emerges from the story's arras as an ancillary character whose inner life makes a claim on our attention, defying the narrative opening in favor of one that begins near the end. Nicely offering up a narrative that points to its own narrative occlusions, Munro reminds us again of alternative ways to tell this story, depending on where we enter it.

Regularly, crises in her later stories of one or another character's experience are buried amid the detritus, the quotidian, the irrelevant gatherings of a life.[9] Which helps explain why the significance of the title

---

9. Coral Howells suggests "a speculative essay might be written on the importance of rubbish heaps in Munro's stories, which sit alongside her well-ordered lists. These heaps

"Haven" pivots midway through: from Jasper's conventional masculine assumption that "A woman's most important job is making a haven for her man" (114); to the narrator's evolving appreciation of the protective haven this family offers, so different from her own Jellyby-like parents in Ghana; to Dawn's success at last in defining her emotional sanctuary, though it remains unclear for how long or how fully. Munro herself seems uncertain of the trajectory her story offers, later remarking on the "caricature" of an "ideal wife" who finally "lets herself be tired of it.—God knows what will come of that" (Treisman). The reluctance to render judgment, moreover, lies at the heart of a generous, sometimes bafflingly equivocal vision.

Munro delights in enforcing that view by disrupting casual assumptions, leading us to abandon all but immediately what we had confidently regarded up to now as true. Her deliberate method of breaking up sequence, introducing judgments less sanguine and assured in the aftermath of events, regularly offers a bracing jolt to our casual habits of routine interpretation.

That seeming advance on chaotic experience, unorganized by conventional expectations, affords once more a shifting template for her later stylistic ventures. "Leaving Maverley" initially focuses on the central figure in Ray Elliott's world, his wife Isabel, only to diverge toward the oddly waif-like Leah, whose life is one of odd turns, abandoned family, lost children, and finally mere saddened circumstances. Still, amid anecdotal conflations and abrupt narrative swerves, the story slowly traces his wife's fatal cancer and the effect it has had, as Ray, staggered by loss, becomes aware of a basic calculus: that "she had existed and now she did not. Not at all, as if not ever" (90). All he can feel is "lack," though that feeling itself prompts him to recollect as if by chance Leah's own grim situation, and suddenly to sympathize with "the loss of her children" (90) as he contemplates her in memory: "An expert at losing, she might be called—himself a novice by comparison. And now he could not remember her name. Had lost her name, though he'd known it well. Losing, lost. A joke on him, if you wanted one" (90). Loss becomes the story's relentless theme, endured variously in a disjointed assortment of neglected times and forsaken friends. Yet

have very little if any meaning in a literal sense, but they are presented as jumbles of signifiers whose appearance is usually deceptive" (Howells 94). Ailsa Cox concurs: "Munro is fascinated by detritus, junk and jumble—for instance, the optometrist's equipment and the sunken car in 'The Love of a Good Woman'" (Cox 41–2).

even as the story recounts the painful experience of evanescence, leaving one with only remnants of memories themselves fleeting and broken, it suggests something of the larger narrative form's own elusive grasp of character. Recollection (and its failure) become the very coin of narrative, reminding us of what so often occurs with stories themselves: of that familiar condition we feel days after reading a story, of being transformed yet because stories are so short, unable to recall details or names. Without quite being aware, we come to realize that this story of half-knowledge and loss is in fact a meta-narrative of the form itself, based on the indirections we nonetheless frantically track down.

That theme expanded is characteristically Munro's own, as she self-consciously avowed in 2004 about *Runaway*, admitting the collection was "darker" than earlier ones: "Memory shapes many of the stories: that relationship between the older and younger selves in a life" (Wachtel 219). Focusing on memory, playing narratives back and forth as a means of registering present and past, she reveals how often the two fail to align. Narrative simply misrepresents as the very basis of its performance, with life offered up as a process of recollection always awry, rarely on track with experiences that prompted the recollections themselves. As Ajay Heble points out about a story from her second collection, already "Munro's fascination with the transforming, fiction-alizing power of memory results in the reader's inability to determine whether or not events presented in the fiction have actually, within the context the story provides, taken place. By invoking a kind of hermeneutics of suspicion, a poetics of mistrust, Munro suggests that nothing in her fiction is as stable or transparent as it may seem" (Heble 82). That "poetics of mistrust," moreover, evolves in tantalizingly convoluted forms through her career.

Ray's initial failure to recall Leah's name, along with his final recovery, offers curiously enough a partial assuaging of his own loss, in the testament memory sometimes offers to the paradox of life always in the process of being forgotten. Intriguingly if ironically, Munro's own memory of the story is itself revealing: "In 'Leaving Maverley,' a fair number of people are after love or sex or something. The invalid and her husband seem to me to get it, while, all around, various people miss the boat for various reasons. I do admire the girl who got out, and I rather hope that she and the man whose wife is dead can get together in some kind of way" (Treisman). Again, Munro appears unsure of what might ensue in her own story, though in expressing this sentimental hope she reveals how even the author can misrecall the deeper resonances of loss she has imaginatively evoked.

V. Designs, Developments, Versions

Repeatedly, stories in *Dear Life* conclude with characters failing to appreciate their experiences or to adequately assess their own lives. Similar as that may seem to earlier stories, the strain of bewilderment has become more pronounced in narrative omissions accompanied by a more dramatically swerving sequence of scenes and temporalities. The effect of "Leaving Maverley" is instructive, with Ray Elliott shattered by a sense of failure that makes him no better able to comprehend the implications of his loss or to grasp its import. His bereavement differs little from the experience imagined elsewhere, of lives upended, with characters confused but rarely achieving peace. Munro's later figures remain as they were, untransformed, which may partially explain why she prefers short stories to novels, admitting to a preference for "people living in flashes." Robert McGill expands on this admission by observing that "although recursion and review encourage one to see things that one has not seen before, they do not necessarily transform one into somebody new and improved. Munro's skill in presenting such anti-epiphanies is one of the reasons critics have noted the significance of the momentary in her work" (144).

The conclusion to "Amundsen" all but makes this observation explicit, when Vivien (jilted years before, long since happily married) bumps into Alister Fox in Toronto: "For me, I was feeling something the same as when I left Amundsen, the train carrying me still dazed and full of disbelief. Nothing changes really about love" (66). And, one might add, about life. Even when an alternative possibility presents itself—in the conclusion of "To Reach Japan," when Greta is finally embraced at the Toronto station by Harris—the aftermath seems mystifyingly similar. Her sense of "shock, then...immense settling" (30) differs little from Vivien's response, as if disappointment in love paradoxically matched love's satisfactions, making the two hardly so disparate as we presume. The story perfectly captures Munro's refusal to believe in "time as brutally diminishing or hurting people. My feeling is probably too random for that. That we are liable to get hurt at any time and that things can get better at any time too. Mostly in my stories I like to look at what people don't understand" (Hancock 201). The comforting notion of some accumulated understanding, some larger vision of who and why we are, is utterly unforthcoming, now or ever. In answer to the question of whether "there [could] be wisdom in looking back," Munro bluntly responded as early as 1982: "No. I don't know if there could ever be wisdom" (Hancock 202).

Again, the arrangement of stories in her collections would seem at least indirectly to address this question, of whether even dissimilar accounts of love, abandonment, death, and the incursions of memory might offer a design larger than the divergent narrative logics that inform a single story. The linked sequences that earlier wove moments together from a single character's history (Juliet Henderson, for instance, in *Runaway*) have faded entirely, broken up into splintered accounts arranged in possible thematic alliances. Given Munro's own notion of sequence as something increasingly adventitious, the absence of linked narratives makes sense as a condition of her later style, though even then one wonders at the particular arrangement of rather different stories. *Dear Life* does seem more self-conscious than earlier collections on the advantages provided by certain perspectives—on who is seeing what and from however advantaged or blocked an angle—which may help explain the malleability of the stories themselves. From a casual reference to Japan, to small-town life in Amundsen and Maverley, to gravel pits and havens and trains: the sequence seems hardly linked or otherwise compelling *as* sequence, making it once again clear that one might well read in any direction, skipping along.

Only the concluding array of four "not quite stories" of autobiography, which move in chronological order of Munro's childhood, seem deliberately staked off, silently asking to be read apart. Their connection to the rest, even with the final entry, "Dear Life," is altogether speculative, as if the author's own narrated memories required being partitioned off from fictional constructions. Yet her final confession of seemingly unforgivable behavior towards her dying mother seems to encompass the dynamics of so many earlier stories, including the swerving reversal of her closing sentence: "We say of some things that they can't be forgiven, or that we will never forgive ourselves. But we do—we do it all the time" (319). And this admission of dispensation and grace, towards others as well as oneself, forms a thread that at last stitches the earlier stories together. Even so, something about the autobiographical sequence of Munro's final accounts resists being read in tandem with her fictional inventions (in contrast, as we shall see, to Lydia Davis's nonfictional creations).

James Grainger has acknowledged this broader, more encompassing view in *Dear Life*, arguing that Munro achieves it via a less obviously structured or prescriptive narrative strategy. Her later turn towards what he characterizes as an "expressionist form of storytelling" represents a more "liberating" account of figures familiar from earlier collections:

Many of the plots are marked by abrupt reversals and departures, premonitions and portents, and personalities twisted by strange religious and secular ideals....By actively suppressing so many chronological and biographical markers, these new works capture qualities of memory and consciousness that, in Munro's earlier stories, were embedded in larger, detailed narratives. The result is a less complete but more startling accounting of character types familiar to Munro's readers. We've encountered these people before, the reader thinks, but not with such stark, almost surreal insight. This is not entirely new for Munro. Her stories often turn on a seemingly inconsequential detail that moves to the fore of a tightly circumscribed life, tormenting and liberating the protagonist. In her new work that progression has become the dominant motif. (25)

Munro's hesitation at nailing down characters via customary narrative constructions is itself, according to Grainger, instrumental in defining a more sophisticated, moderated vision.

This may remind us of Henry James more than a century earlier revealing the ways in which authors like him invariably trapped and contained their characters, who nonetheless strive to break free from their creators' control. And the feeling that Munro's current stories seem more intense, more abrupt and unexpected, results from many of the strategies she had not only explored in earlier stories but held up for modification and revision. That re-examination matches what critics like Ajay Heble have asserted about "the ways in which she subverts and self-consciously renders problematic the very conventions within which her fiction operates" (3). Conflicting meanings seem to proliferate more readily in her stories, matched by fluctuations in time and heterogeneous perspectives. A dozen years before *Dear Life*, Mark Levene had surveyed overarching transitions in her style, arguing: "The sort of dense, complex, elongated structure Munro seems fascinated by now is one that resists, even denies, closure; it therefore reinvents the existential tension typical of the short story that she used to write. What her new fictions present are not so much conflicts between completeness and transience, but endless, parallel narratives to our own, in which not knowing is a shared 'pause, a lost heartbeat'... rather than a source of anguish" ("Vanishing" 854). Clearly, Munro's resistance to closure coupled with her acceptance of dissonance and contradiction works simultaneously at stylistic, narrative, and thematic levels, a method she has long persistently refined.[10]

That suspicion of accepted conventions has long been matched by an equally irrepressible impulse to alter her own stories in a series of different incarnations unlike nearly any other writer today. Separate publications of the same title become an occasion for fresh critical speculation about the meanings idiosyncratically promulgated by each revised version. Partly, this springs from an uncommon conviction that her stories exist independently of her, springing free of her imagining, almost as if nonfictional, thus requiring an adequate representation:

I pay attention to the story, as if it were really happening somewhere, not just in my head, and in its own way, not mine. As a result, the sentences may indeed get shorter, there may be more dialogue, and so on. But though I've tried to pay attention to the story, I may not have got it right; those shorter sentences may be an evasion, a mistake. Every final draft, every published story, is still only an attempt, an approach, to the story. ("What" 333)

Thus stories that require heavy revision are the ones that would seem to matter most, drawing attention back to themselves if only to demand another direction.

Consider "Corrie," which opens as the married architect Howard Ritchie arrives at a small town to advise the local eminence on restoring a church. Howard silently deplores Carlton's visibly lame daughter as conventional—"Spoiled rich miss. Unmannerly" (156)—and later speculates that her "forwardness... would become tiresome" (157). Still, stirred by coy post cards from Corrie's holiday in Egypt, he returns to town "for an unnecessary inspection of the church steeple, knowing that she had to be back from the Pyramids" (158). Just as that

10. Michael Gorra also observes the late change in her style: "Munro has always had an ability to take a narrative corner at speed, to whip a story into a new direction at the last minute. But the corners are now tighter than ever, single words or sentences that seem marked by an epigrammatic impatience with the whole business of endings; as though every tale might allow for an alternative version and no story is ever really over. Fully half the pieces in *Too Much Happiness* [2009] finish with such one-sentence paragraphs, endings that don't feel open so much as jagged or bitten-off. Their edges are sharp, never rounded into smoothness, and I wonder if this abruptness might be something like the formal expression of Munro's own age; a sense of no time to waste, and a sense too that all conclusions are arbitrary."

slyly inserted "unnecessary" adds a tacitly adulterous twist to his visit, suddenly the narrator blurts out: "He hadn't been sure how he would react to the foot in bed" (158). From this unceremonious point, their ensuing affair is chronicled, framed by a need to keep it "secret from his wife" (159) while appeasing the Carltons' blackmailing housekeeper, Lillian Wolfe. "The foot in bed" forms an abrupt revelation, akin to moments in other stories that offer a perspective too precipitously, as a narrator makes a jarring leap in succession. Later, after years of threat cut short by Lillian's unexpected death, Corrie is startled at the funeral to hear her eulogized as a beloved local figure: "The children adored her. Then the grandchildren. They truly adored her" (170). Again, the revelation is unanticipated, though even Corrie is moved to reconsider the familiar past on the basis of everyone's unforeseen esteem.

In a pattern common to other stories, a character is unexpectedly compelled to retrace events and relationships just as the reader must, surprised by emerging possibilities though no clear evidence is available one way or the other. Corrie quietly mulls over the facts, and suddenly "knows something. She has found it in her sleep" (173), wakened into consciousness of what seems to her like the larger betrayal that "There is no news to give him. No news, because there never was any. No news about Lillian, because Lillian doesn't matter and she never did" (173). Abruptly, everything appears to fit into place, with the semi-annual payments explained as Howard's own duplicitous accumulation, not the received story of Lillian's overt blackmail. Corrie "gets up . . . and walks through every room in the house, introducing the walls and the furniture to this new idea" (173) that links the "cavity everywhere, most notably in her chest." Strangely, the architecture of the house becomes her own interior, even as the story's own architectonics twist suddenly in a new direction. Compounding that analogy is the charged coincidence of Munro having made Howard Ritchie an architect, as the focus of a story that unwinds floor by floor, at once unpredictably and reversibly.

Yet this ending hardly forms the kind of "stage-managed" O. Henry conclusion that Michiko Kakutani dismissively blasts, and for two reasons: first, Corrie doesn't actually know for a fact what she configures as explanation; and second, more importantly, her surmisal apparently changes nothing about her own feelings. Indeed, were one to enter the story at any point and read in either direction out of sequence, the result might well surprise by simply making little discernible difference. As Charles May more broadly observes about the inherent incompleteness of short stories, and of Munro's "Corrie" in particular: "Although the novel may focus on cause-and-effect in time, the short story accepts that what makes characters do what they do is often quite mysterious. Munro's short stories deal with moments when people act in such a way that even those closest to them cannot understand what drove them" (May, "Living in the Story" 46). In fact, the story's very premise itself, of deep affection driven by secrecy, seems to founder under the weight of suspense and dread that has galvanized it. By the closing lines, we feel as increasingly uncertain about Corrie's response as does she. Howard's initial irresolution has become hers, remarkably enough, with her final ambiguous musing: "Too late to do another thing. When there could have been worse, much worse" (174). Escaped from the long shadow of blackmail, she now comes to suspect how the man she loves may have exploited her, kept her loyal, even paid for the pleasure, though a painful pleasure she now seems willing to accept. The allure of the story lies once again in our own unassuaged doubt about what we actually know.

Yet "Corrie" compounds these questions in a fashion indubitably Munro's own, since she published three versions of it offering distinct alternative interpretations that each prove challenging. In its third revision in *Dear Life*, Corrie actually sends a brief note to Howard, positive he has deceived her, yet willing to silently let it go ("who cares?"), and agreeing to continue their fractured relationship in the knowledge that his affection for her is still somehow real: "So that's the way they're going to leave it. Too late to do another thing. When there could have been worse, much worse" (174). The sentiment quietly invokes her anxiety at Lillian's supposed blackmail threat years before: "I could not stand for there to be an end of you and me" (162). The story's closing, that is, appears only to reiterate the emotional status registered midway through, with little in the interim having changed. The conditional mood remains fixed, confirming Corrie's uncertainty.

In the initial version in the *New Yorker*, on the other hand, she had deliberately foregone writing Howard about Lillian's death (here named Sadie), as she ponders implications of that knowledge and the uncertain consequences of acting:

But then there is a surprise. She is capable, still, of shaping up another possibility.

If he doesn't know that Sadie is dead he will just expect things to go on as usual. And how would he know, unless he is told? And who would he be told by, unless by Corrie herself?

She could say something that would destroy them, but she does not have to. What a time it has taken her, to figure this out. And after all, if what they had—what they have—demands payment, she is the one who can afford to pay.

When she goes down to the kitchen again she goes gingerly, making everything fit into its proper place.   (101)

The persistent reiteration of the conditional tense ("would…would… could say…would destroy") as she mentally contemplates "shaping up another possibility" at last steadies into a more secure self-possession by the end, with "everything fit[ting] into its proper place." Corrie seems willing, here as later, simply to hold on to the frail, adulterous relationship she already has rather than sacrifice it for something more forthright yet bare. That still falls short of being an epiphany, though it does adumbrate something of Munro's apparently scatter-shot style. Tellingly as well, Munro has altered the story's voice from first to third person, lending the whole a greater uneasiness coupled with a disquieting sense of mishap barely avoided.

Yet the intermediate version offers still another perspective, altogether different and more agitated, as if Munro could not quite settle on a response to Howard's presumed duplicity. Submitted for the *PEN/O. Henry Prize Stories* volume, this version extends the ending, lingering over Corrie as she ponders escaping town for good: "She has calmed down mightily. All right. But in the middle of her toast and jam she thinks, No. Fly away, why don't you, right now? Fly away. What rot. Yes. Do it" (409). The mental wavering back and forth not only points to her indecisive emotional status, uncertain of how she feels about Howard's suspected emotional betrayal, but as well to Munro's apparent unwillingness to end the scene. Teetering between self-possession and -abandonment, Corrie cannot choose between continuing with Howard and walking out intemperately, suggesting nothing has been resolved, leaving us still uncertain about her character and desires. We waver among three different versions—of blinding acceptance, of intemperate rejection, and of a calm willingness to let things continue as they are despite her anger—each of which offers a resolution that fails to satisfy the complicated, conflicting emotions aroused. The productive contradictions among these differing versions work much as the contradictions within Munro's unrevised stories: to reveal the way "dear life" pivots idiosyncratically, with the most adventitious of altered perspectives profoundly altering lives themselves.

It comes as little surprise that Munro openly admitted decades ago her resistance to endings themselves, having "often chopped" final paragraphs in her public readings (Struthers 9). As she once announced, "if I ever do a final edition of all those things, I'll drop the last paragraphs. God knows if I'm right or not. That is just the way I feel now." To which she cautiously added, "the point I'm making is just that it's not even that you are necessarily improving the story. You are telling it the way you see it now. And you have no idea what improvement means" (Struthers 9–10). Nothing else she has said so clearly reveals how Munro's stories exist indeterminately, confirming in revision her refusal to settle on a definitive meaning, opening up instead to contingent possibilities. Compounding that contingency is her preference for reading by starting (and ending) at any point, which alters our sense of them as we realize how skewed they are by our own angles of vision. Finally, that is a tribute to their power, both as individual stories and as part of larger collections. As W. H. New has observed:

Starting with the frame reads the book through a family filter; starting with the sequence probes perspective and arranges issues by gender, time, and disorder; starting in the middle purls outward to the edges in a running conversation about silencing and saying. So what happens at the ends of stories? What story do endings tell, and do they offer another approach to the book? *Endings*, writes the short story writer Clark Blaise, can be interrogative, stoic, rhetorical, judgemental; they can reach out, reassure, accuse; they can turn metafictionally back on a story or scamper playfully away from it.   (New 131)

Of course endings, one might retort once again, depend on where one begins, just as variations and versions of stories have a similar destabilizing effect on our reading. We need here to remind ourselves that the customary pleasures of closure, of personal growth, of life partitioned off into manageable narratives, is precisely the limiting gesture Munro wants to turn us away from.

VI. Conclusion, Understanding

The narratives that constitute *Dear Life* seem as unsettled as Munro's understanding of the titular phrase itself. Ever since childhood, she thought that it expressed a feeling that "you were kind of overwhelmed," even as it also suggested a sense of "joyful resignation,"

maybe of "something precious" (Awano 180). The phrase's very
ambivalence makes it a perfect title for this collection of stories that
often look both ways. Certainly "Dolly" presents itself so, as an account
of an older couple having decided out of apathy that they no longer
want to live, only for the narrator to discover her husband's former
lover arouses in her an intense jealous anger. Franklin gives her absolutely no cause, with the story revealing the irony of niggling irrita-
tions exploding unexpectedly in the midst of a joint commitment to
death—or as he confesses in emotional bewilderment, "Life is totally
unpredictable" (251). In an earlier version, the unnamed wife admits
her realization: "Strange. In the middle of my rage, it had seemed as if
we had gotten time back, as if there was all the time in the world to
suffer and complain. Or make rows, if that was what you wanted to call
it. Whether or not we could spare the time for that had never come into
it, no more than it would have done if we were thirty" ("Dolly" 80).
And that version ends as she calms down, wondering whether she can
recover the angry letter she has already intemperately posted to
Franklin: "That made me think about the conversation we'd had earlier
in the fall and our notion of being beyond all savagery and elation"
("Dolly" 80). Not only are these serene insights dropped from the
later version, but the whole ends with mixed feelings of "rage and
admiration" at Franklin that "went back through our whole life together"
(254). Again, Munro refuses a fixed perspective, much less closure,
registering how rarely that reassuring salve is ever offered in actual life.
What we are left with are conflicted accounts, possibilities that teeter
on the edge of first one, then another narrative sequence, dependent
on little more than a shifting emotional counterweight.

That willingness to vacillate among perspectives, allowing none a
privileged position, is what makes Munro fascinating yet irresolvable,
with serendipity erupting into the midst of ordered events. "Gravel"
exemplifies the mode, with a narrator haunted by the inexplicable
death of a sister, perhaps by mishap, perhaps suicide, in a narrative that
again resists the comfort of closure. The long-ago calamity persists in
defying final judgment, or even an intermediate assessment as the
narrator mulls over what might have precipitated so sharp a cleaving
of her own life. Yet even less wrenching moments can, for Munro, be
equally unsatisfying, with "dear life" disrupting expectation as much
through satisfaction as betrayal. "Train," unlike "Gravel" and "Dolly,"
refuses to depict its precipitating event, offering instead a peripatetic

account of a lifetime of aftereffects. Culminating the collection's preoccupation with trains themselves, it breaks into segments of Jackson's life, beginning as he arrives unexpectedly at Belle's rural farm, hopping off a train just before arriving at his home town for reasons that never become clear. The major revision to the original *Harper's* version is an additional early paragraph of proleptic explanation of all that follows, though it finally (perhaps predictably) seems as tantalizingly evasive as it is instructive:

Jumping off the train was supposed to be a cancellation. You roused your body, readied your knees, to enter a different block of air. You looked forward to emptiness. And instead, what did you get? An immediate flock of new surroundings, asking for your attention in a way they never did when you were sitting on the train and just looking out the window. What are you doing here? Where are you going? A sense of being watched by things you didn't know about. Of being a disturbance. Life around coming to some conclusions about you from vantage points you couldn't see.   (176–7)

The curiosity of that final sentence of life having "some conclusions about you" is a perfect late gesture toward the multiplicity of perspectives we engage, expressed here in a way that embraces metaphorically all the embodied perspectives of earlier stories. Jackson wants to "cancel" a past that keeps re-emerging in his future, caught in the endless loop that so often defines Munro's strategy of reading. That loop will bring him back to an old girlfriend he wants to avoid, though once more no reason is apparent. And again, the story all but demands we reread to make sense of this added paragraph, which evolves into a scenario (of "being watched," of "life around coming to some conclusions about you") that is like the story itself, characteristic of a simultaneously evasive yet engaging style.

Jackson lingers on, refusing to return home, remaining with Belle as handyman, then as platonic partner. The description of his transition to "the man he was now" occurs (as so often in Munro) as a contrast of characters: "Whereas Belle, so far as he could see, was stopped at some point in life where she remained a grown-up child. And her talk reinforced this impression, jumping back and forth, into the past and out again, so that it seemed she made no difference between their last trip to town and the last movie she had seen with her mother and father" (189). Apart from the fact that Jackson also seems "stopped" psychologically, however physically altered, the description of Belle's "jumping" talk reminds us of nothing so much as Munro's own nimble narrative leaps and swerves, not only in this story but elsewhere. The whole succeeds in jumbling time frames among their early years together, with Belle in the hospital being operated on for cancer, then Jackson abandoning her there to take a job collecting rents, followed by a chance eavesdropping on the high-school girlfriend he initially wanted to avoid by leaping from the train, setting everything else in motion. All this leads to recollections that thrust us unavailingly into the past, disorienting us at the turn to these decades-old memories. As Jackson ruminates about his experiences of sexual failure, of shyness coupled with social ineptitude, melding past scenes with present circumstances, he comes to regret having avoided Ileane Bishop. "She'd have forgiven him, yes, right on the spot" (215), he realizes, though his guilt is assuaged only as we vaguely perceive how unearned that guilt actually is, more self-generated than owing to any actual fault. Three days later, he leaves his job once again, to avoid Ileane once more.

Jackson's ceaseless need to move on becomes the story's driving motive, to escape (as we finally realize) from women who might gain an emotional hold over him. Yet we never quite learn why this should be so, rendering the narrative's persistent turn backwards as inexplicable as Jackson's dodging ahead. The story maps a spiraling biographical account that repeats without developing, reminding us of a certain emotional paralysis amid all of Jackson's agitated thoughts. Intentions vie with actions, expectations with events, as "all the time he's thinking this, he's walking in the opposite direction" (176). His initial offer to work for Belle turns into a singular sibling-like relationship, as years pass, then decades of quiet, sexless contentment that end in Jackson's discovery of Belle's breast lump. The narrative leap from the 1940s is announced abruptly, automotively (in an ironic shift), with "the second car that they had owned, a used one of course, that took them to Toronto in the summer of 1962" (189). The transition from a relationship of faux brother and sister to something like a long-familiar marital state has occurred all but unnoticed, though only after breast surgery does she finally admit to a tormented history: of her father's ogling her as a teenager that led to his shamed throwing himself in front of a train. His action had cast a pall over her adolescence: "he had changed us," she admits (197), casting her into "an abnormal state" (198). But we also realize that her revelation has opened up his own past to Jackson, for whom her admission drives him away three years before he reads of her death.

Coincidentally, Ileane reappears in his life, overheard as a voice in the next room that prompts him to ruminate over a lifelong of failures with women. Recalling the cause of his psychological isolation, he realizes he needs once again to sequester himself from Ileane as he successfully did with his stepmother's illicit attentions:

> Things could be locked up, it only took some determination. When he was as young as six or seven he had locked up his stepmother's fooling, what she called her fooling or her teasing. He had run out into the street after dark and she got him in but she saw there'd be some real running away if she didn't stop so she stopped. And said that he was no fun because she could never say that anybody hated her. (215)

But being "locked up" is only to confirm his aversive, recursive behavior, as Jackson once again moves on, no different at the end than the beginning, with Munro adding a concluding sentence to the *Dear Life* version that reinforces a sense of his simple repetition coupled with a lack of self-awareness: "Work there, sure to be work in a lumbering town" (216).[11] Interestingly, Munro's description of the story distinguishes it from her more familiar theme of women oppressed or misunderstood: "'Train' is quite different. It's all about the man who is confident and satisfied as long as no sex gets in the way. I think a rowdy woman tormented him when he was young. I don't think he can help it—he's got to run" (Treisman). But more important than its differences are the story's similarities to so many others: with disordered moments leading not to revelation; with narrative not working progressively, allowing us instead to start anywhere; with the reader left, like characters, in a state of mild (if entranced) bewilderment.

Dear Life forms a capstone to Munro's career, in bringing to fruition a vision honed for decades, perfecting narrative techniques, character development, chronological suspensions, and more as a means of disabling a reader's (and writer's) brazenly self-confident authority over what her characters do and say. Clearly, she cherishes a deference for them, honoring their dignity, resisting imposing some sort of design

---

11. Robert McGill observes that the titular homonym "evokes not only mass transportation but also a train of episodes. In doing so, the title suggests two divergent possibilities: first, that Jackson's life involves preparation for something, 'training'; second, that it involves mere juxtaposition, not development. As the story progresses, it confirms the second possibility: there is no clear line of improvement for Jackson in his life, and his experiences over the course of the story leave him no more prepared to face unexpected challenges or confront his past than he is at the outset" (146).

or judgment on their idiosyncratic motions. And more than the other three authors, she embodies a certain continuity of style that might best be understood as an intensified vision, one articulated early in the 1980s (her fifties) and brought to maturity in dozens of stories over the next three decades: of individual lives lived in a state of somewhat perplexed constancy, with little added sense of intellectual advance or psychological renewal.

Certain insights may be revealed at the end of her stories, but nothing actually changes, either in terms of a character's imaginative construction or our own understanding of what has taken place. The days simply continue incrementally, for all the untoward, occasionally exciting circumstances that entangle us. Contrary to conventional notions of narrative sequence that contribute to developmental gains—of experience leading to wisdom—Munro suggests that we simply continue, whether high or low, up or down. As she has stated outright: "I don't see life very much in terms of progress. I don't feel at all pessimistic. I rather like the idea that we go on and we don't know what's happening and we don't know what we'll find. We think we've got things figured out and then they turn around on us. No state of mind is permanent. It just all has to be there" (Hancock 214). The sole way of evoking that experience without misrepresenting it is through sequences that do not require a sequential mode, through characters who respond fully to events but without any sense that what they have supposedly learned will apply next time. The sign that this is Munro's distinctly late style consists in its ever starker concentration of a vision there all along, with characters adrift in the rhythms of an indeterminate narrative world that paradoxically makes them seem all the more intensely alive.

2

Trauma in *Dancing After Hours*

Were one to concoct a writer the opposite of Alice Munro, Andre Dubus might well fill the bill. And not for the obvious thematic disparities: that his stories explode with violence, or that the rules of Catholicism recur so often, or that alcoholism, casual sex, and military service form the persistent backdrop of his characters' lives. Rather, the most distinctive contrast lies in narrative strategies themselves, with Dubus turning dramatically from Munro's spatial, even architectonic mode of story-telling that defies a conventional, otherwise progressive understanding of experience. Instead, his stories build temporally, often chronologically, though just as often pivoting on a singular, explosive moment that transforms a character's consciousness unalterably. Given his profound spiritual faith, it is hardly surprising that he should be fascinated by the possibility of such epiphanies registered narratively, something entirely absent in Munro's otherwise peripatetic stories. Where she might seem to align with Chekhov's commitment to artful indeterminacy, he seems forcefully to prefer Poe's argument for dramatic *effect*. Unlike Williams, moreover, whose Protestant leanings tend to be citational and literary, Dubus regularly invokes Catholic doctrine itself in his fiction, as injunctions that create a continuing pressure of insufficiency and guilt. "I see the world as a Catholic does," he once confessed. "I didn't really know that that was a whole lot different from other people. I didn't know that there are people who perceive physical reality as the only reality of their lives. The Catholic Church is filled with sacraments, which are physical transactions with a spiritual meaning" (Dubus, "Conversations" 139). The surprise in this admission ironically emerges at how fully he himself was nonplussed that others did not share this presumption of the sacramental aspect of daily life.

Dubus's belief in the eviscerating power of fictional revelation came close to being devotional over the course of his career, expressed by him with ample caution accompanied by calm conviction less than a year before he died:

Wanting to know absolutely what a story is about, and to be able to say it in a few sentences, is dangerous: it can lead us to wanting to possess a story as we possess a cup. We know the function of a cup, and we drink from it, wash it, put it on a shelf, and it remains a thing we own and control, unless it slips from our hands into the control of gravity; or unless someone else breaks it, or uses it to give us poisoned tea. A story can always break into pieces while it sits inside a book on a shelf; and, decades after we have read it even twenty times, it can open us up, by cut or caress, to a new truth.   (49)

That profound belief in the capacity of stories to change us for good (at once fittingly and permanently) became increasingly the sign of the kind of stories Dubus wanted to write. And if more evident late than early, they were also curiously (and paradoxically) akin to Munro's growing notion of a certain mystery residing in her own fiction. Where her evolution defines a continuous lengthy arc in her career as the gradual fruition of earlier efforts, his late style appears as a more decisively abrupt conversion. It is as if he wanted to seize on narrative angles tested decades before in order to probe unexplored possibilities ever more dramatically.

Dubus tended in early stories to adjust narrative strains chronologically, building toward a mounting convergence in the present. Latterly, he more often resuscitates the past through recollection, testing retrospectively a series of still unsettled consequences. As it happens, that turn away from relatively straightforward narrative sequence accompanies a shift from Dubus's early fascination with Catholic doctrine itself (in its insistent behavioral edicts) to a more pervasive exploration of gospel imagery associated with the need for greater spiritual awareness. Violence dramatically escalates in his later work, with narratives focusing intently on insights achieved when expectation and recollection collapse into each other, and where time pauses and characters come to realize what they find genuinely important in their lives. A strangely humanizing quality of violence paradoxically reveals itself in characters reduced to a broadly egalitarian status, differing only in memories of intense, transfiguring experience, as if they were more or less the same except for those wrenching episodes they have been made to suffer. Therefore the most distinctive aspect of Dubus's late vision is the acquired capacity to remain alert, ever attentive to the moment, capable of responding with full emotional intelligence to an experience that words themselves cannot adequately appraise or even altogether recover.

This registers a dramatic divergence from the disturbed acceptance that frequently stamps Dubus's earlier stories, where firm if occasionally questionable Catholic precepts tend to hold sway. It is as if the obligation owed to orthodoxy, to canon law and doctrinal conventions, gradually lost its suasive power for Dubus, at least as narrative subject. The visceral intensity of his later stories hinges not simply on an escalation of violent events, then, but on the tension generated by a perspective less simply religious than profoundly spiritual in orientation, transfiguring common assumptions and pre-empting conventional narrative sequence itself. The cause for this change seems hardly to matter, though the change itself is reiterated variously as Dubus's signature moment, revealed in the possibilities of his concluding narrative epiphanies that persistently defy elaboration. Part of the marvel of his late style lies in the crisp concision with which he at once sums up narrative trajectories even as he finally avoids settling for a secure concluding meaning.

I. Rejiggering Expectations

Other stories illustrate more fully the salient features of Dubus's late style than does "At Night," though as the briefest effort (two pages, four paragraphs) in *Dancing After Hours* (1996), it provides a quick introduction. Everything converges on a flashpoint, compelling us to savor an event that is hardly rare (the death of a spouse) if nonetheless singularly memorable. The very opening consists of an all-encompassing claim that erases the novel to which the story might otherwise aspire: "She always knew she would be a widow; why, even before she was a bride, when she was engaged, she knew, in moments when she imagined herself very old, saw herself slow and lined and gray in a house alone, with photographs of children and grandchildren on a mantel over the fire. It was what women did, and she glimpsed it, over the years, as she glimpsed her own death" (169). In two sentences, a life and a genre both seem snuffed out, with the unnamed figure given a singular insight, somehow knowing she will be widowed almost before she is wed. The subject clearly differs from anything Munro would be drawn to, given the woman's self-confidence, fully aware of what she wants.

Indeed, her firm anticipation of adversity differs entirely from Vivian's bewilderment in "Amundsen" or Greta's addled behavior in "To Reach Japan." What makes this characteristic of Dubus and distinctive of his late style is the way expectation and recollection collapse, together and immediately. Before events are given, before a narrative even quite begins, we already know where it will end and feel deprived of the sequence.

Odd as this gesture may seem, it forms a reiterated salute in Dubus's later work, of inadvertently viewing something still to come even while swiveling obsessively back to scenes already past. Instead of the plausible novel that might unravel from this opening premise, what we get instead are three brief paragraphs, outlining the unnamed woman's entire wedded life as mere preparation for its abrupt demise, since that is the fate she awaits. The revelation she anticipates pre-empts the occasion of an epiphany, as if Dubus were self-consciously alerting us to the habitual practice of many conventional stories: one that has become so commonplace that, as Charles Baxter observes, "The mass-marketing of literary epiphanies and climactic insights produces in editors and readers an expectation that stories must end with an insight. The insight-ending, as a result, has become something of a weird norm in contemporary writing" (62).[1]

Yet here, paradoxically, insight occurs at the story's beginning, upending expectation, with an effect nearly the opposite of what we experienced with Munro: not of being able to enter the story at any point in its brief four paragraphs, but of locking us into a sequence of firmly ordered calculation. A final paragraph then grants us the intensity of a moment the wife has surmised all along, in fleshing out disappointment and desire, in a sustained conflation of dream and reality, anticipation and regret:

She rolled toward him and touched his face, and her love went out of her, into his cooling skin, and she wept for what it had done to him, crept up and taken him while he slept and dreamed. Maybe it came out of a dream and the dream became it. Wept, lying on her side, with her hand on his cheek, because he

---

1. "The language of literary epiphanies naturally has something in common with the rhetoric of religious revelation," Baxter states. "The veil of appearances is pulled aside and an inner truth is revealed. A moment of radiant vision brings forth the sensation if not the content of meaning" (55). Then he adds, "We watch as a hidden presence, some secret logic, rises to visibility and serves as the climactic revelation.... The world of appearances falls away, and essences show themselves" (58).

had been alone with it, surprised, maybe confused now as he wandered while the birds sang, seeing the birds, seeing her lying beside his flesh, touching his cheek, saying: "Oh hon—." (171)

At last, standing imaginatively outside herself, she watches them both in a scene that mysteriously inaugurated their marriage and simultaneously culminates it. They become one in this moment of final dissolution, a moment that at once extols their love and offers a valediction prepared long before. The very resolution she has always imagined for her life, in the death of her spouse, has strangely turned into her most vivid experience, though anticipated a lifetime before.

Dubus's earlier stories, despite their religious conflicts and crises, rarely treasure the kind of spiritual awareness that emerges so often in his late efforts. And the sacramental state of consciousness that emerges in stories like "At Night" seems generated by its author's later realization of the disruptive, even transformative effect of physical violence. Where other writers tend to focus on the aftereffects of violence, however, the recuperative, restorative gestures we make towards trauma, Dubus seizes on such moments as themselves both vivid and cathartic, with a redeeming capacity for personal transfiguration. It almost seems as if the less certain, less concentrated experiences traced so well in his early stories may have contributed to that realization. For as *Dancing After Hours* repeatedly displays, compressed evocations offer life at its most focused, independent of what happens to happen in them. The memorable intensity depends not on the activity itself but on our ability to move beyond the tiresome habits into which we find ourselves submerged. It becomes a matter of not taking anything for granted, living so habitually as to lose sight of the wonder of simply existing, enraptured by the moment. Through his fragmented later narratives, temporal configurations are rejiggered with past and present intersecting in newly transformative ways for the reader, as banal details are ignited by memories that do not let trauma cease but instead help characters find transcendent significance in the quotidian.

This is, once again, the burden of Dubus's own distinctive narrative drive towards epiphany (even in "At Night," paradoxically, which both anticipates and self-consciously inverts that drive). Late stories turn ever more calmly to singular revelatory occasions rather than the Catholic rules that focused his earlier dramas (of needing to attend Mass regularly, or to be in a state of grace to receive Communion, or to obey the marital laws of the Church). His narratives tend to forego grief over what is no longer here, or otherwise to parse the melancholy of loss, instead converging on the suddenly arrested if savage moment. In that regard, the short story's limits themselves are central to Dubus's vision, if only in a formal condensation that allows him to pivot on a constrained narrative arc, effectively leaving details out to create an aura that crucially persists. Yet to gain a better sense of Dubus's late celebration of the convergence of violence and revelation, we need (as with Munro) to turn from the radical brevity of a late story to his earlier efforts, in order to assess how he effectively whittles the form down, and in the process becomes clearer about his central concerns.

II. Earlier Enactments

Dubus's first collection, *Separate Flights* (1975), focuses on suburban unrest and disappointment, apparently taking its lead from John Cheever and John Updike in upending the secret desires and aspirations that puncture middle-class American ideals. As the narrator proclaims in "We Don't Live Here Anymore," "I am surrounded by painful marriages that no one understands" (*Separate* 13). Men lust after other men's wives, who lust for them in turn, as Jack describes his problems with his own wife Terry and mistress Edith; "I felt at the border of some discovery, some way I could juggle my beloveds and save us all. But I didn't know what it was" (*Separate* 25). At 74 pages, the story is actually a novella that traces the shifting relations between Jack, his wife, his mistress, and her husband in a quadrille that gradually reveals all four's mutual knowledge of each other. The narrative wanders and lingers, though the theme remains more or less the same, expressed by Jack as a slow settling of desire and a dissolution of trust: "In a marriage there are all sorts of lies whose malignancy slowly kills everything" (31). That insight is at once gradual and tendentious, though in the wife-swapping negotiation it becomes clear that there will be resolution no time soon (indeed, the story will be expanded into a full novel).

"Going Under" (1975) matches the theme, with Peter Jackman confronting "demons" lurking everywhere in his daily life as he futilely tries to win over a much younger Miranda to abandon her fiancé. The story's otherwise straightforward chronology is disrupted by painful memories of his family deserting him, his and Miranda's infidelities, his naked desire for comfort smothering him as desperation builds. Strikingly, the story offers a turn from Dubus's early style, not only in lyrical landscape descriptions of western Massachusetts but in a series of metaphorical allusions that deftly evoke Peter's fraught consciousness— as "now in the room, demons are about" (124); or as he submitted "with curiosity and hope to the rape of grief" (127), or in wanting to speak to his ex-wife as he "dials the area code of loss" (128) just before once again "demons move in from the walls" (130).Yet this expressionist style also differs entirely from Dubus's efforts later on, as if he were experimenting with ways to evoke a mental collapse.[2] Gradually, in surveying his littered past Peter comes to regret the adulteries: "all were liaisons whose passions were fed by the empty cupboards of the lovers' homes," he concludes, "because there was death in that repetition of lovers" (135). Still, remorse fails to alleviate his pain, leading instead to a panic attack as he calls a new lover to walk him through his forlorn paralysis. Little of greater self-knowledge or control seems promised by the end.

Continuing this early fascination with the breakdown of marital relationships under the erosions of infidelity, "Over the Hill" centers on a tormented Marine private abroad, newly married and already two-timed by his wife, as he learns long-distance. Only eleven pages long, the story divides into six sections, again fragmenting Gale's sensibility, contorting itself as it unfolds chronologically. Having gone AWOL in frustration and later aware of his life's collapse, he reviews his court-martial and prison sentence, followed by a failed suicide attempt, before contemplating a dark future: "All this stretched before him, as immutable as the long passageway where he marched now, the chaser in step behind him, yet he not only accepted it, but chose it. He figured that it was at least better than nothing" (*Separate* 87). In the back and forth rhythms of memory, anticipating his experience in prison, this desultory summation offers a melancholy version of Dubus's ongoing fictional insight, as if no escape might be conceived from the downward spiral of experience.

More explosively, in anticipation of similar moments in his late collection, "The Doctor" (1975) introduces the idea that violence can suddenly obtrude in a life, all in four tightly drawn pages. Like other early stories, the narrative moves in chronological lockstep as the titular physician wanders through his suburban neighborhood, exerting a mild

2. Olivia Carr Edenfield best defines this strain in Dubus's earlier work (see 23).

sovereignty over the land just before narrative and consciousness split explosively in half: "Then something was wrong—he felt it before he knew it. When the two boys ran up from the brook into his vision, he started sprinting" (90). A boy is trapped under water beyond the doctor's efforts to rescue him, an episode that erupts in his life though offering no apparent change in him. All he belatedly apprehends is that one might have been better prepared, making a decision to cut a length of garden hose in order to prevent future such deaths. Where the whole plainly differs from Dubus's later efforts is in offering no psychological or spiritual response to the death, but merely a simple physical precaution that seals off any emotion. The cut garden hose comes to stand for ways in which this torturous episode has been externalized all but completely, left unmotivated and unexplored, with no psychological consequences or considerations suggesting what has changed. Interestingly, for a writer whose late work so often sideslips into epiphanies, here no insight is even marginally intimated.

That focus on constrained behavior rather than personal transformation is confirmed in early stories that map a terrain of sin, with Catholic doctrine invoked to curb purported sexual deviancy. Dubus powerfully evokes adolescent idealism in "If They Knew Yvonne," with a teenager obsessed by needing to confess his self-abuse, only to continue it. Later, he is surprised to feel no remorse in losing his virginity, though still somehow yearning to repent, as if Dubus were exploring the disconnect between religious rules and natural desires, leaving one at last out of tune with oneself.

The opposite of this emotional numbness is revealed in "Miranda Over the Valley," of a woman pregnant too young and committed as a Catholic to keeping her child, though forsaken by parents, a friend, her lover, even the author himself over the choice of abortion. As Joshua Bodwell reports, Dubus "claimed that he was so helplessly enslaved to the will of his characters that he rewrote the ending…three times in the hope that Miranda would act differently—but she would not. 'I didn't want Miranda to be so hard,' Dubus said, 'but that was all she would do'" (Bodwell 24). In this, he strikingly resembles Munro, who also thought of her characters as acting a bit too independently; Davis never found this a problem (perhaps because her characters are too abbreviated), nor did Williams (perhaps because such ethical questions simply failed to intrigue her). The story ends with Miranda gradually having grown into a casual acceptance of her own sovereign self-possession, no longer dictated to by others' dispositions: "She watched him until she didn't need to anymore" (165).

Summing up the collection's focus on pressures of both Church doctrine and marital infidelity is the title story, "Separate Flights." Beth endures an unhappy marriage, no more nor less than anyone else's, though now attracted to a man in a way that makes her feel she has sinned. A lapsed Catholic, she nonetheless suffers intense guilt for having strayed, if only in feelings, not action. Or as Jimmy Carter notoriously admitted in a *Playboy* interview the following year, "I've committed adultery in my heart many times." Beth's faith had dissolved years before—"She had stopped as unconsciously as your face tans in summer and pales in winter" (179)—yet the residue of belief still remains unaltered, shaping her innate reaction not only to the charming stranger but to her daughter's secret affair and her own need to intervene.

The theme is familiar from other stories in the collection, but what emerges in the six parts of this extended narrative is an alteration among different moods, as Beth vacillates in her expanded notion of love and appropriate behavior, of attraction and commitment. Ironically, her censurable efforts to encourage her daughter to use birth control miscarry, since Peggy (we later discover) had actually wanted to end the relationship her mother so carefully tried to assist, in defiance of her own inhibitions, doctrinal concerns, and untoward marital history. What Beth finally realizes, in a moment of insight delayed, is that everything she does is inadequate, misdirected, even wrong, leading to a kind of paralysis, locking her into the irrevocability of action, where onward motion cannot be curbed or eased.

Dubus's early stories tend to end in calm resolution, far from anguish, with a greater confidence expressed in the ways in which conflict can be contained. Granted, his collections through the 1980s extend a preoccupation with Catholic rules, with sexual wandering and hetero-sexual conflict, with parental oppression and filial strife, with bullying and lying and weight loss. But in each of these, a level-headed certainty finally prevails, however tentatively expressed, as if tensions were settled summarily, at least in memory. Perhaps one sign of that assurance is the way narratives unfold more or less sequentially, even in accounting for a daughter's vehicular homicide in "A Father's Story" (1983), moving gradually from a description of the habitual daily routines Luke Ripley performs, to the spiritual reassurance that Church ritual provides, to his higher obligation to protect his drunk-driving daughter whose life is suddenly split in two: "Her brakes were screaming into the wind, bottles clinking in the fallen bag, and with the music and wind inside the car was his sound, already a memory but as real as an echo, that car-shuddering thump as though she had struck a tree" (*SS* 466). After refusing to call an ambulance for the victim, still barely alive, he covers up the accident and ends with his deeply disturbed faith expressed in anguished prayer. Clearly, the kind of transforming violence that would later effect Dubus's own life has here been already imagined—but still, only as event, not as the forms of psychological transfiguration that would become so central to his later fictional vision.

Curiously, Dubus's very first publication in 1961, which remained uncollected until appearing as the inaugural story in *Dancing After Hours*, offers another singular anticipation of that theme of violence, if not of the ways he would find to transform the moment into renewed consideration, indeed into insight. Still, the "The Intruder" seems prescient in registering various aspects of Dubus's late style, in its cross-hatched integration of setting, psychology, disturbed syntax, and temporal circling. Right from the opening sentences, a disquieting late mood is paradoxically established, of thirteen-year-old Kenneth Girard feeling transcendence in the woods *before* any violence occurs, as he waits "for the silence and trees and sky to close in on him, wait[s] until they all became a part of him and thought and memory ceased and the voices began" (*DH* 3). This slightly surreal setting offers a peculiar mix of secrecy, discomfort, sin, and psychological oppression, causing us to realize the woods grant Kenneth imaginative license to indulge in heroic deeds as compensation for the inadequacies he suspects in his life.

The one exception to this awkward adolescent consciousness is his deep affection for his sister Connie, though even that is hard to decipher the evening their parents head out, as he realizes how much "He loved the nights at the camp when they were left alone. At home, there was a disturbing climate about their evenings alone, for distant voices of boys in the neighborhood reminded him that he was not alone entirely by choice. Here, there were no sounds" (7). The passage drums an enigmatic beat on its adverbs, with "alone" and "alone" and "not alone entirely by choice" offered in quick succession, as if somehow opposed, forcing us to puzzle out the meaning of repetitions that seem to contain in their tension an answer to Kenneth's feeling. The very difference under the repetition of the two sentences—of feeling differently in similar situations but in two different places—is hardly clear, though it suggests something of Kenneth's fraught relations with his sister, where Connie is now attracted by the "distant voices of boys." Already, the emotional tensions of the evening are anticipated in Kenneth's partially incestuous feelings of affection, jealousy, and isolation.

Inflaming those feelings is the prospect of Connie's boyfriend soon to arrive, in the shift of the narrative back and forth temporally, registering Kenneth's own anxieties about being passed over "as if he were another chair...paralyzing his tongue and even his mind" (10). Artfully, the story builds this tension as Douglas appears, then leaves, before Kenneth goes to bed only to hear a twig crack, at which point his italicized imagination takes over: "*Get up. Get up and get the rifle. If you don't do it now, he might come to this window*" (16). At this point, emotion drives the action, with incestuous undercurrents dictating a crisis that ends in his blindly, impetuously, irrevocably shooting Douglas: "Then he knew" (18). Those three words propel the narrative ahead to a retrospective view of time collapsed, deferred in the very syntax itself: "Afterward, it seemed that the events of a year had occurred in an hour, and, to Kenneth, even that hour seemed to have a quality of neither speed nor slowness, but a kind of suspension, as if time were not passing at all" (18). The paragraph, jumbling episodes in Kenneth's recollection and his experiencing of them, leads to his father's account that closes the whole by belying the facts, denying the victim was Douglas. Adolescent notions of heroism in the opening are transfigured by the end, as "he stood on a high cliff and for a moment he was a mighty angel, throwing all guns and cruelty and sex and tears into the sea" (19). The suggestion here of pubescent yearning and idealism, if only "for a moment," teeters into the supposed regret represented by unassuagable "tears."

The whole triumphs by treating more abruptly those features that other early stories are perhaps too careful to pull apart or unsort, in a pattern Dubus only much later realized could allow fuller resonance, revealing the repercussions and reverberations forward and back of violence itself. Questions linger: why does Connie fall out of the narrative? Why did Kenneth pull the trigger? What does he in fact believe, and what will be the consequences of manslaughter? Yet instead of addressing these, the narrative deftly focuses on the strange welter of adolescent feelings of resentment, affection, and fear, capping them with a moment of violence that fails to resolve the feelings. While no one is redeemed by violence, the story itself confirms in its fragmented organization, its use of free indirect discourse, its casual uncertainty about antecedents, and its sometimes circular syntax (heading back over ground already covered) that we as readers are to be left disarmed, to experience in our own simultaneous insight and obscure confusion what has occurred. Remarkably, most of the ingredients of Dubus's late style are already present at the beginning, though a series of notable collected stories would test his narrative inventiveness in various ways before he returned to this more intense, less conventionally structured, psychological mode.

III. Revelations of Violence

No story better exemplifies the characteristic cadences of *Dancing After Hours* than "Blessings," whose title itself captures the paradox at the heart of Dubus's late vision, revealing the way in which savage violence can become the means of redemptive grace. Immediately, the reader is bewildered, though in a fashion not at all like Munro, since he keeps us always aware, unlike her, of *fabula* as the driving force of his narrative, in the iron links of temporality. *Syuzhet*, when Dubus occasionally makes us aware of his reorderings, intentionally discloses the emotional, psychological distress over what needs to be kept *away from* memory, a strategy that proves again the opposite of Munro. We begin near the end of a narrative sequence whose consequences seem clear, though the story refuses to identify the looming initial events apparently buried in the past until midway through, in contrast to the more chronological presentation preferred in Dubus's earlier stories. Indeed, the narrative compounds this enigmatic effect in fragmented fashion characteristic of late modernism. Its initial sentence is suitably tantalizing—"Early in the morning on the first anniversary of the day her family survived, the mother woke" (44)—even as pages go by without clarifying what happened the year before. All we have is the simple repetition of a phrase describing herself, now describing her husband: "His family had survived" (47). No further illumination emanates from events for the memory that hangs so oppressively over consciousness.

An experience that has pervaded the life of the mother, Rusty Williams, refuses to be named, not because otherwise repressed but because so otherwise obvious, so altogether ever-present. Her sub-vocalized dialogues with her sleeping husband Cal occur in the opening three pages as slightly slap-happy run-on sentences, confirming all but unalterably her agitated state this morning, the anniversary of something impossible to expunge from memory. "For she knew it was not the birds that had alerted the muscles in her legs and arms and the one beating beneath her ribs, ready to fight the intruder her body was gathered for, the intruder she had known when she first woke was not there; it was the day itself that woke her: the fourteenth of July" (46). Inadvertently invoking the title of his early story here, Dubus actually signals a significantly different late motif with an "intruder" now psychological rather than physical. The ominous specification of that date, three pages into the story, makes us aware of something lurking behind the arras in the shadows of the past. What gradually emerges from the awakening of recollection is that, though Cal and their two children survived a fishing expedition, the captain and mate "were dead" (47), with the flat spondee of that confirmation offering its own tentative closure. Still, no explanation is offered for why or how this happened. Awake now, Rusty recalls her sleeplessness that night in St. Croix, as she also is reminded of the funerals she attended—again, in run-on prose—mixed in with memories of having earlier planned for the holiday. She invokes, repetitively, as if still in the grip of PTSD, the day as well as her family, each of them isolated by his or her memories just as their names ("she and Cal and Gina and Ryan") are isolated by simple polysyndeton every time. Whereas Dubus's earlier predilection was to have the story dictate a character's consciousness, here it is Rusty's psychology that has the effect of dictating the story.

Finally alert as dawn arrives, she walks into the kitchen and the full horrifying devastation of the year-old experience explodes in the single phrase, "saw the fins of sharks":

in this last of darkness and beginning of light her eyes had adjusted to while in bed she listened to birds and saw the fins of sharks.

She still did, standing at the sink in her white gown and looking through the window screen at dark pines, and she heard the mate's scream just after he tied the knot lashing together the two orange life preservers and she had looked up from buckling her life jacket, looked at his scream and saw a face she had never seen before and now would always see: his eyes and mouth widened in final horror and the absolute loss of hope that caused it; then he was gone. (51)

The horror of the past suddenly bursts in on Rusty and at that very moment on us, with the same abruptness the precipitating event had presented at the time. The past is imposed on the present in that astonished coupling of "she listened to birds and saw the fins of sharks," with senses then precariously reversed in her "looking through the window screen...and she heard the mate's scream." Memory merges with sight, precluding her from peering through the darkened window to see what is actually out there.

Nothing in Dubus's earlier stories prepares us for this dizzying depiction, as if the equally tormenting emotional moments had been stripped bare, exposed to the bone. The past here obtrudes irrepressibly, with images that burn Rusty's eyes as she gazes unseeing on her own back yard, until finally "she left the sink and the window and the images between her and the pines of the dead captain in the helicopter, and the first fin" (55). Later checking the refrigerator, she recalls her daughter's bare legs in water as she alternates between the banal domestic detail of a turkey crowding a cold lit space and the frantic recollection of her family one by one lifted into a rescue helicopter, before the Captain reaches down to unwittingly gift his arm to a shark. That unintended gift seems grotesquely to merge with the image of a turkey carcass, in the passage's sensory overload joined with the lack of any further explanation.

Still, nothing clarifies. And while Dubus frequently sorted out the history behind earlier narratives, here his very silence denotes how little avails. The capsizing seems inexplicable, as does the emergency helicopter's arrival; we are simply plunged into memory's whirlpool—casual, violent, unanticipated—with the "downward rush of air from the huge blades. Their loud circling above her made Rusty feel contained from all other time and space save these moments and feet of rope that both separated her from Cal and joined her to him" (53). Description appears somehow isolated from the experience itself, as Dubus focuses on the aesthetic allure of such violence, which offers a clarity of ethical judgment that seems to gleam through trivial details. Deadly moments paradoxically bring us back to life, to the vivid realization of what is important in contrast to making morning coffee or planning a summer holiday. At the same time we become aware of the sheer fortuitousness of events, whether the Captain suddenly loses an arm and his life or Cal is casually, nonchalantly, altogether mystifyingly ignored by a shark.

As central as the story's informing events, recovered belatedly, is the narrative's backward motion, moving from the present to a full year before in a gesture that becomes characteristic of Dubus's late style. The early pivotal day emerges long after the fact, finally leading to the immediacy of being in the water itself, where suddenly memory collapses in a tumultuous run-on sentence that begins in accusation against the captain for his fatal mismanagement and ends with Rusty granting absolution:

He had known why they were sinking, and she knew it was something he had done... and she was about to accuse him... but could not, for his face was like that of landed codfish, resigned to sunlight and air and death, as if they accepted that they had destroyed themselves, feeding on the dark bottom... while she reeled them up, why they were simply weight on the end of her line. The captain's name was Lenny Walters. Watching his face with its look of being caught in a trap that he had set, she forgave him. (64)

The melding together of dire fact and strained metaphor; the slippage among pronouns, he, she, and they; the sudden uncertainty about who might be imagining all this (though it quickly becomes apparent that this must be Rusty); and here, seemingly overdue, the naming of the captain as Lenny Walters (contrary to Dubus's late inclination to get such matters settled at the very beginning): this stream of consciousness dramatizes a prismatic occasion that would otherwise resolve into a simple gesture of forgiveness. Slowly, we learn of the error that led to this disaster, before paragraphs plunge us into the present following these remembered sequences ("Then she was in her body again, in the room" [68]), as we move from sharks in the water to deer in her back yard, aligning animals in jeopardy to her own family exposed in the sea.

All that can save Rusty this day is a hastily swallowed sleeping pill at dawn, helping stave off memories that interpose themselves so forcefully, all but shanghaiing the present.

Soon she would feel it: the dullness in her legs and arms and behind her eyes, so they would see then only what they looked at, objects and doors and rooms and hall; free of sharks and blood, they would steer her to bed, where she would wake a second time to the fourteenth of July, a day in history she had memorized in school; but a year ago, in a sea as tranquil as this lake, that date had molted the prison and the revolution. As when Vietnam had disappeared in 1968, burned up in Gina's fever when she was nine and had pneumonia. (59)

The wonderful melange here unfolds in a series of clauses, images, random past moments that abruptly merge, held together neither by calm recollection nor by self-controlled syntax. We lose a secure grasp of referents, of antecedents, of subject itself as the syntactical clauses abut each other. And with that disarray unfolds a disabling sense of

other horrific moments that cannot be expunged from memory—her
daughter's fever that corresponds to the Vietnam War, and that otherwise
punctuates her thoughts—all in a convergence of recollection, family,
and pain. It is as if an older Dubus were willing to pull back for a larger
view, inquiring into the meaning of events that younger actors, younger
writers, simply assumed. For those who have endured so much, is revelation actually reserved?

Not until late in the story do we fathom the cause of the accident,
even though Rusty had early, rather damningly proclaimed, "And it
was his own fault" (55). The Captain's specific identifiable "fault," however, remains eerily enigmatic until much later in the narrative diegesis,
as if cause itself mattered less than the disaster's effect, with the mind
ever persisting in pursuing some adequate explanation. Afterwards, she
admits: "He had known why they were sinking, and she knew it was
something he had done or had not done, and it should not have happened, should not have been allowed to happen…" (65). The very
accumulation of negations itself registers a fruitless attempt to close off
the past, and close off as well any explanation. At last we learn why,
though Rusty's admission to the investigator of the Captain's presumed
negligence matters less, a year past, than her overwhelming recollection of feeling simply disembodied:

> She saw only Cal, and in his face she saw only herself, and though she felt the
> chair she sat in, and Gina's hands moving on hers, she felt bodiless, too, out of
> the room, as though her spirit and Cal's had left their bodies and were moving
> side by side, above time, above mortality. Then she was in her body again, in
> the room and the cool of the trade winds coming through the window behind
> Cal, and she was aware again of the tall lieutenant.   (68)

So transfigured is her consciousness by the violence of the experience
that there can be no question of recovery, or of somehow returning to
an earlier serenity. Still, the swaying syntax of the passage, tilting from
polysyndeton to a sequence of prepositional clauses, has her apparently
falling into and out of her body along with the recollected trade winds
that accompanied the closure represented by the "tall lieutenant." It is
this revelatory moment that confirms the effect of her experience,
which Dubus reveals as something marked out as transformational.

The story ends with a stunning and seemingly irrelevant scene of her
observing a buck and doe at the lake, then falling back into bed, succumbing to the sleeping pill, allowing us finally to grasp the paradoxical

effects of that year-ago devastation. Rusty sleepily acknowledges to Cal why she got up on this anniversary of "the worst day our family's ever had," though still feeling a sense of disembodiment, she feels compelled to concede as well: "'But it was the best, too,' she said, her voice detached from her body, coming from a throat somewhere above her. She felt his voice close to her face, but she heard one word at a time, then it drifted away from her, and the next word and the next were alone, and meant nothing. 'Do you understand?' she said" (71). Their very voices have become deracinated, threading words together singly one by one, as if marking out a verbal terrain whose semantic contours no longer quite have any leverage over the past. By now, that deracination affects us as well, in the paradoxical conjoining of worst and best, of a devastating near-death experience that has been survived, unscathed. But the title also reveals its ironic resonance in the "blessing" of Rusty's having come to realize what is important in life, and of how the very violence of that experience a year past has given her a sense of immediacy, of vivid consciousness, of transforming revelation. The paradox lies in the wall between horrific experience and earned insight, which recurs throughout *Dancing After Hours* as nonetheless a constantly and necessarily renegotiated exchange.

The epigraph to *Dancing After Hours* seems pointedly addressed to Rusty's newfound willingness to inhabit the moment, as Christ enjoins his disciples: "Therefore do not worry about tomorrow, for tomorrow will worry about itself. Each day has enough trouble of its own" (Luke 10:41). The injunction has larger implications than mere "trouble," as Dubus realizes, revealed in the ways his own imagined violent threats *to* life become themselves moments in which we can be awakened to the marvel *of* life. Correlatively, we become attuned to the powerful resources of narrative in its capacity to register transcendence, signaled by any such transfiguration into a new mode of seeing. This represents a clear development for Dubus from earlier stories in not simply depicting extremes of adversity and pain, anguish and terror, but in evoking for the reader as well as characters what those liminal experiences reveal. We look into the abyss at such moments and step back, but not without being altered. If even Dubus's late stories rarely seem as visceral as "Blessings," each does hinge on this notion of reassessed realization, silently evoking lines from the gospel song "Amazing Grace": "I once was lost but now am found, Was blind, but now can see." Trauma sometimes disables, but it can also wonderfully enable insight not available in our pre-traumatized state.

IV. Opening Strategies

If few writers have envisioned violence as quite so humanizing, it may come as no surprise that only belatedly did Dubus explore the implications of that vision, and did so in very different narrative evocations that remind us how fully pain and insight, violence and transfigured consciousness are linked. Yet for all their remarkable differences, what strangely ties his late stories together is their initial constructions of character, as part of an utterly egalitarian vision. Consider this authorial bio itself, written in Dubus's own later preferred style: Andre Dubus, a bluff, bearded, thrice-married Catholic writer, lost the use of both legs at fifty in an automobile accident ten years before publishing his finest short story collection, *Dancing After Hours*. The sentence consists of a name, a physical description, a notorious calamity, then a testament to his achievement: itself an exemplar of Dubus's own introduction of entirely invented, fictional others. That prefatory pattern was rarely in evidence earlier, but becomes in his later stories something like Dubus's "tell," as poker players like to declare. He immediately defines his main characters in opening sentences through simple, stripped-down details and box bios—giving us a formal noun, a precise age, often a brief bodily description, sometimes even a physical locale.[3] That signature style of beginning with ostensible stick figures suggests a need for scaffolding on which flesh, facts, memories, extraneous fumblings are attached in the form of simple external details and character-laden

---

3. Dubus himself claimed, "I noticed rereading Chekhov that in most of the stories I read that in the opening paragraph we learn what day it was and what season almost right away. I need that as a reader" (Dubus, *Conversations*, 154). Curiously, Alice Munro at times imitates this tactic, as in "Tricks": "Joanne was now thirty years old, Robin twenty-six. Joanne had a childish body..." (237). One might consider how often novels, by contrast, burst on us immediately in their opening sentences. "124 was spiteful. Full of a baby's venom" (Toni Morrison, *Beloved*); "I drove out to Glendale to put three new truck drivers on a brewery company bond, and then I remembered this renewal over in Hollywoodland" (James Cain, *Double Indemnity*); "Strether's first question, when he reached the hotel, was about his friend; yet on his learning that Waymarsh was apparently not to arrive till evening he was not wholly disconcerted" (Henry James, *The Ambassadors*). The interesting aspect of Dubus's introductions is how he deliberately forswears such dramatic identifiers in preference for a standard, even habitual entry.

gestures—something no other short story writer consistently does. Consider a few introductory sentences: "In college, Luann was mirthful and romantic, an attractive girl with black hair and dark skin and eyes" ("All the Time in the World" 83); or, "The retired Marine colonel had two broken legs...His name was Robert Townsend...and now at home he was downstairs in the living room on a hospital bed" ("The Colonel's Wife" 103); or, "Lee Trambath was a fifty-five-year-old restaurant manager, with three ex-wives and five children" ("The Lover" 123); or "Ted Briggs came back from the war seven years before it ended, and in spring two years after it ended he met Susan Dorsey at a cast party after a play's final performance, on a Sunday night, in a small town north of Boston" ("Falling in Love" 27); or, in the collection's powerful titular story, "Emily Moore was a forty-year-old bartender in a town in Massachusetts" (194). Name, age, sometimes occupation or physiognomy or bare-bones setting: the pattern invariably recurs, and in the title story is compounded when he later introduces another character: "Rita Beck was thirty-seven years old, and had red hair in a ponytail, and wore a purple shirt and a black skirt" (198). Multiple other instances might be adduced, confirming how regularly this imaginative habit dictates Dubus's grip on his narratives.

Rarely does he treat figures so summarily in earlier stories, whereas his late mode adopts a new austerity in which character has less to do with an inherently unique personality and more with simple trappings associated with a self.[4] It is as if his very vision of identity had shifted away from the customary notion of lives configured discretely and disparately to something like a one-size-fits-all scaffolding transformed idiosyncratically by events. Still, the question remains what effect is intended by this oddly reiterated opening strategy on the rest of any

4. The pattern did not begin with his last collection, but it is hardly as ubiquitous. Consider the following examples, beginning with an early story in which the introduction is unusual: "Her name was Louise. Once when she was sixteen a boy kissed her at a barbecue; he was drunk and he jammed his tongue into her mouth and ran his hands up and down her hips" ("The Fat Girl" 45, 1977); or "Her name was Anna Griffin. She was twenty. Her blond hair had been turning darker over the past few years, and she believed it would be brown when she was twenty-five" ("Anna" 262, 1980); or "In the summer of 1944 Roy Hodges was back from the Pacific. He was a staff sergeant, a drill instructor at the Recruit Depot at San Diego. He was twenty-six years old, and he was training eighteen-year-old boys. He was also engaged to marry Sheila Russell..." ("The Misogamist" 51, 1980). Or "My name is Luke Ripley, and here is what I call my life: I own a stable of thirty horses, and I have young people who teach riding, and we board some horses too. This is in northeastern Massachusetts" ("A Father's Story" 455, 1983).

story in which it occurs. Hard to say, although perhaps the implications of this guileless method can best be teased out by its antithesis, exemplified in classic stories that refuse to award names at all. The narrators of Poe's "The Tell-Tale Heart" (1843), Stephen Crane's "The Open Boat" (1897) and Jack London's "To Build a Fire" (1908) never refer to their characters formally, as if the three authors resisted the notion of personal identity being collapsed into a sobriquet. That pattern is copied for rather different reasons in Ralph Ellison's *Invisible Man* (1952) and Philip Roth's *Everyman* (2006), both of which envision their central figures as representative.

By contrast, Dubus cuts to the chase, bluntly eager to get introductions out of the way: here's X, she's so many years old, and this is what she does for a living, so let's get on with it. Are these details meant to be taken as essentials of identity, or markers by which we can hang a narrative onto a character? Is the irrelevance of formal identity to the random story that follows the most telling feature of these introductions? It may well be that the very absence of distinctive voices requires identities be defined by arbitrary signs of name, age, and so on—and that otherwise none of us are so different, none so distinctive, except in the things that happen to happen to us. The effect is to highlight a specific identification of the sort made on a driver's license or library card as the locus for whatever story ensues. The violence that so often erupts in Dubus's later narratives is then summarily linked with a particular identity that happens only arbitrarily to be attached to this person, not another. Earlier stories tended to be less imperious about the violence that ensued or that otherwise transformed characters' lives. And introductions to those stories tended as well to seem less peremptory than his later excursions, as if he had come around to a realization of the randomness of violence as well as of revelation.

Consider in this regard an exceptional early story, "Killings" (1979), which anticipates even more than "The Intruders" a pattern that later recurs in *Dancing After Hours*: "On the August morning when Matt Fowler buried his youngest son, Frank, who had lived for twenty-one years, eight months, and four days, Matt's older son, Steve turned to him as the family left the grave and walked between their friends, and said 'I should kill him'" (47). The temporal descriptor, the names, the relative ages, the locale: all are finally unnecessary details whose irrelevance enhances the unsettled feeling introduced by clauses that confirm Matt Fowler's confusion in the face of a dismayingly violent, troublingly debilitated world. The very logic of naming itself—enforced through description of experience duly ordered, thus predictably known—is already challenged syntactically by the disarmingly rational sequence that anticipates the heedless plot that ensues, of a senseless murder and the cold-blooded killing it inspires.

This pattern is repeated throughout, moreover, in introductions given to other characters: "Richard Strout was twenty-six years old, a high school athlete, football scholarship to the University of Massachusetts where he lasted for almost two semesters before quitting" (49). Name, age, skill-set, history, though again none of it explains the man Strout will become. "One night he beat Frank. Frank was living at home and waiting for September, for graduate school in economics, and working as a lifeguard at Salisbury Beach, where he met Mary Ann Strout, in her first month of separation." The important point is that the very inability to explain Strout, or Frank, or Mary Ann through a set of familiar descriptors itself contributes to the unsettling power of Dubus's story, which hinges on the dramatic divide once again between the rational, ordering principles we adopt for understanding our world and the disjointed, savage transformations that can so often, so suddenly, so unexpectedly erupt. Coherent patterns dissolve amid the anguish of Frank's murder, and Matt from that moment "had not so much moved through his life as wandered through it, his spirit like a dazed body bumping into furniture and corners" (54). The story seems to anticipate a pattern that will become more familiar later on, as if once again Dubus foresaw a late style whose possibilities he was not quite ready to test any further.

By the time of *Dancing in the Dark*, however, earlier qualms had dissipated, with Dubus no longer hesitant about stripping his style down to something that only at first seems more rudimentary but actually offers a more comprehensive vision of possibility. Partly, this seems to owe to his characteristic dependence on a generally undemonstrative narrator who reports in the third person, usually through free indirect discourse, lending a sense of characters being shadowed even as their distinctive voices are muted. In that regard, Dubus differs from other late modernist authors. In fact, paradoxically (given his openings), he is less concerned with fleshing out distinctive characters than with identifying vivid moments of consciousness, shorn of all the inessential elements of apprehension involved in habitual activities, thoughtless experiences, the simple waiting for something to happen. Unlike Munro or Davis, Dubus can readily ignore the apparent trivialities of dear life, or the everyday perspectives so often shaped by such experience. For him, the particular inflections a voice gives, the ways it defines a psychology, matter less than moments in which a sensibility itself is transfigured.

The striking undercurrent of Dubus's conception is that he might agree we all sound more or less alike in our petty concerns, our strivings and disappointments and customary behaviors—no matter our culture, or gender, or ethnicity, or even class. Much rarer, however, is the moment of breaking with that sense of habit, learning anew to value the here and now, becoming transformed. That helps explain the collection's second epigraph (from the gospel of Luke): "Martha, Martha, you are anxious about many things. There is need of only one thing." Looming over the stories is the sense that too often we are easily distracted by needless annoyances, daily trivia, garden-variety unease. Instead, we need to aspire to an almost Zen-like acceptance of the travails of life. The paradox, of course, is that the caution occurs as an epigraph to a collection of stories desperate, distraught, deeply traumatic. The point is that Dubus seems to believe that only the centering drama of violence can actually alter consciousness, having the effect of concentrating our thoughts on essentials.

That contrast between triviality and trauma, dull daily habit and instantaneous dire horror animates "Out of the Snow," the third in a trilogy of stories told from the viewpoint of LuAnn Arceneaux.[5] "On a dark winter morning, upstairs in her new home, LuAnn woke to classical piano on the clock radio; she was in her forty-fourth year..." (172). Again, the signature sentence has little to do with the untoward day to come, in its understated description of a woman we already know from earlier stories. The effect is to return us to solid descriptors that have already failed to root LuAnn in a predictable life, one that has been upended at least twice before. The whole is depicted again in free indirect discourse, from her perspective as stay-at-home mother, encumbered with the clashing demands of housekeeping, homemaking, parenting, shopping, and washing.

5. "All the Time in the World" presents LuAnn Arceneaux as a college student; "The Timing of Sin" depicts her as a married mother with children, contemplating adultery. That trajectory of a life amid separate stories reminds us of Munro's own pattern, occasionally of Davis, as well as Dubus's earlier stories about Peter Jackman's tormented love life, in "At St. Croix," "The Winter Father," and "Going Under."

Suddenly for no reason, amid the converging pressures of the day, LuAnn realizes she is not immersed in her world but living somehow outside it, as she reflects on her displacement from her own life in one long sentence, divided mostly by semi-colons that themselves delay her a step longer than commas might signal, having the effect of making us pause unnecessarily in concert with LuAnn's own constantly inter-rupted daily pattern:

Her mind was eluding her; it was living the day ahead of her; it was in the aisle of the supermarket, it was bringing the groceries into the house and putting them away; it was driving to the gym for aerobics and weight training; it was home eating lunch, then taking clothes to the dry cleaners and getting the clothes that were there, and driving home before three-forty when the school bus brought the children to the driveway; it was lighting charcoal in the grill on the sundeck. (176)

Unlike many Dubus characters, LuAnn is prompted out of herself by the simple gesture of self-reflection, realizing how her mind keeps tricking her into thinking *outside* the present to apparently pressing considerations rather than *in* whatever should be focusing her attention. The welter of activities she performs seems displaced by anticipation and recollection, introducing a wedge of thought between herself and the immediate present.

Yet as she gradually presses her thoughts, she comes to realize a way out of this buffered sensibility, wrapped up in dull expectations and tedious memories. And the escape ironically emerges from her own initially unheeded advice to herself, expressed in dialogue with her husband in a scene central for Dubus:

She had told Ted she must learn to be five again, before time began to mean what one could produce in its passing; or to be like St. Thérèse of Lisieux, who knew so young that the essence of life was in the simplest of tasks, and in kindness to the people in your life. Watching the brown sugar bubbling in the light of the flames, smelling it and the cinnamon, and listening to her family talking about snow, she told herself that this toast and oatmeal were a sacrament, the physical form that love assumed in this moment, as last night's lovemaking was, as most of her actions were. (177)

The religious imagery is compelling, and clearly different from those arbitrary doctrinal injunctions that so dominate early stories focused on young, impressionable minds. Indeed, the imagery suggests some-thing far more uplifting than sexual prohibitions and marital dictates, with brown sugar and cinnamon, snow, toast and oatmeal serving as a sacrament, the material expression of *caritas*. The diffusely spiritual aspects of this gesture attest for LuAnn to something found nowhere in the other three authors, though they are each in accord with Dubus on the need to attend to the local and immediate, on refusing to ignore the details that structure our lives. Rarely does that insight occur even for Dubus in earlier stories, and certainly not as a driving initiative. The contrast then in this story, and the question that persists, is how the stilted quality of its opening introduction of LuAnn that morning has prepared us for this, except to suggest that settled openings of stories (as of days) are equally unavailing in preparing us for the days and stories to come.

Of course, the sacramental moment can never be sustained or preserved, as is all too soon evidenced in her beginning to worry about Ted on the plane, her children in dark woods and danger, confirming how difficult it is to stay rooted in the present, how often and easily our anxieties distractingly loom. Dubus makes us realize, even shy of external threat, the terrors that psychology provokes unexpectedly, catching us unawares, as a feature very distinctly part of his later achieved vision. And the closing scene of "Out of the Snow" serves as confirmation of how inadequate our everyday patterns must always be. For here, the story's title takes its significance, as "doom walking out of the snow" occurs in the assault by rapists in her own kitchen (185). Unanticipated, the attack leaves her strangely even more thoroughly connected to herself as three pages glide by in the anxiety, terror, and vicious speed with which she responds. The scene of her fiercely fighting back unfolds straightforwardly, no longer disjointed or disconnected. Instead, it achieves a vital intensity for LuAnn and the reader in the uncertainty of the outcome, the focus on details that tilt self-preservation her way as she swings a skillet: "The sound of the blow filled her; the shock of it danced in her. She swung again, hitting his hand and face; and again, smelling blood and saliva from his mouth" (188). The sibilance of the description at once hastens the sequence and somehow uncannily eases the violence, as if the perception of what she is doing were at one with the doing itself.

LuAnn's astonishment at what she has become, the reinforced link between body and self that recalls her earlier decision not to commit adultery: all confirm the precarious balance between evil and rapture, threat and self-validation. As she later fiercely rebukes her husband's pacifying gesture of support and calm: "I didn't hit those men so I could be alive for the children, or for you. I hit them so my blood would stay in my body; so I could keep breathing. And if it's that easy, how are we supposed to live?...And we do this with rapture" (193). Ted's misplaced reassurance is attuned to conventional expectations that LuAnn has completely transcended, confirmed by her rhetorical question. If the passage's closing confirmation leaves as many unresolved issues as not, by the conclusion we (and LuAnn) have gained a sense of her now fully secure, self-contained, able to pull her separate selves together, having found a vocabulary commensurate with the unavailing vicissitudes of life (quite a different notion than Munro's "dear life"). She ends "amazed at my body" (192), at its capacity for unrestrained violence only minutes after she was simply buying groceries.

What confounds LuAnn (and us) is the idea that enduring rape might actually have been preferable to responding as she did in sheer defense of her body, since that response has so completely transformed her sense of herself. The revelation she has is a perfect confirmation of the epiphany one feels at the end of the story, in defiance of the rape itself. More to the point, LuAnn now seems aware of the odd disconnect between the story's conventional opening description of character and the discovery she makes of her own more complicated identity through the violence that has erupted into her life. As Elliot Eglash has observed:

what terrifies LuAnn is that evil lurks within us, waiting for the right moment to express itself, a moment when it can be written off as familial love. It haunts her that she doesn't know what the men wanted, and seems to think that if they had "only" wanted to rape her, it would have been better to simply endure it.... Or at least, it would have accorded more with her image of herself as a good, religious woman. The root of the dilemma seems to crystalize in her last word of dialogue, "rapture," which has strong religious connotations. It seems terrible to her that the moment when she should actually feel rapturous does not occur during her normal, quotidian activities, but rather in the process of nearly beating two men to death. A god who sanctions this kind of ecstatic response to violence does indeed present serious moral qualms. But in another sense, the violent encounter was a sort of cleansing, or confession. It made LuAnn, who before was "far removed from nature," now re-appreciate the sheer normalcy of her day to day life.   (Eglash)

As well, the very process of reading the story makes us aware of the asymmetry between our own retrospectively constructed narratives and the conventional descriptors we customarily invoke. Dubus all but self-consciously calls into question the very ploy he (and we) use to identify one another—the conventional earmarks of identity itself. LuAnn's realization becomes ours, in the dissociation between violent causational episodes and the narratives we comfortingly tell ourselves, trying vainly to constrain uninhibited occasions within civilized plots that supposedly proclaim our humanity.

V. Against Expectations

Dubus was fully aware of this pattern in later stories, having come increasingly to express identity through violence, sometimes physical, at others via psychological pressures that can seem almost as eviscerating. It is as if he realized how fully we needed to project identifiers into identity, grasping figures presented to us in all the ways detail allows. That self-consciousness may be evident most fully in the stories that occasionally play against it, countering the basic confirmations of character he so often provides. In "A Love Song," for instance, he offers a strange twist to his characteristic opening: "Call her Catherine. When her heart truly broke, she was thirty-seven years old, she had two teenaged girls, and her husband loved another woman. She smelled the woman's love on his clothes" (20). Instead of instant, secure identification, we are offered a shape-shifting imperative—"Call her Catherine"— which forms an odd nod to *Moby-Dick*'s opening of "Call me Ishmael." Much as with that novel, the story's narrator appears to engage an issue of privacy, deliberately keeping secret "Catherine"'s actual identity. Immediately, we wonder about this rather odd suppression (certainly in late Dubus), the unusual need for concealment. Why not, as in other occasional openings, simply refuse to name her, or postpone this imperative naming until later in the narrative? We never learn, even as the story tells us right off that "her heart truly broke" and can no longer be healed, given her conviction of being unable to begin over again.

Yet while the opening three words are *not* characteristic, the rest of the paragraph *is* familiar in laying out her situation, once again proffering information before we can possibly know what it means. This seems somehow typical of his late style, leaving the reader in uncertainty, enforcing a curiosity about why these details of identity should matter. In fact, the view of words we are given suggests they cannot grant us further knowledge, nor accord Catherine any amelioration of her situation. Consider how the four opening sentences bring us into this situation, first via a brief identification that is actually a concealment; then a second sentence that outlines her betrayal and sums up the plot; followed by a third that focuses on the lingering scent of perfume that revealed her husband's adultery. And all leads to the final sentence that forms an untethered run-on, tumbling out of the unassuageable need to go over again what cannot be repaired:

Even the woman's name, when she learned it from her husband's lips, was not large enough, only two words for the breath and flesh and voice and blood of only a woman, only part of what she had traced by smell on his sweater one night, his jacket another, and traced by intuition and memory when he was with her and when he was away at his normal times and when he was away on the evenings and weekend days he lied about; and what she had not traced but simply known long before she smelled another's love on him.   (20)

The suppression of "Catherine"'s actual name is finally given a near explanation, mirrored here in the unrepeatable name of her husband's lover.

More importantly, the anguished sentence unfolds amid clauses that map the terrain of Catherine's dismay, gathering us into the woman's appalling emotional paralysis, registered in the circling-back syntax itself—its grasping repetitions and anaphoras ("only," "traced," "when he was"), its water-treading polysyndeton ("breath and flesh and voice and blood"), its staggering breathlessness. The sentence moves less forward than backward, reverting to the scent she smelled only two sentences earlier, crashing into consciousness as the demise of devotion, the death of a marriage. The whole captures the irrevocable quality of betrayal, of love outraged, no longer reciprocated, closed down. And just as the story inverts Dubus's habitual conventions in some ways, it also confounds his usual celebration of violence as restorative. Here the psychological carnage leads to no resolution and little reprieve, though the effect is clearly recognizable as part of his later style. Still, the story establishes a rhythm nearly the opposite of "Out of the Snow," with its simple, straightforward chronicling of a life apparently somehow unlived, of consciousness ruthlessly untethered, until violence finally redirects LuAnn to essentials.

Here, the violence has already occurred, leaving "Catherine" shattered, deracinated, unable to move on. Even more fully, the second paragraph clarifies this in a hopeless spiraling outward into the universe, as at first language fails, then body, then earth, and finally light itself. A reference to "the woman's name" seems initially to refer to Catherine herself but

then becomes apparent as her husband's lover. Yet strangely in a story
by Dubus, we discover that a name that means nothing, that does not
"refer" to the pain she is feeling, that fails to intersect with her in any
significant fashion except as a sign of eviscerating loss, is nonetheless the
center of her emotional vocabulary, her entire psychological panorama:

> The woman's name could not encompass what was happening. Nor could the
> words *love* and *lie* and *sorry* and *you*, nor could her own name on his tongue,
> on the night he told her in the bright light of their kitchen the color of cream,
> while upstairs their daughters slept. Nor could tears, nor any act of her body,
> any motion of it: her pacing legs, her gesturing arms, her hands pressing her
> face. The earth itself was leaving with her sad and pitying husband, was drawing
> away from her. Stars fell. That was a song, and music would never again be lovely;
> it was gone with the shattering stars and coldly dying moon, the trees of such
> mortal green; gone with light itself. (21)

Again, in this very short story, the heart-destroying beat of her syntax
("nor...nor...nor") tends to wrench everything apart, confirming
the opening claim that "her heart truly broke." The description is
hardly literal, of course, but it does come to seem more than simply
figurative, more than a casual momentary setback.

    The cumulative weight of the prose underlines a sixteen-year-
marriage suddenly gone up in smoke, even as each successive paragraph
seems only to add to the anguish, as if she could not let it go, or rather
it could not release her. Sentences break down into clauses, as she reviews
the calculations presumed, over and over, in the two-hour discussion
with her husband early the morning after. Now she's dried out, saved
only by the occasional bonds with her daughters when it's possible for
her to feel present, in the moment. And yet a strangely deracinated
quality pervades the story, infusing a largely absent voice with intense
pain bordering on hysteria. That apparent paradox centers the whole,
as Elizabeth Ussery has observed: "the narrator gives us her name and
access to such intimate moments throughout the narrative, yet we
aren't allowed her voice aside from a single thought, *I am here. Now.*
(22). It seems fascinating that the one thought we have access to is a
thought that contradicts the entire narrative."[6] This observation gets to

---

6. As Elizabeth continues: "When she says *I am here. Now,* however, she's almost permanently lost all sense of light, of color, even the ability to speak certain words. Where is
   here, exactly? This is an instance (similar to other works) where the meaning of words
   doesn't quite fit. One of my favorite lines is at the beginning when the narrator says;
   'Even the woman's name...was not large enough, only two words for the breath and

the power of Dubus's late prose in focusing on a moment of trauma that cannot adequately be expressed, or somehow fails of suitable representation; that very ineffability itself speaks to the emotional trauma, making clear how little narrative can help either Catherine or us. In short, the story's unusual opening somehow anticipates the problem once again for Dubus of making words, descriptors, identities all match an experience that evades them.

Time does pass, of course, but it regularly lacks any genuine healing power, defying conventional platitudes. Her husband remarries over the next year and spring's promise reliably returns, but instead of revival the season reminds her how little has actually changed. In an astonishing evocation, she feels reduced to no more than a passive part of nature, first figuratively and then somehow progressively in an almost literal fashion:

She sat on the patio, drinking a soft drink without sugar, and knew that she longed for spring even as she watched it; she was last April's leaves fallen in autumn, then frosted, then frozen under snow, and in March wet again and becoming part of the earth, while spring was moving before her eyes, leaving her with the other dead it gave life to a year ago, when not only her skin but her heart felt the touch and light of the sun.   (24)

The very possibility of love renewed is something denied, sequestered off. At the earliest sign of another's interest, she becomes even more self-contained than the seasons in their cycles, closing down any possibility of opening up or out. Yet for all her self-control, for all her self-denial, the story ends with a strange, almost unearned evocation of joy at her daughters' weddings: "filling her, so her body felt too small for it, and she deepened her breath to contain it, to compress it, to keep it in place in her heart" (26).

In barely six pages, the narrative encapsulates a life defined by nothing but the devastation of betrayal, shorn of lingering hope though finally the emergent prospect of love itself cannot be suppressed. As elsewhere in the late stories where a dramatic moment appears to change the

flesh and voice and blood of only a woman, only part of what she traced by smell on his sweater at night . . . ' (20). The repetition of 'tracing' is continued in the sentence a few times, which I thought was a nice way to think about not only the power of the eight spoken words in the narrative, but also that first line. Along with Catherine's thought, there are four other italicized words: *love, lie, sorry, you*. While it's clear they are the husband's words, they are out of context and detached from meaning. They trace perhaps the gist of what the husband felt but don't adequately root the reader in his remorse. Why should we believe him? We don't even know his name."

direction of a life, any epiphany comes to seem almost crueler than its absence, evidenced in the failure of life's traumatic pain to stymie an ever irrepressible faith in possibility—if not for Catherine herself, so-named in hiding her pain, then at least for her daughters in the feeling of joy that bubbles up. In short, even in manipulating his opening sentence in order to bury Catherine's identity, Dubus again challenges usual assumptions about identity itself. We feel, if only retrospectively at the end, that Catherine could not be named because she is no longer whole, held together, identical with her body, her memory, her assumed self-assurance.

Repeatedly, Dubus returns in his late stories to fraught experience that seems to collapse into moments, whether Rusty's anniversary of a vicious shark attack or Catherine's memory of a tangled marriage reduced to the stark realization of loss. Even in scenes far less dramatic, a similar transition defies our interpretive calm. Take the figure in "Woman on a Plane," whose dread of flying to visit her brother is upended by anguish over his fatal illness. "Fear scattered her grief" (99), she realizes, even as he counsels her:

embrace your fear... They could have been sitting at her kitchen table, drinking wine. He could have been saying: *Read Tolstoy; lie in the sun; make love only with one you love.* He had told her that, drinking wine at her table, years ago. She looked at his face on the pillow, wanting to see him as he had seen himself, holding his fear in his arms. She saw her brother dying.   (101)

The wise admonition does little to ease her feelings—admonitions rarely do in Dubus. But the more important realization is that the story focuses on moments of conscious recollection from an unusual perspective, one that tends to abridge the past and instead offers a spotlight on various intersecting events. Here, the convergence takes place as a merging of imagination, memory, and desire that confound our usual temporal reconstructions, confusing expectation and recollection. As Cameron Platt observes of the woman's circling in on the obsession she at last sums up as bare observation ("She saw her brother dying"):

These associations move in the opposite direction from what we might expect: Rather than bloom outward from the moment of experience, they precede it; they seem to compose the fact of experience as they accumulate and culminate. Dubus appears to resort to his simple, declarative final sentence only as he cannot adequately express the complex—and perhaps more real—transformations of consciousness that underlie it. In the free indirect discourse of his narration, he also transfers the subjects of these sentences from "They" to "He" to "She," as though his central female character tries to enforce mutuality and empathy in consciousness but finds that she must return to the singleness of her own experience. (Platt)

Again, his pointed late style tends to work its perspectives more intently, in this case questioning from various syntactic angles our readerly understanding of who constructs experience, and how the past is to be sympathetically understood, whatever pain it has caused.

That intersection of perspectives, whether internal as here or the result of mutual relations, informs not only the most violent of Dubus's stories but also those less inflamed, with an equally revelatory power. Take one of the more retrospective of his final stories, "The Colonel's Wife," whose very title already displaces its subject one remove. And though the narrative emerges as a more subdued and domestic investigation than most, it opens in characteristic late fashion with name, rank, and nearly serial number, offering rather woodenly the bare essential facts. The story surveys the way accident not merely cripples lives or hijacks imaginations but how it compels us to reassess pasts, learning to accept them as well as each other. The colonel has been left no longer ambulatory with the cause unexplained for pages. Unlike "Blessings," however, which returns obsessively to horrible life-altering conditions, here the narrative simply assumes them, focusing on the transfigured consciousness created by the brutal accident and what it means for a man whose military career had never revealed to him what violence could actually effect. Now nursed by his wife, Robert thoughtfully contemplates his recurrent fears of fire, of falling, of simply excreting without assistance, ending in the absence of all desire.

Yet desire is not so readily quenched, as he discovers in realizing his wife has a lover. Immediately, he suffers emotional turmoil, forced repeatedly to review his self-confident career abroad and a life apart from her, when "he had believed he knew where she was" (117). Finally, he "listened to the house" (116) and pulls her to him in a gesture that seems akin to "Blessings," of deep pain—in this case emotional, not physical—that has its own fierce intensity, but that opens Robert to an insight into Lydia, to love, to aging and to his reduced self. Her admission of the affair now well past forms a gesture that paradoxically binds them closer together, freeing him to open up to her, to share his own infidelities, to make him even accept the fundamental realization of a Dubus story: "I'm glad that damned horse fell on me. It made me lie still in one place and look at you" (121). Violence leads once again to a transfiguring revelation, an epiphany utterly unlike Munro's treatment of a similar theme in "Dolly."

Again, Dubus does not settle into a predictable pattern, whatever shared stylistic and thematic strains emerge in his later career. Indeed, a final example demands attention if only to offer a converse perspective, one that seems to invert his usual concerns. "The Lover" ends by offering a different version of Dubus's late style, though it opens characteristically—"Lee Trambath was a fifty-five-year-old restaurant manager, with three ex-wives and five children" (123)—and then sums up a history in which pain, loss, and betrayal no longer hurt (unlike Catherine): "time had healed him, had allowed him to forget whatever he and the women had done to each other, or removed the precision of pain from his memory" (123). Lee does, in fact, accept responsibility for that history, without feeling hampered emotionally or otherwise cautious about trying again to connect, if only out of a naive faith in love, a word that recurs in his thoughts.

The story tends to work subliminally, as the simple impulse to go for a cup of coffee in the rain leads him to a café—though he is led as much in paratactic prose that embodies his disconnected emotional state as he is prompted by the simple physical desire for coffee in a café. There, he plays out a scene with the attractive waitress Doreen that we imagine he has repeated with others, even though he refuses to allow that failed past to dictate his present. From one perspective, Lee recalls William James's intriguing philosophical claim that "Fear doesn't cause running away. Running away causes fear" (131), which nicely inverts Dubus's recurrent emphasis on transfiguring violence to suggest that effects conversely can actually create their own causes. As if defying Dubus's more recumbent late vision, we are offered a magically inverted program, in which "Acting the way you want to feel" (132) may serve better than responding to life's injustices. Of course, that is hardly a simple possibility in Dubus's world, presuming one can actually make a choice of the kind of life one desires instead of succumbing to traumas and habits that otherwise dictate a future.

Clearly, however, Dubus can imagine just such a narrative trajectory, with Doreen attracted to Lee, and him wanting to create possibility rather than simply reacting. "He felt the cool plume of a lie. 'I want to feel you,' he responds to her question of 'What is it you want to feel?'" (132). Immediately, "The lie spread upward, but light was in her eyes, and she was standing, was saying softly: 'Let's go'" (132). The wonderful gesture of a "cool plume of a lie" that he wants to make into a truth leads to their emotional union as he opens up. What becomes compelling, however, is his realization that "His life was repeating itself, yet it felt not repetitious but splendid, and filled with grace" (133). Flannery O'Connor, an important influence on Dubus (and not only as a Catholic writer), has argued that "All human nature vigorously resists grace because grace changes us and the change is painful" (307). But "The Lover" reveals Lee's increasing awareness of what it is he wants from love, as a form of transcendence and actual "grace," which is always, necessarily disruptive. The love he seeks with Doreen forms, as he realizes, not a retreat from pain but an opening up to the possibility once again of being hurt, throwing oneself once more into the fray by extending oneself to another, leaving oneself always at risk. It may not be too derivative at this point to recall Dr. Johnson on second marriages as invariably "the triumph of hope over experience," which finally becomes the triumph of life over death.

VI. Conclusion, Pre-Modernist?

Dancing After Hours collects stories together that often open similarly and move via disruptively violent moments toward startling epiphanies: all parts of Dubus's distinctively late style. It is as if we can see a convergence of vision and treatment both, sometimes anticipated in earlier stories but come to fruition only in his final years. At this point, however, it is worth addressing the ordering of stories in his collection itself with a series of questions, especially in contrast to Munro, for whom starting with any story was presumably the same as starting with any other, much as her attitude to reading individual stories themselves. Dubus clearly differs, both within his stories and among them. Why open with "The Intruder," written decades earlier of a teenager's manslaughter of his sister's boyfriend, then turn to the ironically titled "A Love Song" about a woman tormented by her husband's infidelity? Why spread LuAnn's and Ted Briggs's three linked stories so broadly, interrupting them with others? Indeed, Ted's separate bachelor story comes temporally earliest, though third in overall order, before the three of his and LuAnn's marital experiences that then follow in chronological succession. And that story seems nearly to reverse the arc of "A Love Song," ending with Ted emotionally crushed by his actress girlfriend's abandonment of him, aware of how much his love for her has undone him: "feeling only helpless now; and ashamed, knowing what a woman could do to him, knowing she could do it because he wanted her to" (42).

On the other hand, why include "Sunday Morning" and "The Last Moon" in this collection, about brutal, remorseless homicides, when their tone seems so different from the rest? And why end with "Dancing After Hours," about Emily's tentative return to the possibility of being involved, embraced, awakened from hibernation—a theme that has woven throughout the whole, perhaps especially in "The Lover"? After all, sequence almost always matters (for anyone other than Munro, that is), with not only collected stories, but novelistic chapters and books of poems. Yet Dubus's intention does not quite reveal itself, nor does the collection's arrangement clarify how we are meant to pull the whole together.

If the questions raised by his story sequencing continue to stand unanswered, we can at least observe another aspect of Dubus's late style in the intersecting narrative rhythms, themes, and counterpointed strains that weave through *Dancing After Hours*. That is certainly different from earlier collections, which seem less concerned with a shared focus or intertwining a mutual set of concerns. In fact, Mitchell Hammer has argued that Ted and LuAnn's experience seems

written even by the stories that did not mention them. For example, after "Falling in Love" comes "Blessings" and then "Sunday Morning." Neither Ted nor LuAnn are in these stories, yet after we read "All the Time in the World" we are struck by the sense that despite their absence, their story was still in a way being told. In "Blessings" we discover the selfless and all-consuming love of a mother over her child and the tenacity of family; in "Sunday Morning" we feel the fear/mistrust Ted feels after Susan's betrayal (in the form of the abortion). These sentiments are repeated in the beginning of "All the Time in the World" by LuAnn, who becomes weary and shut off from love. Even though the stories are not about them, Dubus develops their narratives in these stories so that the reader reads their relationship with all the themes picked up along the way in stories where they are not present. Another function of the separation of the Ted/LuAnn narrative by other stories is to mimic the passage of time that occurs between each blip of their lives we get.   (Hammer)

That forms a provocative reading of sequencing, of the interleaved stories in the collection and more generally of the process by which Dubus succeeds in linking lives, in melding consciousnesses, in recognizing a brotherhood among figures drawn together by trauma and disappointment, desire and expectation. As Ted Briggs realizes midway through, in a remarkable confession he makes to LuAnn: he had "stopped believing people wanted advice; they wanted to be looked at and heard by someone who loved them" (173). And that claim seems genuinely to embody a vision Dubus has struggled to embrace throughout *Dancing After Hours*.

Munro is more likely to leave us bewildered in her late stories; Williams to leave us on edge, between this world and the next; Davis more likely to offer snippets of insight, some marvelous, others banal. But Dubus views experience with a certain religious seriousness that becomes clear in later stories variously sharpening the implications present earlier: through replicated introductions; through a more dramatic focus on isolated, violent incidents; through a prose pitched less chronologically and more toward an emotional register. Even when characters fully embrace the epiphanies they experience, as Rusty Williams and Lee Trambath and Colonel Robert Townsend succeed in doing, others like "Catherine" remain unmoored from their lives, far from the rapture experienced by LuAnn Williams.

That seems to be the point, as Dubus's modestly disjointed late narratives unsettle the intersections of past and present, igniting mundane facts with inflaming details that intersect in transformative ways— sometimes keeping trauma alive, at others simply reminding us how fragmented our lives actually are, but always to help us find transcendent significance in the everyday. Keep in mind that the famously modernist mode (depicted so convincingly by Henry James, Franz Kafka, and Samuel Beckett, among others) is of life as a matter of patiently waiting, hoping against hope for something simply to happen, lingering with expectation that is frequently unfulfilled. Dubus seems relatively uninterested in such an accommodating view, and returns in his stories to a more familiar pre-modernist terrain of unsettling occasions and eruptions of violence, precisely because those compressed experiences seem to be where life is lived most vividly, most intensely, most as *life*. In that sense, narrative is less about residual grief over what is already long gone, or about parsing feelings of loss, than it is about capturing moments where everything suddenly converges, coming together in a starburst of self-realization.

By that token, how one begins the narrative of one's life hardly matters. The commonplace triggers of identity (name, age, description, vocation, and so on) rarely get at the emotional core that makes each of us immediately identifiable, even special. For that is, of course, what Dubus's stories end by revealing, having begun with an egalitarian view only to shift to the devastating particularities that make us us. If his late stories so often begin all but exactly alike, their extraordinary revelations just as often emerge by ending quite differently (in simple events, of course, but more importantly in emotional repercussions). Even when their revelations seem more or less akin, it is only to remind us variously of what we all knew so well as children, though have long since forgotten: that the violence of the world is everyday, and that *in* that violence we find ourselves transfigured, removed from habitual comforts, compelled anew (as if for the first time) to recognize how fragile and miraculous the gift of consciousness is, or can be. Where other writers may placate us by avoiding the effects of dislocation, turning us back to comfort in the long familiar, Dubus warns that we are always exposed, never secure in the identities we supposedly secure so tightly for ourselves.

3

Disjointedness in *The Visiting Privilege*

O f the four writers studied here, only two include epigraphs for their late collections, both coincidentally drawing on the New Testament. As observed above, the Cajun-Irish Catholic Dubus seizes on Christ's injunction to attend more fully to the present, warning against being distracted by mere duty and petty anxieties, alerting us to stories marked by epiphanies that reorient our spiritual compasses. Intriguingly, Williams as a Protestant likewise anticipates scenes of revelation and transfiguration, citing St. Paul's announcement that "we shall all be changed, In a moment, in the twinkling of an eye" (1 Corinthians 15:51). Yet though the epigraphs sound alike, the religious tenor of their separate collections turns out to be radically different: Dubus focused on the way that lives should flourish day by day, in spirited heedfulness; Williams fascinated not by how we comport ourselves but instead by the resonant aesthetic claims of the Bible, as an exquisite literary performance that resists casual interpretive gestures.

Time and again, biblical echoes spring to mind for her readers, alerted to how deeply her writing is shaped by the Gospel, saturated with scriptural references and allusions—indeed, part of an entire exegetical and imagistic tradition.[1] As Williams herself acknowledged about its verbal hold over her imagination,

---

1. Daughter of a father and grandfather who were both ministers, Williams admitted inheriting her father's Bibles: "Oh, yes. He had lots of Bibles. I kept them all. I've got my father's notebooks, his sermons. One of these days I'll get them organized. My mother always said she was going to throw them out. They're not meant to be read, they're meant to be heard, she said. But I've still got them" (Winner 36–7).

The Bible is constantly making use of image beyond words. A parable provides the imagery by means of words. The meaning, however, does not lie in the words but in the imagery. What is conjured, as it were, transcends words completely and speaks in another language. This is how Kafka wrote, why we are so fascinated by him, why he speaks so universally. On the other hand, there's Blake, who spoke of the holiness of minute particulars. That is the way as well, to give voice to those particulars. Seek and praise, fear and seek. Don't be vapid.   (Winner 54)

Yet even more than "the imagery" of Williams's stories, or "the holiness of minute particulars," what makes us realize we are firmly in her fictive realm has to do with her delight in provoking uncertainty: about what is genuinely true and what is otherwise merely imagined; about bizarre, otherworldly events and what they might otherwise actually mean. That strain as well, perhaps even more powerfully, was shaped by the Bible, whose transformative effect during her childhood she has recently acknowledged: "The Bible influenced me because all those wonderful stories—about snakes and serpents and mysterious seeds and trees—didn't mean what they seemed. They meant some other thing...that began my preoccupation with what a story can do...the literal surface is not important" (Bradley 574). Disorientation deeply characterizes Williams's vision, inspired by the Bible's transcendental contrast between surface detail and hidden meaning. Or as she has confessed, "my real interest lay in illuminating something beneath or beyond the story itself" (Winner 46).[2] As we will see, this fascination was to grow more dramatic and intensively concentrated in her later work.

Of course, the Bible did not alone shape the contours of Williams's stories, which more than most raise questions about other possible influences: Who inspired so peculiarly mixed a vision, at times hideously violent, at others eerily comic? Where can we find so grotesque and invasive a psychological inventory anticipated by other writers? She hardly resembles Chekhov, though drawn to inessential details deftly woven into revelations of lives ridden out day-to-day. And while Flannery O'Connor yokes together gallows humor and Christian sacrament, she fails to adumbrate Williams's darkly wry perspective, which is as unmistakably verbal (if syntactically sprained) as it is a product

---

2. Paul Winner claimed that "your characters seem to struggle to interpret the world's detritus, trying to make sense of ominous signs. A window opens for a moment, but then the window is shut. Is that a fair description of the writer's consciousness as well?" Williams responded: "I think the writer has to be responsible to signs and dreams. Receptive and responsible. If you don't do anything with it, you lose it. You stop getting these omens" (Winner 44).

of weirdly structured plots. Perhaps the writers with whom she most shares affinities are modernists like Beckett and Kafka, notable for their artfully disjunctive techniques, bizarre predicaments, and surreal effects, anticipating Williams's own unsettling narratives that likewise focus on liminal situations quizzically represented. Transitions seem notable more for their obvious absence than their suppressed presence, leading to what has been called her conspicuous "jump-cut effect" (Schutt), an abrupt turn among characters, scenes, sometimes clauses themselves that ends in not quite bridging banal moments with the memorable reversals they precede.

Clearly, Williams delights in the surprise of sheer disjointedness, with deadpan pronouncements erupting cheek by jowl amid mundane events, often set off by an uncommonly loose splash of exclamation points. Indeed, Dan Kois has observed of that punctuational preference: "When they appear, they hit like hammers. They suggest a kind of wonder at how she, and we, ever could have ended up in all these strange places" (26). Her wrenching, dissociative style offers a vision of experience at an angle, with familiar and otherwise settled aspects of life appearing (at least for the moment) utterly alien. Disarmed, dismayed, we enter a realm where customary rules no longer seem to apply, as if in a nightmare where borders dividing danger from security simply dissipate.

That evocative aura, obviously far from accidental or inadvertent, is central to the vision Williams has always conjured out of materials redolent of nothing more than the everyday. "Mystery seems to be the very soul of her stories," Neel Mukherjee argues, "whether it lies in their interpretive indeterminacy, in the surreal turn some of them take, or in their frequent gestures towards, or the incursion of, the metaphysical; they remain irreducible and inexhaustible" (Mukherjee). In explaining that alluringly enigmatic effect, he finds himself compelled to resort to the paradox of nuclear physics somehow paired with the dangers of mountaineering: "Like some subatomic particle, Williams can be in two states simultaneously: compassionate and ruthless. Her vision is angular, undeluded, astringent. The blank space between each of her sentences is loaded with intelligence and surprise, because you can never tell what the next sentence is going to be, or bring. Reading her is exhilarating and dangerous, as if you're poised on the brink of a canyon" (Mukherjee). That stance of hesitant instability, hovering expectantly above contradiction, characterizes Williams's persistent effort to induce in readers a mood of tremulous mystification.

The author herself is on record as craving fiction at once "exhilarating and dangerous," admitting of stories she enjoys by others as well as those she expects to write in tones that echo Munro's similar confession: "I want to be devastated in some way" (Kois 27). Elaborating further, she argues for a large measure of wily insincerity in her craft: "What a story is, is devious. It pretends transparency, forthrightness. It engages with ordinary people, ordinary matters, recognizable stuff. But this is all a masquerade. What good stories deal with is the horror and incomprehensibility of time, the dark encroachment of old catastrophes—which is Wallace Stevens, I think" (Winner 40–1). That invocation of "the horror and incomprehensibility of time" helps explain what links so many of her stories together, early and late. Defining the terms of that vision and how it has evolved, however, is hardly straightforward.

From the beginning, a wavering tension between elusive mystery and spiritual unease marks Williams's stories. Like Munro and Davis, her later style intensifies those qualities of voice, meaning, and verbal performance that have been present throughout, in her case lending a more clearly barbed aspect to depictions, with disorientation sharpened both syntactically and thematically. Ever more indiscriminate violence reveals a more deeply disquieting tenor to experience, edging toward liminal moments that disrupt our normal sense of determinate borders. Indeed, consciousness is increasingly tipped into an inanimate world, with the paranormal treated as normal, the mystical accepted as commonplace, even as ordinary relations between people become progressively frayed. As well, Williams increasingly invokes an array of familiar texts, from the Bible to Kant, from Rimbaud to Chekhov and Kafka, but ever more often in odd allusions and wacky innuendos.

One late example, taken from a conversation between strangers on a ferry, may lift a curtain on this later eccentric propensity:

It's apparently why Rilke left his wife, why he left home. Because he wasn't allowed to "go into the dog." Or if he did he would have to attempt to explain it, which spoiled everything. He loved easing himself into the dog, into the dog's very center, into the place from which the dog existed as a dog, the very place, he said, where God would have rested when the dog was complete, to watch him.   (405)

The seriousness with which Williams entertains this strangely skewed possibility is enough to distinguish her vision from anyone else's.

Moreover, like Davis, she offers the advantage of allowing the reader to assess her career-long arc in a single volume. *The Visiting Privilege: New and Collected Stories* (2015) gathers up nearly all her earlier efforts followed by recent stories, making it clear how her perspective and expression have become more astringently aligned over time.[3]

I. Indeterminacies of Narrative

As emblem of that late style, take "The Country" (2014), which intensifies the hallmark features she has steadily honed for decades: of death as well as bewildering incomprehension; of the intractable problems of communicating not only with living loved ones but well beyond the grave; and in prose that keeps the reader precariously on edge, unnerved, as if cast into the midst of an alien yet somehow eerily familiar world. The narrator's spouse has left for unknown reasons, though the reader is stymied much as characters are confused, leaving it unclear for pages whether the speaker is male or female, adult or child. When it finally becomes apparent that he is a husband and father, description still fails to keep pace or otherwise set the scene, with his other relationships now revealed to be as indeterminate as his identity had been at the story's beginning: "things have become more volatile. We live alone, you understand, the child and I. He's nine, and the changes in this decade have been unfathomable. Indeed, it's a different civilization now. My parents, with whom we were very close, died last year. My wife left in the spring. She just couldn't feel anything for us anymore, she said" (463). Generalizations about volatility, about civilization itself being somehow different, seem yet unearned. And the narrator's aphoristic claim (again, a familiar Williams gesture) about "The tree that bears the fruit is not the tree that was planted. He knows that much, it goes without saying" (463), remains fumblingly enigmatic, though with definite biblical echoes, both Old and New

---

3. "Woods" was dropped from *Taking Care* (1982); "Gurdjieff in the Sunshine State" and "The Route" were dropped from *Escapes* (1990); and "Claro" was dropped from *Honored Guest* (2004). Her most recent publication, *Ninety-nine Stories of God* (2016), takes a radical swerve that seems to have been influenced by Lydia Davis more than Williams's own earlier work (which explains why it is not addressed in these pages). The stories are each at most a few pages, offering a mix of theological, nonfictional ruminations.

Testament.[4] But what does it mean here in its slightly mangled form, and what does his son's professed knowledge consist of?

Next day, the man's wife surprisingly returns to "cut back the orange tree" (464)—a gesture apparently if inexplicably linked to his aphorism—though she then abruptly, unexpectedly departs before finishing. Their young son Colson remains phlegmatic: "He's through with her. I wonder if somehow I have caused this latest unpleasantness. I have never known how to talk about death or the loss of meaning or love. I seek but will never find, I think" (464). Again, the final sentence is a biblical quote, of Christ's warning to his disciples about the afterlife, as if the father were quietly conceding that Colson has access to that world beyond death, access denied to him.[5] But how to measure the tone of slightly stilted, somewhat pretentious self-dramatization—or is it something else? The paratactic rhythm of successive anaphoric sentences seems mildly troubling, without coalescing into any clear reckoning of the situation. This is the imaginative world that Williams weaves, although our customary uncertainty in reading her has become more extreme as we teeter between states of consciousness, either bound by a peculiar psychosis or simply baffled by a son's condition.

What we soon learn is that the paternal narrator has discovered his son is a medium between two worlds, a fantastic condition he has learned to treat as by now routine if emotionally taxing: "When he enters these phases I become exhausted. Sometimes, I admit, I flee. He doesn't seem to need me to fulfill his conversations with the dead, if indeed they are conversations. They seem more like inhabitations. And they're harmless enough, if disorienting" (466). Colson speaks to him in different but recognizable intonations, with the narrator ruefully conceding that this ghostly intercession has had the salutary effect of improving past relations: "I find it easier to be with my father when Colson brings him. Though he always seemed rather inscrutable to me he now doesn't sadden me so" (466).

---

4. This seems to invoke Psalm 1:3: "And he shall be like a tree planted by the rivers of water, that bringeth forth his fruit in his season; his leaf also shall not wither; and whatsoever he doeth shall prosper." Though it also resembles Matthew 7:18–19: "A good tree cannot bear bad fruit, and a bad tree cannot bear good fruit. Every tree that bringeth not forth good fruit is hewn down, and cast into the fire."

5. John 7:34: "Ye shall seek me, and shall not find me: and where I am, thither ye cannot come." Reiterated in John 8:21: "Again He said to them, 'I am going away, and you will look for Me, but you will die in your sin. Where I am going, you cannot come.' "

Yet as Colson continues to channel the dead, the narrator grows restive, resisting these odd spiritual interventions in a deepening state of disquietude. He finds familiar domestic patterns placed perpetually at risk, the predictable become somehow capricious, even if Williams's characteristic perspective renders his hesitations wryly amusing: "I never know whom I will be coming home to, whether it will be mother, father, wife or son. Often it is just my son, my boy, and matters are quite as they should be" (463). This ghostly incarnation of family members seems at once preposterous yet perfectly natural, as Williams converts the logical language of realist description into an evocation of experience few of us have had, or even believe possible. Colson himself seems simultaneously adolescent and curiously avuncular, intoning his oracular observations in recognizable deliveries: " 'We are here to prepare for not being here,' he says in my mother's soft, rather stroke-fuddled voice" (466). And we are reminded again of orotund biblical phrasings, even though it is "my mother's voice of wonderment" (466) that lingers for the father.[6] Bringing the dead alive, putting us in touch with those who have gone before (as Colson does), is of course what Williams likewise achieves as an author, and like her the boy clarifies what had seemed inscrutable all along. Ironically, the narrator's demand that Colson desist, having become inflamed at those irrepressible figures and forces who want to intrude from the other side, only confirms his failure to realize that one can never keep the dead at bay. Like troubling memories, they persist willy-nilly, embodied in the articulations we hear, or otherwise overhear.

By the end, we feel compelled to reconsider the story's murkier aspects, beginning with the narrator's initial meeting of a group that regularly discusses issues of some philosophical import. Jeanette responds to the formulaic opening question "Why Are We Here?" by claiming that "her purpose was to be there with the dying in their final moments. Right there, in attendance. Strangers for the most part. No one she knew particularly well. She found that she loved this new role. It was wonderful, it was amazing to be present for that moment of transport" (460). The prose rhythm itself is once again mildly disturbing, signaling in its broken paratactic cadence something of the uncertainty of the narrator's reaction. For a further unknown reason,

---

6. Luke 7:27: "This is he, of whom it is written, Behold, I send my messenger before thy face, which shall prepare thy way before thee."

her explanation appalls the narrator, who considers Jeanette distinctly "evil" as he ponders her response, walking home afterwards through a landscape become "this wasteland" (463).

As if to explain his dour impression, he adds, "I would like to move to the country but the boy refuses. Besides, 'the country' exists only in our fantasies anymore" (462). The admission once again invokes a recognizable biblical reference, even as the seemingly stark, passing remark that "country" no longer exists anticipates questions raised at the end about the narrator's uncertain condition.[7] Still, given the story's title, we are alerted to the importance of fantasy voices themselves. Only Jeanette alone appears at the next group meeting, with the narrator finally unable to suppress his inexplicable outrage at her: " 'It's disgusting what you're doing, you're like the thief's accomplice,' I say. 'No one can be certain about these things.' Suddenly she appears not nervous or accommodating in the least" (469). His reference to a "thief's accomplice," religiously inspired, leaves us with figures rendered all but allegorical. Yet her unerringly calm demeanor in the face of his verbal assault becomes itself disconcerting, another instance of behavior slightly awry, leading us to wonder at the larger context they inhabit.[8]

As confusion coalesces around these untoward, seemingly transformative exchanges, the narrator announces: "A few days later my father is back. He was a handsome man with handsome thick gray hair" (470). How does one understand this disconcerting reference to a man long dead? Colson channels his grandfather's voice, though he "doesn't seem to have heard me. He runs his fingers through his shaggy hair" (470), at which point we begin to wonder who the spectral presence is. Our doubts even arouse a suspicion that the narrator himself may be in an afterlife, already in limbo, unable to contact either the quick or the dead. Compounding that odd possibility is Jeanette's final behavior in the calm face of his incommensurate anger at her, insinuating the faint possibility that she may actually be a ghost helping to "transport" the living (as she earlier described her role), explaining his vituperative reference to her as "the thief's accomplice." The story's closing lines only confirm our uneasy response to all that has occurred,

7. Malachi 1:3 New International Version: "but Esau I have hated, and I have turned his hill country into a wasteland and left his inheritance to the desert jackals."
8. Proverbs 29:24: "Whoso is partner with a thief hateth his own soul: he heareth cursing, and bewrayeth it not." New International Version translates this as "The accomplices of thieves are their own enemies; they are put under oath and dare not testify."

matched by the father's own sense of suspense and untowardly eerie expectation: "I begin to speak but find I have no need to speak. The room is more familiar to me than I would care to admit. Who was it whose last breath didn't bring him home? Or am I the first?" (472). Once more, scriptural echoes reverberate through the prose, of Christ himself speaking, all but ventriloquizing the narrator.[9]

His own consternation reinforces a sense of being immured in a space between, unresolved, ill-defined. The story's title itself echoes *Hamlet*'s reliance on ghostly inferences in "the undiscovered country from whose bourn no traveler returns," all of which informs Williams's enchanted narrative vision of some possible world beyond our ken. Her fascination with biblical surfaces never becomes transparent, however, in contrast to Munro, who delights in starting her narratives anywhere simply because no temporal site is conceivably prior. Williams instead moves in a single narrative direction, if only to stress its own instability, its mild hold on all that fails to make sense. Only at the end do we consider the halting possibility that the narrator may actually be dead, his son in fact stranded in limbo, with a wife having left their garden so abruptly because both he and the boy are now gone. Thinking back, we come to realize how this possible scenario might help explain his attendance at meetings he never addresses, indeed where he is never acknowledged (save for Jeanette, the Charonesque ferry-woman), just as his lack of any gender or age in the story's opening pages emphasizes an eternal spiritual self at the expense of explicit bodily identification. In Williams's characteristic, compelling mode, none of this is at last resolved or otherwise lent confirmation. In short, she celebrates the indeterminate in ways altogether unlike others of the quartet, making us wonder at any confident assumptions of what we have read, deviously introducing an exhilarating and dangerous aspect to the story, leaving us in suspense long after it is over.

II. Early Tiltings at Consciousness

Turning back from "The Country" to earlier stories helps reveal the emergence of Williams's narrative preferences, and the way in which she has sharpened and shaped them into a singular imaginative vision.

9. Mark 15:37: "And Jesus uttered a loud cry, and breathed His last."

Her later calm acceptance of paranormal experience forms simply an extension of less radical strains explored long before, while the more darkly troubling aspects of psychology she later investigates have already been anticipated in less starkly pronounced ways early on. In "Summer" (1982), for instance, a wife on vacation with friends cannot stop mulling over her husband's heart attack or the transfiguring effect it has had: "Things appeared different now to Constance: objects seemed to have more presence, people seemed more vivid, the sky seemed brighter. Her nightmares' messages were far less veiled" (22).[10] Despite the echo of the Apostle Paul, less explicit than Williams later becomes (the language less clearly borrowed), and despite the similarity of this traumatic memory to many such in Dubus's stories, nothing here will become at all redemptive. In that regard, she resembles Munro, though more intensely fascinated by the "teeming, chaotic underside" of consciousness (Bradley 574). A fascination with psychology, both ordinary and extraordinary varieties, permeates even her early stories, though it never extends to particular curiosity about individual characters' fates. Indeed, while her stories establish situations open to psychological readings, narrators themselves resist intervening with either explanation or commentary, refusing to lend the reader an explicit hand in fathoming motivations.

Still, Williams's signature style early and late has the effect of quietly revealing the effects of strange attitudes and strained emotions. Altered consciousness in "Preparation for a Collie" (1982) is embodied through a spasmodic paratactic syntax, alerting the reader to the romper room mentality that reduces parents' tired mentality to their children's broken thought processes. "The house is always a mess. It is not swept. There are crumbs and broken toys beneath all the furniture. There are cereal bowls everywhere, crusty with soured milk. There is hair everywhere. The dog sheds" (33). Family life is viewed catawampus, extricated from conventional bromides, with the story ending nonetheless as "Jane kneels and kisses her soiled son. David does not look at her. It is as though, however, he is dreaming of looking at her" (37). That final clause reaffirms Williams's melding of psychological possibilities, of dream and reality somehow linked and mutually interdependent.

10. 2 Corinthians 3:13–14: "We are not like Moses, who would put a veil over his face to keep the Israelites from gazing at the end of what was fading away. But their minds were closed. For to this day the same veil remains at the reading of the old covenant. It has not been lifted, because only in Christ can it be removed."

The stakes seem rather different for a divorced mother in "The Wedding" (1982) desperately eager to remarry, finally achieving her wish with a much-divorced lover. Yet the grammatical resolutions sound characteristically Williams's own, suggesting emotional affirmation is little different for her from domestic disruption. At the reception after the ceremony, her new husband finds her alone in the bathroom where they share an "animistic embrace" whose ecstasy emerges in the repetitions and anaphoras leading to a certain magical release: "Sam kisses Elizabeth by the blue tub. He kisses her beside the sink and before the full-length mirror. He kisses her as they stand pressed against the windowsill. Together, in their animistic embrace, they float out the window and circle the house, gazing down at all those who have not found true love, below" (46). While Williams regularly resists epiphanies, or other moments of transfiguring insight, this unusual scene teeters right on the verge of one—in its floating, swooping blissfulness resembling nothing less than a reverie by Chagall. That sheer delight in all states of consciousness, whether in pedestrian struggles or mystifying enchantment or simple calculated confusion, again sets Williams apart from the other three writers if only because she resists trying to explain. And when characters do so, the result is often a mixture of grotesquery and wry comedy. In "The Blue Men" (1990), a driver discloses why she continued down the road after her car flipped over twice: "I thought it was just a dream, so I kept on going" (212). That barmy logic might well be taken as summing up the entire collection.

Williams's interest in the serendipitous turns of psychology seems to underwrite her willingness to conjecture that nature itself is variously conscious, as evident already in earlier stories. The titular figure in "The Yard Boy" (1982) admits to feeling sad, after which the narrator adds: "The fern can feel it too, which makes it gloomier than ever. Even so, the fern has grown quite fond of the yard boy. It wants to help him any way it can" (54). That kind of "help," asserted so casually, alerts us to Williams's strangely preternatural sense of the reach of consciousness. At other times, as in "Woods" (1982), the suggestion is rather more muted, though the description likewise verges on attributing agency to horticulture: "The forest was so thick it seemed static . . . and she heard branches falling on the roof and tapping against the aluminum siding" (*Taking Care* 56). Even daylight itself is described evocatively in "Train" (1982), casting itself indiscriminately over a richly assorted landscape: "It fell without prejudice on the slaughterhouses, Dairy

Queens and courthouses, on the car lots, Sabal palms and a billboard advertisement for pies" (76). Likewise, in "The Little Winter" (1990), a very different species of landscape looms ominously: "The land falling back from the highway was green and still. It seemed to her a slightly lugubrious landscape, obelisks and cemeteries, thick drooping forests, the evergreens dying from the top down" (166). The description is meant as expressive, but with Williams one forever waits for uneasily strained pathetic fallacies to somehow become comprehensively literal.

Weather itself seems capable of deliberately guiding, sometimes ordaining events, as in "Winter Chemistry" (1982): "The cold didn't invent anything like the summer has a habit of doing and it didn't disclose anything like the spring. It lay powerfully encamped—waiting, altering one's ambitions, encouraging ends" (89). Moreover, narrators *within* stories recognize the atemporality of their experience that readers *outside* the stories register stylistically, as in the moment in "Rot" (1990) when "Time wasn't moving sideways in the manner it had always seemed to her to move but was climbing upward, then falling back, then lurching in a circle like some poisoned, damaged thing" (147). The idea of temporal slippage, climbing, falling and lurching, exemplifies the corkscrewing perspective Williams characteristically adopts toward impersonal forces and features.

This tilting of consciousness might well seem a more appropriate condition for children than adults, and it comes as little surprise that Williams's first two collections, *Taking Care* (1982) and *Escapes* (1990), frequently focus on juveniles and adolescents. The latter's title story seems at first less astringent or abrupt than Williams's other work, though it nonetheless anticipates her wayward approach to emotionally devastating events. The narrative self-consciously foregrounds the dis-locating, peripatetic trajectory of Williams's style, as Lizzie recounts in random sequence her childhood efforts to come to terms with a father's abandonment and a mother's alcoholism, both futile "escapes" from something unnamed yet clearly inconsolable. The severe disjunctions of her later stories are already evident here, with a weirdly engaging narrative thread that slowly builds on irrelevant memories: of forgot-ten anecdotes; of a "nightclub that had a twenty-foot-tall champagne glass on the roof" (124); of a description of Houdini making elephants disappear; of a bear with a woman's pocketbook in its mouth. Arbitrary, disconnected moments establish a rhythm of their own that at times mildly resembles other contemporaries.

But unlike Munro, for whom episodes do not contribute to a forward temporal movement (hence allowing readers to start anywhere), and unlike Dubus, for whom violence invariably erupts unexpectedly and irrevocably, Williams elaborates a series of random episodes that register a child's still-nascent sense of sense-building. Munro, that is, thinks of narrative itself as inherently disconnected, always disrupting the accounts we give; Dubus instead considers life as unpredictable, always shifting abruptly before accounts can somehow account; Williams suggests, in a downward step, that it may be a matter of childhood development. For her, character is the turning point, whereas for her colleagues artistic principle and worldview are the central pivots. Each of Williams's depictions forms only a momentary narrative escape, sometimes all but into death itself (Houdini; the bear), even as they collectively register the haphazardly rambling experience of growing up the daughter of alcoholic disorientation.

Bewildered, Lizzie conveys a guileless incomprehension in her short sentences, her simple syntax, her predictably anaphoric expressions of desire for knowledge: "I wanted to see… "; "I wanted to know… " Indeed, the insistent repetition reveals a psychology plagued by anxiety and fear, although one might also construe it as an expression of guilt from the girl now grown up looking back on her younger self and mother, trying retrospectively to capture her psychological state at the time. Still, nearly everything that might explain the past eludes her inquiring eye, her desperate gestures, as she realizes how fully her mother's abiding habit of disappearing into books may have served as self-preservation but also effectively formed a *cordon sanitaire* quarantining the daughter she otherwise seems to love. As Lizzie first recalls, reading was "a place I could not go. My mother went back and forth to that place all the time" (125); later, "My mother looked up from the words in the newspaper. It was as though she had come back into the room I was in" (127); and later still, when her intoxicated mother disrupts a magic show by walking on stage: "She probably thought she was still in that place in herself, but everything she said were the words coming from her mouth" (132). Books seem to define an emotional wall between parent and child, maturity and adolescence, rationality and emotional deprivation.

Grown, Lizzie realizes her alcoholic mother had cared for her within the constraints of inebriation, and much of the story tries to recover that caring past even as Lizzie recalls her mother's warning that "a happy memory can be a very misleading thing" (130). The decided dislocations of her narrative presentation themselves thwart any coherent account that might reduce the past to a straightforward emotion, a conventional love, a typical suburban childhood. Williams refuses here to settle for an accommodating vision. Even so, Lizzie's interrupted reveries serve both as inadvertent escape from the discomfort of the past and inadmissible confirmation of that daily distress. At one point, her suppressed unconscious strikes back as she dreams of hair sprouting on the convertible her mother bought after her father's departure, leading to a poignant realization: "My mother and I were alone together as we always were, linked in our hopeless and uncomprehending love of each other" (126). Nothing more than a hirsute hallucination aligns them, even if that is enough for the moment.

Lizzie ends by looking back over the decades since mother and daughter escaped from the magic show, curiously able now to admit that her mother "was not able to pull herself through, but this was later. At the time, it was not so near the end… " (134). That staccato admission that "this was later" while then "it was not so near the end" comes as a characteristic formulation for Williams, one that springs us out of the moment only to turn back in without actually explaining the disruption or its effect. Finally, two sentences enforce a sense of relief from childhood incomprehension even as they forestall that possibility of escape for years, with Lizzie's careful salute toward the life she has sorrily led since the story's events: "I felt as though I must be with her somewhere and that she knew that too, but not in that old blue convertible traveling home in the dark, the soft, stained roof ballooning up as I knew it looked like it was from outside. I got out of it, but it took me years" (134). A life lived in revolt from escapes that had been recklessly navigated by parents has been captured with the all but parenthetical silence looming ever since the end of those "years." That silence constitutes at last all the leverage we will gain out of scenes we have witnessed—scenes that have, for better or worse, shaped the narrator.

As well, "Escapes" silently comments on much of Williams's own concerns to be adumbrated more fully, more precipitously, more disjointedly in her later work: of stories themselves posed as escapes; of reading as a process that can magically remove us beyond the habitual to a realm buffered from present pain; of details that at the time seem important but finally do not quite interconnect, as in most everyday lives; of love that seems too often amiss or awry, expressed ineffectually, in a family unit reduced to its final minimum; and finally, of Lizzie's closing realization of the effects that her own broken narrative will continue to have on herself long after. In all these respects, the story seems inimitably marked not only as Williams's own, where much that is unsaid bubbles up through sundry particulars, but as continuing to intensify through her later work. What began with efforts to reveal how decentered we can so often feel, unable to bring the separate parts of our lives together, will transition into ever more unsettling narratives of lives free of the all-too-familiar mental bulwarks.

At one point in the story, moreover, a self-reflexive moment seems to occur in a gesture that ironically defines a frequent aspect of Williams's own practice: "The usher said that the magician was not very good, that he talked and talked, he told a lot of jokes and then when you were bored and distracted, something would happen, something would have changed" (129). The magician and Williams are clearly unalike, with the exception that something magical so often appears unannounced, unanticipated in her stories that changes all we have read. That uncanny, enigmatic quality experienced by Williams's readers is achieved by narrative strategies much like those of the incompetent magician, though remodeled and highly refined. In that light, they may be best clarified by Neel Mukherjee: "Nearly all of her stories turn around a transformative moment, often mysterious to the point of acquiring a metaphysical valence, and often occurring outside the margins of the pages.... We have grown used to the invisible presence of the unsaid in the short story, but Williams's genius is to have it suddenly bubble up, giving us a momentary glimpse, then letting the surface settle again; everything is now changed, both for the reader and the characters" (Mukherjee). That fascination with the precariousness of consciousness helps explain part of the centrality of children to so many of Williams's early stories, which foreground the disquieting state of developing psychologies.

Yet settled adult psychologies can also be agitated, perhaps most intensely by the death of a loved one, which transforms settled points of view profoundly, even desperately. "Taking Care" (1982) speaks to the wavering possibility of effective human intercession in mortal affairs, though later Williams would apparently become less comfortingly assured about earlier affirmations. Jones, a preacher, is unsettled by his wife being medically tested, preparing for an operation that promises little, leaving him adrift in fear as he hopelessly offers her pills. Again, Williams's description of objects anticipates a character's psychological state, as the appearance of the pill cup closes down possibility itself: "The cup is the smallest of its type that Jones has ever seen. All perspective, all sense of time and scale seem abandoned in this hospital. For example, when Jones turns to kiss his wife's hair, he nicks the air instead" (4). That loss of perspective, that sense of bafflement at the fruitlessness of medical cautions and polite discretions, disappears in the misalignment of his wife's presumed fatal illness, as he thinks of their daughter's mental breakdown occurring at the same time, abandoning her own young daughter to him at this terrible moment of marital crisis. Consumed by fears that keep multiplying, Jones falls into an all-consuming terror that leaves him unmoored. Waiting for results of his cherished wife's operation, he silently despairs: "Has there ever been a time before dread?" (10).

Later, appalled by his feelings, he continues to envisage his beloved in terms of radical transition itself, from one complete state to another, as the narrator describes: "In the hospital, his wife waits to be translated, no longer a woman, the woman whom he loves, but a situation. Her blood moves as mysteriously as the constellations" (8). Prudent judgment is altered by the intensity of his prospective loss, as he returns home to clean house, depicted in Williams's characteristically reduced syntax punctuated by powerfully isolated moments, with the physical world once again radically unsettled: "He sits down. The room is full of lamps and cords. He thinks of his wife, her breathing body deranged in tubes, and begins to shake. All objects here are perplexed by such grief" (11). Again, that pattern of projecting emotion onto inanimate things, making them somehow conscious, will intensify in later stories, though here the "perplexed" objects seem little more than a metaphorical effect of his own distressed mentality.

Nothing avails, here or hereafter, exemplified in his own bootless, otherwise phatic injunction to "*Take care*," of which we are immediately informed that "Jones uses this expression constantly, usually in totally unwarranted situations, as when he purchases pipe cleaners or drives through toll-booths" (5). Only at the story's end, preparing for her return from the hospital, does he realize that "His wife's sickness has changed everything" (12), with the story itself subsiding into a more serene concentration on his own consciousness rather than shifting wildly between responses and confusion prompted by objects surrounding him. The point, of course, is that everything *has* been transformed unalterably by his fear, though that "everything" is only his own emotional balance. If the understandable moderation in Jones's imagined response forms a dramatic contrast to Williams's style, it is because knowledge and customary formulations simply break asunder in the extremity of grief.

III. Towards Death

Clearly, Williams has long been drawn to liminal moments, intrigued as a child by Bible stories and the disjunction between surface and depth and as an adult by the dissolution of life into death. In this latter, she again resembles Dubus, captivated by the drama of experience foreshortened by violence, though coupled for her by the uncertain prospect of an afterlife. Moreover, the idea of death self-inflicted looms increasingly large in her career. The once-suicidal narrator of "ACK" (2004) opens his account unable even now to fully abjure his self-destructive past, admitting the "rough years...I only managed to live through" by invoking the "tragedy" of Nantucket whales annually grounding on shore: "It's their fidelity to one another that dooms them, as well as their memories of earlier safe passages" (310). This repeated calamity is a reminder of years before, of "the dangerous imminence of an unendurable stranding" (312), with whales compelled to follow others into perilous shoals, serving as an admonition of the limits to human endurance as well. The narrator's past coupled with this annual cycle of cetacean deaths somehow punctuates the otherwise petty pursuits detailed in the story, whose title seems initially odd as simply the air-port code for Nantucket. But it also stands for "acknowledged signal" (in the mobile radio communication system), apparently referring to the frantic terminal exchanges among whales but also among people— of the anonymous narrator, his prickly spouse Pauline, and an array of casual acquaintances.

The story opens haphazardly at a dinner party where desultory conversation keeps us off balance, bringing to mind Williams's penchant for narrative disjunctions as relations begin to unravel. A local mother arrives, daughter in tow, whose mildly irritating behavior angers Pauline beyond patience, compelling her to leave the party as her hus-band ramblingly recalls an account of whale hunting they had earlier heard—his memory enhanced by Melvillean echoes from the chapter "Stubb Kills A Whale":"Pauline had been quite right about the whales. Had they not cried out in the days of their destruction with exquisite and anguished song? Yet their pursuers wanted only to extinguish them. Indeed, many had reveled in the fine red mist that rose and then fell, as though from heaven, from the great collapsing hearts to herald the harried and bewildered creatures' deaths" (317). The style here evolves into a dramatically powerful peroration, however unearned, as if the story's opening prospect of whales self-destroyed coupled with its ending account of their cruel slaughter were meant as telling contrast to a dinner party upended by trivial expectations. Interweaving the banal with the momentous, Williams again reveals a fragile, sometimes eerie balance as we navigate between liminal states of consciousness and oblivion, this world and the next.

Regularly, much like Munro and Dubus, Williams exposes the presumably clear-cut design of our lives—the familiar characters that wallpaper our days, the mundane behaviors that criss-cross our hours, the commonplace holidays and brokered expectations that punctuate the months we otherwise plan—as always provisional, ever capable of shifting suddenly to reveal a landscape awry, a universe alternative to our own, operating with the same casual efficiency and effectiveness. But unlike her contemporaries, she fully embraces this view of an alternative landscape, conceding it may proffer more incisive narrative explorations of our condition than the silent, realist, conventional understandings to which we have otherwise become accustomed. And she ranges in tone between melodrama and the grotesque, veering at times into realms of kooky verbal disruption.

Among her more cross-hatched combinations of tone and sentiment is "The Other Week" (2004), which opens with pages of wacky dialogue between unemployed husband Freddy and his wife Francine. Unpredictably, the two seem driven by obscure motives, talking past each other, concerned about rattlesnakes and finances, illness and fire department charges. It is as if Williams has given in to the whimsy always nibbling at the edge of her stories, willing to probe the humor for a vision more substantial. Francine wakens from a nap to find herself fending off an unexpectedly ardent gardener, who woos her solely because she happens to resemble an old girlfriend. Later, having escaped his fondlings and successfully driven away, she encounters an unduly suspicious gas station attendant who declines to accept her twenty-dollar bill for payment:"I'm using my discretion" (330).

The cast of characters, like Flannery O'Connor's, seems more than one tick shy of normal in behavior, speech, and perspective, inhabiting a setting that likewise appears garishly fantastical, at least as depicted in Williams's characteristically abrupt, somehow surreal prose: "Dusk arrived. A dead-bolt gold. Francine maintained an offended silence as vermilion clouds streamed westward and vanished, never again to be seen by human eyes. Freddie made drinks for them both" (321). Little that Williams's characters do or say is more exaggerated than her own descriptive angle of vision, as here, in the hyperbolic admission of "never again to be seen" that, however unneeded, reinforces a sense of perfect if improbable evanescence. And with the addition of "by human eyes," that sense is subtly controverted, introducing the whimsical notion that other animate eyes might be different, possessing fuller or more perfect sight.

In bed, watching a bizarrely acted film, Freddie and Francine try to communicate, with her explaining why she's "upset" by offering the kind of weird pronouncements that sometimes emerge in such untoward, forgettable moments. As she explains, "Kant said our senses were like the nightclub doorman who only let people in who were sensibly dressed," to which Freddie responds, "Something's been lost in your translation of that one, Francine. Why does one want to get into the nightclub anyway?" (322). Who knows what Francine might here have in mind, though it may be nothing more than Kant's declared view that "the senses do not err, not because they always judge correctly, but because they do not judge at all."[11] They simply react to what is perceived or felt. That of course would form the basis of Williams's own evocation in the story, and despite the zaniness of this exchange, it seems in context more or less believable, as the narrative careens: through Francine's attempts to fire Dennis the gardener; then searching for Freddy, only to be told by strangers that he had "A swift closure" (331) while walking their shelty; leading her briefly to mourn his supposed demise before again encountering Dennis and wondering "what could be the harm?" (333) of hooking up. The whole hinges on absurd miscommunication and goofy misinterpretation as Pynchonesque characters hardly attuned to each other ricochet off broken conversations in a fashion flaky yet perfectly possible. Williams, that is, incorporates a certain postmodern style without reducing characters

---

11. Immanuel Kant *The Critique of Pure Reason* Introduction, I.

to two dimensions, simply offering a different angle of vision on suburban, middle-class life.

Words emerge in Williams's stories as quirky and amusing on the one hand or askew and endangering on the other, with initial settings never there to reassure us about either possibility. The suicidal high-schooler Helen in "Honored Guest" (2004) has a relationship with her dying mother Lenore that is so taut she shies altogether from bedtime conversations. Convinced that "she shouldn't try to say anything at night. Words at night were feral things" (235), Lenore presumably believes nighttime conversations possess a different valance from those uttered in daylight.[12] And the story's style itself corroborates this conviction in offering intimations of a disquieting, nearly deranged dimension to life, with consciousness extended out into the world, making our sense of projection once again almost ontological. At one point, the mother mulls over her curious past, only to realize that "now she did not know what to do with time at all. It seemed more expectant than ever. One couldn't satisfy it, one could never do enough for it" (229). Again, nature acquires a strange agency while temporality appears somehow animate, a decisive force field rather than a neutral dimension in which we abide.

Later, Helen's mother Lenore reveals she shares this belief, repeating her hairdresser's casual expression by converting it into a strangely independent essence that defies its own logic: " 'An honored guest,' she said aloud. To live was like being an honored guest. The thought was outside her, large and calm. Then you were no longer an honored guest. The thought turned away from her and faded" (237). The moment embodies the story's premise that somehow, if fleetingly, consciousness seems transformed, seeping out into the world it perceives in a fashion peculiar to Williams. Adopting a Poesque vision associated more often with madness and male hysteria, Lenore (whose name itself registers a

---

12. In her story "Health" (1990), a similar fear of language emerges that seems distinctive to Williams's practice and vision: " 'There's a way to do things right,' Morris told her, and when he said this she was filled with a sort of fear. They were just words, she knew, words that anybody could use, but behind words were always things, sometimes things you could never tell anyone, certainly no one you loved, frightening things that weren't even true" (184). Conversely, from a more touchingly humorous perspective, "Charity" (2004) presents a scene of a couple driving past a family with a sign "printed in crayon PLEASE: NEED GAS MONEY. The colon in this plea touched Janice deeply. 'Richard,' she said, 'we must give that family some money' " (289). Of course, this being a Williams story, Richard refuses to even slow down.

debt to America's most self-conscious story practitioner) reconfigures that vision as a normal if mystifying aspect of the way in which we all at times experience ourselves and others. Of course, at liminal moments we also can feel as if perception, judgment, and self-reflection have been projected outside ourselves.

More and more variously, Williams explores implications of a vision rarely held for long by most of us in which things become aware, capable even of relating to us as humans. "Congress" (2004) most obviously pursues that angle of vision in the attention given to irrelevant details, simply lending them an importance through a depiction of the meaningless minutia that constitutes daily routines. Miriam lives with Jack Dewayne, a forensic anthropologist so renowned he is often approached by admiring strangers, usually the family relations of victims he has identified. In a grocery store, a customer impulsively confesses her gratitude: "The woman waited. In her cart was a big bag of birdseed and a bottle of vodka. 'If it weren't for Jack, my Ricky's body would probably be unnamed still,' she said" (242). Clearly, birdseed and vodka chart the woeful parameters of this mother's mourning, as an alcoholic reduced to feeding resident wildlife. We likewise learn that Miriam pilfers bedsheets from stores and swipes distressed shrubs to replant: behavior irrelevant to the story yet revelatory of some unnamed emotional instability. Even Jack's attraction to her evokes a peculiar emotional residue (especially given his academic specialty): "He liked Miriam. He liked her bones. She had fine bones and he loved tracing them at night beneath her warm, smooth skin, her jawbone, collarbone, pelvic bone. It wasn't anything that consumed him, but he just liked her was all, usually. And he liked his work" (243). That odd insertion of "he just liked her was all, usually" serves to alert us to his own slightly defensive self-presentation, reinforced immediately by the next sentence offering a further dislocation: "And he liked his work." When Jack's favored student Carl arrives, we are told that he "smelled cleanly if somewhat aberrantly of cold cream and celery" (246), as if the disparate, oddly conflicting smells revealed something of Miriam's sensibility, and Carl's.

Casual details clinch the story's ironic credentials, which elsewhere turn into gallows humor that offers a release from morbid scenes. While bow-hunting, Jack nods off in a tree and falls on an arrow that punctures his brain "like a knife thrust into a cantaloupe." That abrupt analogy is compounded in the aftermath: "He emerged from rehab with a face as expressionless as a frosted cake. He was something that had suffered a premature burial, something accounted for but not present. Miriam was certain that he was aware of the morbid irony in this" (246). Not only the simile of "frosted cake," but the larger conceit of knowing how to identify the long-dead while immobilized himself, suggests a weirdly incongruent perspective. Later, Jack "was gaunt and his head was scarred, and he tended to resemble, if left to his own devices, a large white appliance" (248). Emotional distortion slyly matches physical deformity, culminating in Jack and Carl abandoning Miriam the narrator, driving out of the narrative altogether into a homosocial relationship. Grotesque as these odd crises and perverse descriptions are, they weave together skewed events via a curiosuly disruptive style. The narrative slides us into gradually accepting a hallucinatory vision of something like a biblical ethics of an eye for an eye that Williams has latterly made at once less accommodating and apparently more ordinary.

The story continues peripatetically, tracing a narrative of cockeyed psychology in which consciousness itself becomes suspect, or at least indeterminate. Miriam has already informed us that she "had once channeled her considerable imagination into sex, which Jack had long appreciated, but now it spilled everywhere" (245). And here the story's ill-defined title comes slowly into focus. For "congress" had initially hinted at a sexual connotation but her newly "channeled" imagination suggests a further meaning that ranges outward from physical to something more fantastic. Strangely prompting this possibility is Carl's oddball gift to Miriam of a buck's forelegs as the makings for a lamp, which initially appalls, then intrigues her: "Miriam, expecting to be repulsed by the thing, was enthralled instead.... She often found herself sitting beside it, staring at it, the harsh brown hairs, the dainty pasterns, the polished black hooves, all fastened together... It was anarchy, the little lamp, its legs snugly bunched. It was whirl, it was hole, it was the first far drums. She sometimes worried that she would start talking to it" (245).

The experience registers something akin to "Taking Care" eight years before, but here Williams raises the stakes by translating feelings fully into the world, with external objects themselves becoming "perplexed" rather than having a husband simply lament his wife's condition. We now are meant to wonder whether the lamp is somehow actually conscious or if Miriam is just delirious. She packs the piece along as she travels, plugging it in at different motels, slowly coming to realize how special it is when "the lamp and Miriam had their first disagreement.... The lamp had witnessed a smattering of Kierkegaard and felt strongly that thought should never be confused with existence" (247). The defiant surrealism of the moment makes it hard to know how to respond, except that the reference to Kierkegaard silently invokes a consciousness of dread, of characters who experience the feeling even as they suffer untoward disruptions. His very name insinuates the possibility of existentialist horror, along with the "leap of faith" that defies rational doubt—itself a necessary condition for the very possibility of achieving faith.

Suddenly, accompanying the obscure metaphysical allusions, we find ourselves thrust into a world well beyond our ken, where lamps presumably think and disagree over philosophical riddles with those who feel the singular need to respond. "Back in the room, Miriam sat with the lamp for some time.... Even if she slurred her words when she thought, the lamp was able to follow her. There were tenses that human speech had yet to discover, and the lamp was able to incorporate these in its understanding as well" (254). Her receptiveness becomes a sign at once of higher consciousness and something like mental hysteria: "Back in the room, the lamp was hovering over *Moby-Dick*. It would be deeply involved in it by now, slamming down Melville like water. The shapeless maw of the undifferentiating sea! God as indifferent, insentient Being, composed of an infinitude of deaths!" (257). Immersed repeatedly ("back in the room") in this weirdly estranged world, only finally are we given something like an explanation: "The odd thing was she had never been in love with an animal. She had just skipped that cross-species eroticism and gone right beyond it to altered parts" (258). Here, sheer assertion (mixed with batty and whimsical descriptive play) finally confirms the naturalness of a scene we had all but dismissed, with the slightly transgressive style of Williams's similes coupled with her curiously punctuated narrative of equally odd events all slowly convinces us that Miriam's experience may actually be credible.

The whole ends with a renewed understanding of "congress" as inter-relational, of animate and inanimate somehow communicating, having captivated us by a world in which such affiliations are perfectly possible: "She looked at the lamp. The lamp looked back at her as though it had no idea who she was. Miriam knew that look. She'd always felt it was full of promise. Nothing could happen anywhere was

the truth of it. And the lamp was burning with this. Burning!" (258).
Williams manages to massage realistic detail into resonances that are
clearly inconceivable yet nonetheless emotionally explicable. Where
Munro had quelled expectations for narrative sequence in order to
recoup a sense of wonder at life's capricious energy, bewildering readers
in the process, Williams is more interested in sheer enigma, focusing on
the mysterious aspects of lives transformed by what seems incompre-
hensible. "Williams evokes a visceral fear of chaos as she tells secular
tales of spiritual crisis," Jane Bradley has observed. "Usually recovering
from the random and often freakish deaths of loved ones—death by
ant bites, bat bites, pieces of bread—her characters have given up trying
to make meaning of life. Instead, they try to live with meaninglessness
and to distract themselves from sorrow" (Bradley 574). Not only distract, moreover, but as the enumeration of "freakish deaths" confirms,
doing so with a mischievously mordant twist.

Progressively, Williams turns from more or less familiar domestic,
adolescent situations to odd paranormal encounters—to kooky dream
situations and haunting probes of the afterlife. Even less outré stories
still hug the coast of surreal possibility. "Hammer" (2004) depicts a father
expired before the narrative begins, the mother Angela deceased by
the end, but teenaged narrator Darleen posed fiercely, in adolescent
rage against her mother in between these book-ended deaths. The
narrative again, as often with Williams, seems more than mildly
peripatetic, involving accidents, animal deaths, characters at cross
purposes, unprovoked outbursts, madcap dreams, lambent memories,
and passers-by harboring their own anxieties. That vagrant pattern
makes it hard to know how to interpret the central tension Darleen
feels with Angela, who finally reaches out with a maternal, entirely
undeserved (but quietly welcomed) "I love you" (349). What do we
make of Darleen's friend Deke, in his cavalier superciliousness toward
mother and daughter both? What is the proximate cause of Angela's
earlier drinking?

What, more importantly, is the titular hammer, along with various
threads otherwise unrelated? All seem vivid reminders again of Williams's
eye for the bewitching, irritating, ever engaging waste of life, its unbut-
toned verve and bottomless energy. As Stephen Metcalf observes of
her: "the world is such a cool, obdurate and sometimes grotesque place
that her credo might be an upended version of the famous Forster line:
'Only disconnect'" (Metcalf). A chocolate lab falls off a ferry, though

when it is rescued the owners claim it is actually not theirs. Angela dreams of a furniture salesman trying to sell her a bed, but when his heavy head "began to resemble something more like a brown dog's head, she woke up" (338). Darleen arrives from boarding school with Deke, who begins with criticisms, then later "casually resumed his litany of the inadequacies of Angela's housekeeping: 'Carpeting not particularly clean'" (340); and later still, "From the kitchen, Angela heard him excoriating the rust on the gas jets, the lime buildup around the sink fixtures, the poorly applied adhesive wallpaper" (347). Only then do we learn, as Angela does, that her daughter hired him to accompany her as a relational "buffer" on this family visit (340).

All these spirited scenes seem minor or otherwise unrelated, though when Deke admires a painting of beavers that Darlene spitefully reveals was stolen from a roadhouse by her mother, the description suddenly turns not only lyrical but chimerical, as Angela recalls the reason for her theft. It as if we were invited to a strangely imagined realm in which prospective fantasy and past memory intersected wondrously:

Sitting and drinking, pretty much alone in that unpopular place, she would watch the painting with all her heart. Slowly her heavy heart would turn light and she would feel it pulling away as though it wasn't responsible for her anymore, freeing her to slip beneath the glittering skein of water into the lovely clear beaver world of woven light, where everything was wild and orderly and real. A radiant inhuman world of speechless grace. This was where she spent her time when she could. These were delicate moments, however, and further weak cocktails never prolonged them. (342)

That startling depiction of "the lovely clear beaver world" where "speechless grace" is ephemerally possible becomes a transcendent image, and as with other stories, we are reminded of mental spaces to which one can at last escape. Deke appreciates the power of such art, however derivative, for as he blithely claims: "'At first it appears to be realistically coherent and pleasantly decorative, but the viewer shortly becomes aware of a sense of melancholy, of disturbing presentiment.' Angela wondered if it was possible to desire a drink any more than she did at this moment. It couldn't be" (347). With only a slight dislocation, we realize Deke could be commenting on Williams's own more recent stories and their strange mix of half-realistic, half "disturbing presentiment" (347).

Equally equivocal (and puzzling) is the story's title, referring to a moment in Chekhov's "Gooseberries" (1898) directly invoked in the narrative but alluding as well to James Agee's "A Mother's Tale" (1958), silently acknowledged by Angela. Deke recalls the Chekhov story, allowing "that there should be a man with a hammer reminding every happy, contented individual that they're not going to be happy forever" (343), even as Angela rightly points out that he has misremembered the whole, since no such man actually appears in Chekhov's story. Yet the imagined man with a hammer is invoked precisely as a persistent reminder of all that is not as it appears, that lurks beneath the obvious surface of seemingly pleasant details to resonate troublingly. More obscure is the reference to Agee's narrative, where cattle are slaughtered by a man with a hammer in an account narrated by the mother cow of "one who came back," warning others not to bear calves.

The teetering reference to a hammer is appropriate in a story itself so divided between coruscation and affection, teenage anger and adult confusion. Yet more intriguing is the narrative's final turn "several years later," with Angela dying as she recalls Deke making a witticism on his visit: "Angela wanted to laugh, even now. What a night that had been! 'Most enjoyable evening,' Deke agreed" (349). The sudden proleptic leap in time, the humorous recollection of a night we as readers experienced so differently, offers a strange twist to the narrative and a dubious confirmation of memory's misplaced power. Yet Williams then deflects understanding with another narrative strain entirely, as Angela passes away and a new nurse overhears her dying words, recounting them to a more experienced colleague: "It sounded like, 'Did you bring the hammer?'" And her co-worker silently responds in the story's final lines, thinking: "She didn't care for this one. She was awfully eager and still being evaluated. It was quite possible that ultimately she wouldn't get the job" (349). The conclusion comes as something of a small surprise, as Michael Schaub argues: "The story ends with an abrupt time shift and a shocking ending that calls into question everything that preceded it. That's one of Williams' favorite techniques: Straightforward, declarative writing punctuated with razor-sharp observations and twists that seem to come out of nowhere, but fit perfectly" (Schaub). Williams cannot seem to help but move us into other dramas, other rooms, other consciousnesses, where desires, antipathies, and emotional rumbles cause their own new versions of envy and pain, consternation and confusion.

And here occurs another intensifying swerve in Williams's late stories, in the increase in the tension among people familiar with each other—the weird disjunction between those who know and should sympathize, and those who do not. It comes as little surprise that in a community dissociated by death and mortality, by fractious marital strife and parental discord, the alignments we normally strive for emotionally tend so often to break asunder. That that should become the center of Williams's attention is likewise predictable, as becomes clear in her mid-career story "The Girls" (2004). From its opening, it turns to a less serious tone than usual in Williams: "The girls were searching Arleen's room and had just come upon her journal. The girls were thirty-one and thirty-two." (388). In the ensuing description of these bubbleheaded, disarmingly self-assured cases of arrested development, we slowly realize their archly affected destructiveness. Both make fun of the priest Father Snow, and his maudlin depression over a dead lover; then they move on to another house guest, Arleen, revealing their ghoulish bond in a macabre private world. Blithely defending their pets as "sweet cats, old stay-at-home cats," knowing they "had slaughtered no fewer than a dozen songbirds by visible count" (393), they confirm our vision of a slightly demented, largely conspiratorial social alliance.

The verbal concoctions Williams elsewhere delights in, meant to release characters and readers from banal expectations and familiar assumptions, have taken a strange turn here, as if the story were casting a self-conscious eye on the actively destructive capacity of words so often earlier treated playfully, or whimsically, or with little affect accompanying them. In this story, the stakes of impish inconsequentiality are painfully raised, as rhetorical fabrications mutate into a lexical dungeon devised by demented sisters, imprisoning the narrator with others in a symbolic snare from which they cannot escape, revealing how words themselves not only expose pathology but generate it. And the reversal occurs as we realize actual parents are being appropriated by the sisters into psychological pawns:

They talked about Mommy and Daddy. This they did not usually do, preferring to keep them inside themselves in a definite and distinct way, not touching them with words not even inside words, but just holding them inside—trapped, as it were—and aware of them quite clearly without thinking about them, fooling around with them in this fashion.

But Mommy and Daddy were changing. In the girls' eyes, they seemed to be actually crumbling. This was of concern.   (393)

The sisters, blithely immune to social or ethical mores, remain unaware of protocols much less of feelings, revealing themselves as monsters of communal alliance.

Later, they demand to hear aloud their father's proposal to their mother in a scene that Williams milks for its daft black humor:

> "Tell the whole story," the girl squealed. "We love the story. Tell how Daddy ran over that man who was standing beside his disabled car on the highway that winter night, but Daddy didn't stop even though he knew he'd very likely killed him because you were going to a concert. It was the night Daddy was going to propose to you and he didn't want your life together compromised or delayed. You had your life before you!"
> Father Snow visibly paled. (396)

Their giddy, graceless pleasure becomes a childish night vision, as Williams evokes an emotional world that might have seemed simply puerile in her earlier narrative mode but here resonates in an unsettlingly spooky minor key: "The girls closed their eyes and hummed a little. They loved the story—the night, the waves of snow descending, the elegant evening clothes, the nonexistent girls, some stranger sacrificed" (396). The sequence of clauses offer at once a poetically evocative past (as the girls respond) and one oddly disquieting in a fashion that seems a darker version of quintessential Williams. The unfolding, back-and-forth exchange between sisters allied in a shared memory becomes itself—in the weighted agreement—a disquieting sign of invincible judgment. The skittish medley of tones, characters, and psychologies seems initially comic though verging as well on a distressing, dread-filled perspective, ominous and alarming. Before we can decide, the story simply ends, precluding us from knowing how things will happen to turn out.

IV. Death, Silence, Stylization

In Williams's recent stories, the fascination with consciousness deformed, even mystified, and often as not reconfigured through otherworldly scenarios, becomes ever more focused and stylized. From the beginning, death occurs less as morbid occurrence or tragic event or even seriously painful end of process (evoking Dubus's vision) than as a neutral, normal, expected part of process itself. But Williams seems to take increasing delight in mortality's demise, evidenced in vivid evocations that defy what one character describes as "death's drear uniformity" (346): whether mothers of serial murderers meeting in group counseling sessions or casual animal torturers; whether victims of cancer and choking at meals or solitary suicides, both successful and failed; whether described by forensic scientists or retiring taxidermists or caretakers cleaning road kill; whether whales grounding on beaches or simple thoughts of Kafka's gravestone. The subject persistently arises as worth addressing.

Of course, one might adduce the very premise of short stories as a matter of bringing short-lived figures to life, then effectively killing them off (at least in narrative durations). And Williams increasingly contemplates this generic aspect of story-telling in the plots of her stories themselves. Remarkably, few critics have moved beyond the commonplace judgment that Williams happens to focus on mortality to inquire instead about her rationale for that recurrent choice. The very mysteriousness of her vision rests on a willingness to challenge conventional assumptions about safe havens and protected lives, in stories that disrupt predictable cycles and in descriptions that dismantle our idea of how things happen. Her recent stories, moreover, have a hard-bitten, less equivocal, even blunt bearing, appearing to take for granted assumptions (and integrated styles) registered less abruptly in earlier work.

That perspective is declaimed self-consciously in "Dangerous" (2014), which depicts an alcoholic daughter whose father dies when she is only twenty, to her dismay: "I find it difficult to believe that my father no longer exists. He lives in something I do not recognize" (425). Yet as she later adds in more expansive tones: "My point is that however fortunate your life or—considering the myriad grotesque ways one can depart from it—your death, it's usually strangers who have their hands on you at the end and usher you down the darkened aisle" (426). The story continues in a characteristically itinerant mode, though with an even more rambling survey than usual of a life stymied by drink, of neighborhood fatalities, of a mother obsessed with first building a tortoise enclosure, then destroying it: all amid the daughter's own lingering uncertainty about the day-by-day approach to the end, the relationship finally patched together with those no longer here. Her summation at the conclusion seems valedictory, reaching out to the reader in a vague gesture of social accommodation: "Eventually I moved out of the shithole, though I still go to AA. I've even stopped drinking. I would say then that all is continuing here. Is it the same way there?" (432). Amid her disabling emotional waywardness, the story's gesture is simply to define a comforting narrative trajectory on which to hold: "Maybe that's why I go to AA as much as I do because at least people are telling stories, pathetic and predictable as they may be, and all manner of reassurances and promises are being made" (428). That humane need for the mild reassurance and suasive denials of narrative itself has come, for Williams, to stand warrant for earlier efforts, in contrast to the trio of other writers in this book. Yet we never lose sight of the schizophrenic quality of her vision, a disjointed breakdown that often occurs at the level of the sentence itself.

Williams's stylistic turbulence increasingly finds its correlative in a more frequent thematic and narrative vision of actual indiscriminate violence (absent random acts of kindness). As "Cats and Dogs" (2015) announces peremptorily: "Lillian was telling her daughter about the period in her life when she killed cats" (438), catching them with traps, drowning them in a pool. The callous behavior conforms to its terse description, as the story wanders among forgotten moments and desolate settings. The narrator, Toby, has sold her parents' former home to an eager couple—who desire it precisely because a murder had occurred there and they had also "had a loved one murdered" (440)—and now is unloading the rest of her father's acquired real estate. If Williams's early stories rarely focus on description, here she reveals a deft eye for the uses of metonymy:

She was at present occupying an oddity built decades before that had never been remodeled. Its roofline was angled like wings. The ceilings were crazed and water-stained, an avocado green shag covered the plywood floors, the bathroom wallpaper depicted toreadors and bulls, rather a single toreador and a single bull over and over again. The wood was biscuit-colored and flimsy, the rooms small, the foundation cracked, the malfunctioning kitchen appliances a grotesque shade of ruby. The yard was large. There had once been flower beds, all in ruin now, and a small pond was spanned by a concrete arch from which a concrete fisherperson "fished." The place was a hoot, though Toby felt it worsened her sinus condition.   (441)

It is as if the grotesqueness of behavior in Williams's earlier stories, often the focus of humorous dismissal, had been transferred onto this ramshackle "dump," with decrepitude surveyed and itemized in a series of ever more outlandish details. Irrelevant as they seem, their sheer prepositional accumulation reveals Toby's silent judgment of her father (coupled with the tense relation with her cat-killing mother), all culminating in the combined casual "hoot" and worsening "sinus condition" that suggest her conflicted family feelings. Again, as in earlier work, the house itself seems animate: "though it was unlucky. It was aware that it was unlucky" (441). Enforcing that invigorating conclusion is the earlier offhand observation that "the house appeared to be making every effort to be charming and forthright" (440).

The story slowly unfolds to embrace the buyer who wants this house of death because she happened to be raised in it, and who then recounts a story of her father teaching young Billy Crawford to drive. The boy inadvertently kills a dog, whose owner angrily attacks the truck, climbing into the bed: "There was a can of turpentine in the back as well and it wasn't long before death triumphant placed it in Rockford Wiggins's hands. He drenched himself and all those rags were like a hundred wicks so when he set himself off with a packet of matches, the whole truck went. I was told that it looked like a parcel of hell burning, in the manner that hell is popularly pictured" (447). Williams has perfected a style of grotesque violence depicted with a sardonic smirk, drawing together disparate events only to end by circling back to Lillian now repeating the story of killing cats: "She had meant no real harm. What if everything one did mattered. Thank God, it could not" (449).

The narrative suturing here is intentionally less seamless, the integrity of the whole is deliberately more dubious than Williams's early work. For precisely that shift creates an aura of aloof indifference towards death (whether of cats, dogs, or their owners) that beguiles us much as do Stephen Crane and Flannery O'Connor, with much the same reinvention of straightforward narrative style. As the narrator of "The Mother Cell" (2014) remarks of the group meetings of mothers of "serial rampage" murderers, lending a logic to nearly all Williams's late stories: "In general they believed that the dead remained around, fulfilling all but the most technical requirements of residency on earth, yet relieved of the banality of daily suffering. In this respect, they could argue, though they never did, that their children's victims weren't as bad off as commonly assumed" (474). The casual accommodation of brutality attests at once to a mother's overriding love and to the bizarre underlying suspension of ethical considerations required to maintain that love.

Perhaps a clearer measure of Williams's escalation of effect in her late style emerges in the differences between two versions of "Another Season" (2014): the original published in 1966, and its revision a half-century later retracing a narrative that is everywhere altered in language, character, and scenes. The former establishes right from the opening a distorted psychological terrain, of fading memory and lost desire summed up in a sprawling, sometimes broken syntax (stressed through its notable abundance of dashes, so unlike Williams's late efforts where dashes disappear):

He was an old man and like all old men, he could no longer remember what it had been that he wanted most. He could no longer see which town it was that he wanted to return to—which of the years of youth had been good years. He had lived in no other time than age and the memories that he lived were three—the island, the furry feathered mounds of the road, the snow falling into the black waves. He suspected that once he had wanted something he could touch—a wallet, a woman, a fine Buick, black, with power and a silver pointer dog on the hood—but he had been weary of possessions now for many years. (123)

The man remains unnamed throughout, having arrived years ago at an unnamed island that seems to match the metaphorical island of his inner being: "he had always contained one within himself—carried one about with him" (123).

Gradually, we learn of his walking the roads, picking up carcasses of dead animals: "This was his task, his dedication—the protection and preservation of silence, the birds that no longer screamed, the cats whose padded paws no longer crept over walks. He stroked the clotted fur, arranged the limbs, the still talons, wrapped them in scraps of sheets and placed them in a box" (125). It never becomes clear why he feels the need to do so, though Williams describes his years in prose evocative of John Hawkes or Cormac McCarthy, drawing attention to its own evocations. In a half-dozen pages, the man's life is summed, his death at last described just after he has gained a young apprentice in "the protection and preservation of silence": "He struck a world at every turn, a new terror, and with his hands flailing out to touch no wall, he saw the crushed animals beyond bone in the road, gone beyond love, mangled beyond touch. His sleep made circles he could not enter and crying in rage, he clawed his chest" (130). It is as if the man's psychological pressures, projected onto the island of dead animals, finally had become too much.

Five decades later, Williams overhauls the basic premise, revealing how fully her late style is a deliberately chosen vehicle meant to press resonance and meanings out of the mystery of "another season" of silence. Her deep-seated biblical insight on the divide between "surface and hidden meaning" emerges in the later version's selective renaming of characters with the old man now identified as Nicodemus. The Gospel stresses his centrality in two ways important for Williams's story that were unclear in its earlier telling: the first, as Nicodemus pedantically questions Christ's encouragement to be spiritually reborn: "Can he enter his mother's womb a second time to be born?" (John 3:4); and the second, as he anoints and binds up Jesus's corpse (John 19:39). In short, the name signals a twofold fate presented immediately on Nicodemus's arrival at the island: "He remembered the first night being the hardest, as they say the first night of being dead must be. But he was not newly dead, he was entering for the first time what would become his life" (416). The story's theme of death and rebirth is only strengthened by its biblical subtext, as the earlier plot newly acquires a certain shimmering resonance, part of a hallucinatory vision once again identifiably Williams's own.

Appropriately, landscape description is now less purely psychological, if more evocative and elusive, as though Nicodemus on the island now inhabits a dreamscape commensurate with his own emotional fluctuations. Before he arrives, we are told:

In the southern dusk, the dark grew out of the sky like a hoof of mud dissolving a clear pool. But on the island, dusk seemed to grow out of nothing at all. Dusk and night being a figment of fog, an exhaustion of wave, the time when blackness sank into the town as if buildings and trees were a pit to be filled.

A deer fell on the once friendly hillside, the crack of the gun sounding a playful instant later.

His benefactor died on the mainland in a traffic accident.   (416–17)

That strange simile of dark "like a hoof of mud dissolving a clear pool" sweeps us once again into a surreal mix of abrupt, dislocating images. Dusk and darkness serve as backdrop (and prelude) for death that seems all-embracing, if seen from afar (as heard long after the fact), as both imagery and as fate, of animals, pets, and benefactors. Occasionally, Nicodemus realizes his own liminal state, on the border of exhaustion: "He could no longer work as he once had. Sometimes, he couldn't catch his breath and at those times he would think, You're my breath, you belong to me. We have to work together" (418).

Yet at the same time, the narrative itself moves through a surprisingly more straightforward chronicle of his experience on the island, finding work, angered at reckless vacationers wantonly killing wildlife, hired as shepherd for highway carcasses by a rich booster "to make the island appear as though death on the minor plane were unknown to it" (419). Again, "the minor plane" seems initially an odd phrase, though the booster explains it as a contrast to "the prep school boy suiciding by his daddy's basement table saw in June just as the season was starting, or the stockbroker all over the news who was found with an anchor line tied around his ankle" (419–20). Death accidental is no less troubling than intentional self-annihilation (in the odd neologism of "suiciding"), and Nicodemus becomes something like the guardian spirit of dead animals—kind, concerned, questioning, refusing to concede dissolution's demands. Of course, old Nicodemus himself must die in the course of events, leaving his "epigone" to take over, though "they had to say that the boy managed to keep the island just as clean" (422).

Death and rebirth, coupled with a need for the appropriate care and observance of corpses, has emerged from this revised story as its central theme, with materials recast according to the suggestiveness of biblical naming. It can hardly be said that, in the intervening half-century between first and final version, Williams had at last discovered her subject, since her subject has perpetually kept changing. But by converting the simple plot structure and narrative voice of the original into a more mysterious, magical meditation on the ongoing link between life and death, she does unfold a signature element of her later interest, merely implied in earlier work. "The unnamed old man" has been transformed into Nicodemus, from simple character into something more like honored island presence, the patron saint of terminal silence.

V. Incomprehension

Given how fully Williams's late stories tailor consciousness according to various perspectives (real and surreal), and focus increasingly on the anxieties of death (anticipated and experienced), it comes as little surprise how often they engage situations where community fails, where shared assumptions break down and common discourse fractures under the pressure of those whose impressions can be so bizarre. That breakdown of mutual consideration seems matched in later stories stylistically, as discordances in diction or syntax register an inability to hold together at the surface of discourse, much less the depths of feeling and meaning. Characters may feel they understand circumstances or otherwise fathom their lives, but that assumption dissipates when they try to convey their insights to others. As Rand Cooper observes of the rabbit-duck quality of so many claims in Williams's stories, which appear trenchant one moment and the merest persiflage the next:

> As with the auto-body repairman in the story called "Rot," who turns a routine estimate into an existential monologue, the act of speech becomes an occasion for revelation. But most of the time, this revelation turns out to be no more than a passing insight. "A window opens for a moment," Ms. Williams said of her characters, "and they are able to see and say things that they couldn't before. Then the window shuts again." (Cooper)

Cooper continues, arguing that her stories "take place in a perilous world, swirling with inexorable forces—lost love, illness, death. Any form of expression comes to signify a sort of triumph. 'When you realize what's out there,' Ms. Williams said, 'it's amazing we can have conversations at all'" (Cooper). And yet her characters regularly do converse, if sometimes only to talk past one another, at others offering a comic dismantling of shared or otherwise supposedly mature assumptions.

Williams's investigations of the gruesome obliterations of death, or of consciousness more than marginally awry, or of bizarre intersections of the mysterious and the mundane, often occur in narratives of simple incomprehension, with characters failing to understand events or relations, reduced to seeing things from a precariously attenuated perspective. "Brass" (2011) forms a nicely skewed example of this strategy, in a perfect instance of her own hewn late style, building slowly through casual episodes that are once again scattered, seemingly disconnected, even as all pulls abruptly together and into focus by the end. In its combination of wry throwaway lines and profound emotional dismay, of horrifying crises and patently banal events, of human blindness and readerly incapacity, it exemplifies the gnarled vision that Williams has by now perfected.

A first-person, stay-at-home father recounts the whole in sarcasm-laden tones, expressing contempt that seems unearned for his son, for reasons not at all apparent. Clearly, the mother's opening unease about feng shui in their house registers a preoccupation with consanguinity that exists nowhere else in the story—as if to underline or offset the emotional incoherence to follow. Odd exchanges occur with the son, as the father regularly comments about a lost generation, the need for firmer rules, kids now "in a different lane. Slow" (382). Meanwhile, the son's anguished lack of self-confidence emerges only briefly, in his lament, "Daddy, you don't think I can do anything" (184). The mother pleas for tolerance in the face of their boy's erratic behavior, with the father merely expressing an unearned derision that continues to mystify.

In a story built out of distinct, detachable sections, nothing becomes clear until the ending's detonation, when a helicopter thunders over-head "and I think whatever I was thinking a minute ago is the last peaceful thought I will ever have. Though sometimes now I try to pretend he's still in the house ... I pretend he's still with us and eating with us and getting by with us. But of course he's not and he isn't. No, we were never afraid of him. Afraid of Jared?" (387). Something violent has ripped through the fabric of their lives, though not until the final word, a distinctly spoken name, does Williams unfurl an explanation. The perfect balancing act of diverse parts and suggestive alignments ends with the singular reference to "Jared," filling in our understanding (by historical confirmation) that "the congresswoman" mentioned on the last page must be Gabby Giffords, severely injured by Jared Lee Loughner in Tucson on January 8th, 2011, during the mass shooting where he killed six people. As Michael Schaub has observed of this fictional transformation: "It's a gut punch that few writers could pull off, and Williams executes it absolutely perfectly—she's nothing if not unsparing. Nobody escapes her stories unscathed" (Schaub).

Still, the story's title itself remains obscure, appearing to refer to Jared's class reading of Arthur Rimbaud's letter of May 15th, 1871, in which he stated oracularly: "*For I is someone else. If brass wakes up a trumpet, it isn't to blame. To me this is evident: I give a stroke of the bow: the symphony begins to stir in the depths*" (305). Jared happens to repeat the lines twice, emphasizing their importance for him in their dissociation of identity ("*I is*"). In the actual letter, Rimbaud goes on to remark on "the *false* meaning of the Ego," and the need for "the knowledge of himself, complete" (307).[13] But the lines that Jared cites take little allegorical pressure to be read more locally, with Gabby Giffords as "trumpet" and Jared as "brass," murderously spewing Parabellum rounds with his 9mm

13. The importance of this syntax and imagery for Rimbaud can be measured by the fact that his May 15th letter reiterates a similar expression made to another friend two days earlier (305), as if Rimbaud were working through its implications. And later in the second letter, Rimbaud claims: "I say one must be a *seer*, make oneself a *seer*. The Poet makes himself a *seer* by a long, gigantic and rational *derangement of all the senses*. All forms of love, suffering, and madness. He searches himself. He exhausts all poisons in himself" (307).

Glock. By a gruesome irony, Rimbaud's call for spiritual conversion is converted into a murderous gesture, revealing Williams's vision as once again "devious," dealing with what she characterized as the basis of all good stories: "the horror and incomprehensibility of time, the dark encroachment of old catastrophes."

Perhaps an even more exemplary instance of Williams's late narrative disjunctions, bound up in her increasingly stripped-down evocations, is "The Bridgetender" (2015), which offers a more intense investigation of mutual incomprehension, presenting a brilliantly mysterious encounter with another that begins in confusion about the self. That confusion is launched economically in its opening lines, even more perplexed and muddled than "Brass": "I am trying to think. Sometimes I catch myself saying just those words and just in my head. It seems I got to start everything in my head with something in my head saying I am trying to think. I remember how it begins but can't remember how it ends. Even though it's over now" (450). That elliptical admission places us inside a consciousness much like the one Jared's father observed from the outside, as the narrator initiates a five-day affair with a strangely mysterious woman. His very anticipation of their meeting turns out to be mystifying: "What it is I think is that before she came I knew something was going to happen and now that she's been, I know it ain't" (450). Their days together, moreover, end as abruptly as they began: "She was like smoke the way she went away. She was like that even when she stayed. She'd cover me up, wrapping herself around me tight" (450).

Repeatedly, Williams relies on the anaphora of "So" to propel the story along, since narrative logic itself is woefully insufficient, until he finally admits: "So it's over but I can't help but feel it's still going on somewheres. Because it hasn't seemed to have ended even though it's stopped. And I don't know what it was she gave me" (456). If the inexplicable encounter may be "going on somewheres," that possibility calls to mind so many of Williams's surreal scenes, echoed as the story ends with his profound confusion about death and deliverance: "I don't really even know if she's dead and it's me sitting here in the pilothouse or if I was the one who's been dead all the while and she's still going on back there on the gulf with all them birds" (456). The narrative's brevity, its enigmatic lack of determinate borders, combines with a joyful but uncomprehending exchange between the two figures, challenging our familiar assumptions about mortality, even temporality.

As if to confirm Williams's long-standing fascination with mental confines—those dividing people, but also those collapsing skewed subjectivity with a neutral perspective, animate with inanimate— "Craving" (1991) offers another dramatic anticipation of her late style, if just in the way that that version is only modestly revised for her 2015 collection. Again, she focuses on characters befuddled, though it weaves together eerie aspects reminiscent of other stories in its focus on an alcoholic couple. Told from Denise's point of view, the title elaborates all the permutations by which inside and out, desire and will can merge. We learn that their "clothes had let them down" (481), but also that she believes her compulsions can be transferred to Steadman, whom she loves: "She gave them all to him. This was not as difficult as it might once have been because all her thoughts concerned Steadman anyway" (481). Regularly changing hotels, spending time in local bars, they then "return to their room. The room was not welcoming. It had seen too many people come and go. It was wearying to be constantly reminded that time passes and everything with it, purposelessly" (482).

The craving Denise cannot satisfy is projected outward, converted into a disgust that mirrors the presumed self-disgust motivating their drinking: "she hated this room. It, it just didn't like them. She could hear it saying, Well, there's a pathetic pair, how did they ever find each other? She'd like to set fire to the room. Or beat it up. She could hit, no question.... The room stared at her lidlessly" (483). Loathing emanates from a room that seems akin to many other animate spaces in Williams's earlier stories, though now even more actively and with an overbearing weight: "This annoying room was listening to every word she uttered. And what did it know? It couldn't know anything. It couldn't climb from the basement into a life of spiritual sunshine like she was capable of doing" (484). The next day, awakening with broken hands, she presumes that in her sleep "the room had fought back. It made one think, really" (485). Desperate to quit drinking, she realizes she needs to "start stopping" (485), which requires ignoring the craving she feels. Finally, she and Steadman leave, speeding into the night, racing another car, as the story ends disastrously: "before the car swerved around them and turned in inches beyond their front bumper. Then, whatever was driving it slammed on the brakes" (490). We presume the end is theirs as well, with craving finally assuaged by death, offering a caustic conclusion perfectly appropriate for Williams's vision. What in the earlier version is defined as "The road ahead was empty" (245) becomes

"Before them was nothing" (490), as one of many similar revisions that translate local details into larger emotional claims, qualified description into figurative possibilities (or their lack, as here). It comes as no surprise that this should be chosen as the final story of *The Visiting Privilege*, in its vision of lives enigmatically collapsing into themselves.

VI. Conclusion, Macabre Swerves

For all the strains in Williams's late obsession with death that match her early concerns, for all the stripped-down syntactical registers that become ever more severe, she imaginatively succeeds in avoiding any similarity among plots or even narrative strategies, slyly challenging readers' expectations in inventively different stylistic deflections that become more elliptical, more vivid, more disruptive. Returning to macabre scenarios with a gimlet eye, she focuses regularly on terminal moments that offer a foil to the jewel-like qualities of life she otherwise celebrates. Moreover, she revels in the ways consciousness itself seems less stable, less fully self-confident than we too often presume. Increasingly, her stories unsettle our assurance in common-sense understanding and tacit expectations, summed up incisively by her predictably scriptural epigraph as the miracle of self-transformation: "Behold, I tell you a mystery; We shall not all sleep, but we shall all be changed, In a moment, in the twinkling of an eye." From the beginning, her narratives have celebrated just such radically decisive moments, which in that regard at least strangely resemble Dubus's stories, different as they are in plot and enactment. As she once remarked of Richard Yates, her teacher at Iowa's Writers' Workshop whose novels she much admired: his "stories touched me not at all. They seemed old-fashioned, resolving themselves on small matters" (Winner 39). The larger drama that ensues when death is at hand could hardly be ignored, and her writerly ambition had always been to capture that critical tension.

Williams weaves essential and irrelevant details into the fabric of life we find riveting (much as do Munro and Dubus), but clearly transects a different emotional and narrative universe from them, exploring behavior skewed at right angles to theirs. Her deadpan humor; her odd, strangled outbursts; her strangely broken relations between parents and children, lovers, husbands and wives; her focus on peckish habits and amusing desires, credible assumptions and spectral possibilities: all become fodder for a weirdly disorienting point of view that seems to enjoy teetering on the customary boundary between what are more generally taken to be clearly sequestered terrains. Williams delights in trespassing the borderline between living and dead, between lively memories and dulled expectation, between conventional realist description and colorfully surreal possibilities, and increasingly over her career, these infringements define her preeminent concerns. Additionally, her often minimalist style is broken up by similar shifts into lyrical, even chimerical uplifting sweeps. In all these ways, Williams has carved out a unique place in the short story form that is every bit the equal of any modern practitioner, but also perfectly unexemplary as a model.

4

Less Time in *Can't and Won't*

If nothing else, the quartet of writers here have thoroughly altered narrative conventions and done so inventively, confirming singular visions in the enriched prospects of their later work. But no one has so revamped expectations of what the short story can be and do as Lydia Davis, boldly and idiosyncratically. Not only has she radically abbreviated the form into "short short" stories, now more regularly known as "flash fiction," but she has raised the stakes on moments laid out with a philosophical playfulness. Among other factors, the very brevity of her fictional imaginings has fed their continuing power, just as her often anonymous first-person accounts tease us with larger implications of the kinds of trivial incidents we all experience at one point or another every day. Davis swerves from a more centrist tradition that has continued to focus on unfolding temporal sequences in order instead to embrace a very different agenda, one more circumscribed and fleeting, out of what seems like greater confidence in the magic contained in evanescent events and negligible dramas. Abandoning the allure of untoward reversals (even more, of physical violence) that has been a recurrent subject of short fiction from the beginning, she focuses instead on the inconsequential occasions when nothing seems to happen, filling our lives with brief interruptions forgotten all but as soon as they occur, part of the noise and shadow in which we are customarily immersed.

Helping explain this deftly skewed vision is the fact that Davis derives from a literary tradition different from most American writers, though like Williams what is intriguing about her are the recognizable influences on her development. In Davis's case, they were two: first, the decisive impact of poetry rather than prose on her conception of short stories; and second, her intrigue with unusual directions taken by French rather than American prose writers. Of the first, she can date exactly her earliest awareness of the kind of fiction she was drawn to emulate: "I read the stories of Russell Edson, an American poet. He would call those stories poems, but I wouldn't. They are bizarre little narratives, absurd and strange, and I suddenly saw that I could try pieces of writing like this and that it would be great fun. I was happy trying something new. So from then on I felt no compulsion to write something traditional" (Aguilar). Or as she added in another interview, ironically revealing the way her own experience would mirror the flashes of insight her writing so regularly celebrates: "Edson was the one who jolted me out of my stuckness in long conventional stories and into one-paragraph freedom. Not only freedom of length and form but freedom of subject matter: some of his stories were so uninhibited, or so absurd, that I saw that anything was appropriate and anything was possible. That revelation happened very specifically in the fall of 1973 when I was twenty-six" (McCaffery 67).

Clearly, Davis's choice of the more etiolated of narrative subjects as well as her starkly abbreviated presentations sets her vividly apart from either Dubus and Williams on the one hand (with their eviscerating moments of violence) or on the other from Munro (with her peripatetic traversals and enigmatic auras). Enamored of very different possibilities, Davis continued for years to dismiss her own creations as stories at all, since so deliberately undeveloped, so often lacking in dialogue, and finally just too fleeting: "Most of [my work] I wouldn't call short stories, even though many are very short. Some you could call poems—not many" (Aguilar). The emotional turmoil that so often engages other writers is notably absent in Davis. And if she regularly turns to an array of ordinary, middle-class figures little different from those central to stories by the other three, she barely sketches those characters; her situations are rarely impassioned, relying instead on tight-lipped narrative understatement and occasional deadpan dialogue. In fact, it might be said that she succeeds in turning the modern short story away from drama altogether, discarding evocative details, casting off what had always seemed to lend a saving intensity to the allusive verbal distillations brewed by Hemingway and Joyce.

The other shaping influence on Davis has been Francophilic, exemplified in her celebrated translations of major French novelists and in her enthusiasm for Samuel Beckett's fiction. As well, her immersion in French post-structuralist theory has had an odd effect, certainly setting her apart from story writers but also offering a directional signal for her willingness to make the autobiographical itself at once philosophical and literary. The sheer abstruseness of her brief philosophical speculations (based on French intellectuals she has spent a life translating into English, Michel Leiris and Maurice Blanchot) underwrites a fictional turn unfamiliar to her contemporaries. In this regard (among others), she maps a powerfully individual trajectory for the short story, pressing the limits of what it can do, bouncing off of Williams's interest in liminality to raise even more unsettling questions about common understandings—not, as with Williams, about mortality or developed psychology but tending instead toward a speculative strain of philosophy and linguistics. As Davis herself admits, this has led to a predictable confusion about the scope of her own ambitions:

> I'm interested in a different kind of premise about what so-called "fiction writers" can be doing—a formal change that moves right out of the fiction genre and enters other genres at the same time, so that a text can be partly autobiography, partly fiction, partly essay, and partly technical treatise...partly poem—*and*—partly story. Confusing the distinctions seems like a very healthy thing. Writing without those boundaries is what increasingly interests me most.   (cited by McCaffery 76)

The commitment to ranging outward with the story format is clear, in embracing generic realms previously bisected and turned out to pasture. Here, the very commitment to confused categories becomes exciting, in the engaging claim of "poem—*and*—partly story" that comes to seem so central to her effort.

Davis exhibits an intense self-consciousness about consciousness itself, which draws her repeatedly to unfinished pieces, mere remnants, the starkest slivers of narrative. And here is where her reading in French theory inspired her, as she once explained in describing Blanchot's breakthrough revelations: "Constant interruption, fragmentation, [which] also keeps returning the reader not only to the real world, but to a consciousness of his or her own mind at work" (Form 324). Blanchot's deliberations about the conflation of thought with its object and ways in which the two intertwine has also become a continuing source of delight to Davis, as she embraces implications in his pursuit of the "misunderstanding" intrinsic to "ordinary language." His willingness to compress abstraction with concrete details resulted in enigmatic narrative impressions that tantalized Davis, not by extending descriptions but by occluding them: "What happens in his novels is often very mysterious....He manages to go very deeply into very

small moments—someone going from one room to another.... He'll
say something like, 'It was as if the thought itself had moved into the
room and done this and done that.' And then the *thought* which we think
of as abstract, becomes a concrete part of the interaction of the story, a
character in the story" (cited by McCaffery 68). Even more, the very
word "thought," having begun as a concept turned into a character,
just as regularly turns back into simply a word among other words,
acting out its symbolic logic.

That fascination with the shape-shifting fungibility of language is
actually an interest in the play of "the word as physical presence,"
explains Marjorie Perloff of Davis's efforts: "vocabulary is stripped
down to a bare minimum, words—frequently function words and
pronouns—being put to the test through a series of permutations that
yield, not knowledge of the signifieds to which they refer, but precisely
the absence that Blanchot talks about" (205–6). Elliptical as Davis's
stories can sometimes seem in their abrupt abbreviations, she views
narrative concision itself as emblematic of an existential condition.
Insistently (if perhaps inaccurately or mistakenly), she reiterates: "What
is certain... is that we are more aware of the great precariousness and
the possible brevity of our lives than we were in the past, our lives
being actually more precarious than they used to be, and for this reason,
perhaps, we express not only more despair but also more urgency in
some of our literature now, this urgency also being expressed as brevity
itself" (Davis, "Lydia" 230). Urgency, brevity: both are linked as well to
Davis's special concern with the fragility of lexical selections, of language
itself as ever unstable, part of the accrued residue of her years spent as
vaunted translator in search of *le mot juste*. Combine all this with an
occasional but growing fascination with nonfictional moments, and
her stories cover a range (however diminished in each case) from sheer
imaginative construction to something better appreciated as *objets trouvés*,
as dreams, as actual experiences transformed into tantalizing imaginative possibilities. That range, moreover, becomes part of the intriguing
allure of her vision.

Linking Davis's condensed style with her eclectic thematic choices
compels readers to focus on fully stopped moments. Curiously, that effect
defies narrative progression in a way that can be seen to complement
Williams's as well as Munro's disjointed, sometimes discontinuous
stories. Like them, she often isolates sections of longer pieces with
white space that actually does enforce a narrative suspension or temporal

disruption. That pattern may in fact owe to specific magazine constraints, with *New Yorker* stories regularly partitioned this way as a matter of house style. Moreover, it is worth noting that Davis resembles Munro in not caring about the order in which her stories are read: "jumping around is a good way to do it. It really doesn't matter. I think so hard about the order, but then in the end I don't mind how the reader takes it!" (Halford). Conversely, unlike Munro, Davis makes only occasional minor changes to stories before they are brought together in volumes, and none from earlier publications included in her *Collected Stories* (hereafter *CS*).

Yet oddly, unlike these writers, Davis rarely elicits formal appreciation from critics despite her own nuanced translations and sustained scrutiny of others' styles. Her essays on stories by Jane Bowles and Clark Coolidge offer exemplary close readings while her more general considerations of "Endings or Order" and "Very Short Stories" similarly prove formidably attentive to diction, syntax, and rhetorical flourishes. As well, she has pointedly revealed her own aspirations in confessing to the most decisive figure for her in terms of bravura verbal performance: "Beckett amazes me stylistically.... The amazing things he could do within legitimately structured sentences. He does so much with ellipsis and inversion—'Of it ride they too would be.' He stands on his head but still keeps a nameable grammatical form" (McCaffery 66).

Elsewhere, as if anticipating creative choices yet to come, she has spoken of being impressed at thirteen with Beckett's "narrow focus, and such plain language and no attempt at lyricism or flowery language, that he would spend a page or two talking about how he dropped his pencil, and what kind of pencil it was. This just seemed utterly strange to me, and wonderful, just so simple and clear" (Wachtel 131). That fascination with the possibilities of "such plain language" would continue to evolve throughout her career, as well as the narrative opportunities presented by simply a dropped pencil. The following proposes to unfold her crafting of stories so short they sometimes seem defiantly *not* stories at all. Further, as in earlier chapters, I want to develop the claim that her late volume, *Can't and Won't* (2014), has refined and extended strains evident earlier in *Collected Stories* (2009), though hardly in dramatic ways. Indeed, there occurs less an intensification of earlier strategies in her later work (as I argue for the three other writers) than an introduction of new ploys not guessed at before, meant to achieve a similar end.

Structurally, this chapter also follows the lead of earlier ones by beginning focused on innovations in Davis's more recent style, if via a slightly anomalous interweaving of early stories with innovations pursued in *Can't and Won't*. In the absence of significant narrative reversals and developments, I want to pay close attention to her relatively ignored verbal craft—her lexical choices and their resonances, her syntax and the rhythm of sentences, indeed the microscopic skill by which she induces a fascination with the mundane minutiae of life by converting it into art. Like modernist and postmodernist painters who have turned our attention from narrative scenes toward representation itself, Davis invites us with increasing inventiveness in her late work to revel in the effect created by an emotionally pared-down style with an eye surprisingly less for character than human types, and in turn less for types than for typographies and verbal shapes.

I. Crucial Trivial Considerations

Davis would reduce the short story to single sentences or less, though the embrace of such flash effects hardly occurred at the outset of her career. The earliest gesture occurs in "What She Knew" (1986), half a dozen entries into her first collection, consisting of four condensed sentences describing a woman "not really a woman but a man" (*CS* 32). Embedded among much longer stories, it signaled a decisive turn to concision, matched by six other brief imaginative excursions through the volume that anticipated her later signature mode. Those lightning-like bursts invariably leave the reader in uncertainty, or bemused, or simply to ruminate more fully *after* finishing a too brief account— treating the prose as prelude with titles almost as long as what follows, tantalizing us with imagined after-effects. But the full skid into such succinctness was neither obvious nor immediate, and not until her second collection did Davis seize the imaginative gesture in "Love": "A woman fell in love with a man who had been dead, a number of years. It was not enough for her to brush his coats, wipe his inkwell, finger his ivory comb: she had to build her house over his grave and sit with him night after night in the damp cellar" (*CS* 178). Only with her third collection would that two-sentence story be followed by a one-sentence micro-story, "The Other." It is as if Davis were experimenting ever more economically with transitory narrative reckonings.

By the appearance of *Can't and Won't*, she clearly understood the unexplored interest in narratives that refuse to nail down details or otherwise close out imaginative venues. In doing so, these ventures also play with philosophical puzzles and symbolic ideas as if they offered themselves up for narrative display. In "Judgment" (2014), a word becomes somehow physical, imagined as inhabiting a space, in a bizarrely intriguing reflection on the intersection of symbolic representation and experience all in one sentence: "Into how small a space the word *judgment* can be compressed: it must fit inside the brain of a ladybug as she, before my eyes, makes a decision" (*C&W* 112). And "The Results of One Statistical Study" (2014), which divides like a poem by lines, makes us pause long enough to consider again the ramifications, even the truth of the claim: "People who were more conscientious / as children / lived longer" (*C&W* 208). In that pause, moreover, we linger over the implications of the past tense spread across the sentence.

Such line-by-line performances sometimes consist of cloistered sentences, most notably in one of the later stories in the collection, "Local Obits" (2014), which culls together some eight pages of largely single-sentence "stories," each summing up a life. The cast of characters parades before our mental screens, snippet by snippet ("Henry enjoyed woodworking" [*C&W* 270] or "Ronald, 72, former fire chief and retired truck driver, was an avid duck hunter" [*C&W* 277]), leaving us simply to ponder implications, devising fuller narratives for ourselves prompted by bare, initial provocations. At times in other stories, titles seem to do battle with the minimal narratives they stretch themselves across; at others, stories simply unfurl from the colorful promise their titles bestow. The customary conventions by which authors convey consciousness are quietly abandoned, as figures are introduced who seem centers of a single obsession, or in Dan Chiasson's words, have become "dilemmas of focused attention: how to translate this French verb, how to spell Nietzsche, what to make of a smudge on a note or a discrepancy in handwriting" (Chiasson).

Yet more than a few of her later stories spread out (back to earlier strategies) from sentences to a few pages, as Davis reveals an ear attuned to personality and a voice that only gradually unmasks the character at hand. Consider "Eating Fish Alone" (2014), which opens all but predictably but then settles in: "Eating fish is something I generally do alone. I eat fish at home only when I am by myself in the house, because of the strong smell. I am alone with sardines on white bread with mayonnaise and lettuce, I am alone with smoked salmon on buttered rye bread, or tuna fish and anchovies in a salade Niçoise, or a canned salmon salad sandwich, or sometimes salmon cakes sautéed in butter" (*C&W* 40). The repeated reversion to the first person, the anaphora of "I am alone," the singular detail expended on the precise fish meals: all encourage us to imagine a narrator fixed in curiously hidebound ways, if precariously self-conscious: "When I eat alone, I have no one to talk to and nothing to do but eat and drink, so my bites of food and my sips of wine are a little too deliberate. I keep thinking, It's time to take another bite, or Slow down, the food is almost gone, the meal will be over too soon" (*C&W* 42). The rigid aversions and tightly prim manners, the fastidiousness coupled with a quaintly tepid view of adventure (eating root vegetables as an alternative possibility that becomes "unexpectedly exciting" [*C&W* 42]): all combine to reveal a personality awkwardly captive to set expectations. Choices, decisions, and worries center in what we realize are trivial considerations that nonetheless take on a kind of grandeur simply through the narrator's first-person absorption in minutiae, the self-satisfied expression of preferences and personality.

The details may appear Chekhovian, as if their accumulation will momentarily unveil more of a sketchy psychology, but they end by seeming to exist for no such reason, certainly not as foil for more important considerations. And by the brief story's conclusion, with the narrator's mild guilt at being unable to finish the restaurant special, fearful the slightly anxious chef might mistakenly suspect an aversion to his cooking, we have been persuaded by the stylistic repetitions and hesitations that we somehow know this timid figure, without being at all certain of age or gender—a figure simply worried about making a bad impression or inadvertently causing a stranger passing pain. If plot normally reveals character, here its absence has the effect of focusing attention on the narrator's mental pivots, the paradoxical combination of unselfconscious mental assurance with social insecurity, commanding our attention despite the absence of any larger explanation for our interest. More generally, Charles Baxter has ventured that Davis's late stories "are not so much developmental as permutational; they do not advance on a line so much as spin on a point, and report on what is glimpsed from that particular angle before turning to a different angle on the same point. They are not revolutionary so much as rotational"

(Baxter 71–2). As he adds: "In these stories there is a gradual freezing of the narrative frame. It seems to me to involve a stop-time effect but without the accompanying discursive enlightenment" (73). His rationale for this is intriguing: that they depend "on the resources of quarreling. The quarrel is not resolved; the quarrel goes on; the quarrel becomes the life" (73).[1]

Perhaps it goes without saying that Davis has always differed from Dubus, Munro, and Williams in having relatively little interest in exploring character or psychology, and less so than ever in her later stories. For her, increasingly, the more compelling venture involves those manifold ways in which diction itself at once reveals and disguises desire, informing her fascination with particular words and grammatical expressions. In early memories, she has admitted: "I *loved* learning the words 'look' and 'see': 'Run, Jane, run. See Jane run.' It was so clear and easy and unconfusing and neat." (Prose 83). Then, being thrust as an academic child into foreign environments where German and French were automatically assumed: "Gradually the words began to have meaning. But first I heard the language as rhythm." (Prose 83). Many have assumed that as an accomplished translator of French, she must prefer that language to others, yet when asked, she has expressed a decided preference for English in a response that helps explain her characteristic style (reminding us again of her fondness for Beckett): "The plainness. I love the Anglo-Saxon words as opposed to the Latinate. Bread, milk, love, war, peace, cow, dog. The English word 'and' seems much more solid, like an apple. Maybe it has to do with those early Dick and Jane books again. Words beginning with 'a,' 'and' and 'apple' are somehow healthy" (Prose 92). Regularly, she focuses on the evocative vagaries of the English lexicon itself.

Christopher Taylor aptly recalls that "Paul Klee famously thought of drawing as 'taking a line for a walk,'" then notes that Davis "seems to have a similar approach to what she does. Sometimes she takes a word

---

1. From another perspective, Dan Chiasson has claimed: "Davis's method has always been reiterative rather than narrative. Writing very short stories is a way of starting over again and again, and her longer stories are often just clusters of short ones, multiple views of a single event rather than a sequence of events from A to B. It is fascinating to watch her work within these conditions, which some writers would seize as a chance to be lyrical, rhapsodic, impressionistic—all of the things people mean when they call a piece of fiction 'poetic,' intending, I suppose, praise. Though she has allowed that she considers some of her stories poems, it is really better to think of them as stories, or, better yet, as tactics toward—or perhaps against—the story."

for a walk" (Taylor). Taking that "walk" for Davis involves going around the block, looking over walls, investigating the multiple, conflicting possibilities that lie hidden in verbal alleys and linguistic mews. "The stories are often sparked by an odd piece of language or a paradoxical situation," she admits. "Like everyone else I live with a number of ongoing problems that don't get solved and that don't even get addressed regularly or directly, consciously" (cited by McCaffery 69). This helps explain her narratives' typical anonymity, seizing scenes (often in brief bursts of description) that might apply equally to everyone or anyone. If this seems counterintuitive or otherwise impersonal for a short story writer, it is worth observing that Davis differs little from Stephen Crane in her acknowledgment that "I've always felt that naming was artificial" (Aguilar). In this, as well as other preferences, she differs dramatically from Dubus.

Accompanying her late focus on brevity, character types, and the casual quirks and whimsical delights of grammatical expression is Davis's equal curiosity about the minor vexations of daily experience, the tepid dissatisfactions she treats with as much consideration as Dubus does in attending to singularly traumatic and violent forays. It would be hard to imagine Dubus writing a story entitled "I'm Pretty Comfortable, But I Could Be a Little More Comfortable" (2014), which unfolds like a Roz Chast cartoon with separate entries that consist of single-line complaints. Each attests to another trivial dislocation or ephemeral irritation, of feelings that weigh little in any larger accounting but still produce faint anxiety and exasperation for each of us, sometimes every hour, and by their frequency if nothing else are rendered compelling. They chronicle a world of more than expected abundance and laughably negligible conflict where "The shower is a little too cold" (*C&W* 105) or "This apple has brown spots on it" (*C&W* 107), confirming in their very banality how such complaints form all but invisible signposts in our days. In earlier collections, Davis focuses sparingly on the vexations of childcare or owning a cat or simple irritability; the title story of her third collection, *Samuel Johnson Is Indignant* (2001), consists of simply the explanatory clause: "that Scotland has no trees" (*CS* 353). By *Can't and Won't*, she repeatedly takes a rubber-necking pause over the most trivial of druthers and dissatisfactions. Even moderately embarrassing behavior—minimally selfish indulgences or otherwise petty resentments that mar our lives—make us recognizable to ourselves, and sometimes to others.

"A Small Story about a Small Box of Chocolates" (2014) is, as its title doubly discloses, trivial as both subject and treatment, all leading from a character conflicted by impulses of charity and consumption, revealed in the story's repetitions ("She thought of sharing...She did not open the box...She thought of having...She thought of sharing..." [*C&W* 247]), as faltering moral conscientiousness rubs abruptly up against heedless appetite. And the very doubling of the prose reflects the back-and-forth indecisiveness of the woman herself. Realizing "she did not want to share the remaining chocolates" (*C&W* 249) with others, the question of guileless generosity shifts to one of deliberation overcome by desire. Davis perfectly captures the trivial scene of vacillation in halting phrases that trace a temporal progression met by backtracking:

When at last she ate a chocolate, by herself, it was very good, rich and bitter, sweet and strange at the same time. The taste of it remained in her mouth minute after minute, so that she wanted to eat another one, to begin the pleasure all over again. She had planned to eat one each day until they were gone. But now she ate another right away.   (*C&W* 249)

The sequence teeters on a gesture of restraint defeated by pleasure, reflected in the structuring transitions ("When...at the same time...minute after minute...another...to begin...each day...right away"). This scenario is matched by other late stories characterized by simple sentence rhythms offering access to common emotion, as Davis refuses to bow to a conventional valuation ascribed to major versus minor moments. If we pause to wonder whether this makes a story, it is only because Davis seems to raise the question in the very process of answering it, nimbly engaging our interest in what happens next. Aptly capturing the magic of a transforming gift, that transforms in turn our notion of taste, the story results in the most undramatic of gestures, lending a voice to all we have been habituated to stow away, to hide in emotional corners.

II. At Their Simplest: Flash, Dreams, and After Flaubert

Finding a discernible trajectory in Davis's oeuvre is less easy than it may seem, if only because she makes it hard to know where to start among stories that move in so many alternative directions. But that tendency in itself might well be seen as part of a larger pattern that comes to shape her own distinctive late style, which consists of spreading ever further, ever more inventively, ever more briefly in directions already anticipated by earlier collections. The best entry into such a reading of *Can't and Won't* may be "Five Stories" (1995), published together by Davis out of what seems an otherwise arbitrary interpretive gesture, one that seems hardly self-evident.[2] After all, as Marjorie Perloff again observes, "the question of interpretation is Davis's real subject" (208), or as Jonathan Evans more specifically argues: "The central characters of Davis' fiction tend to spend their time listening to themselves think, thinking about themselves thinking, trying to understand. Davis' fiction revolves around understanding and interpretation, suggesting that even when translation is not explicitly invoked, it is never far away" (4). This intersection of interpretation and translation, of understanding and paraphrase, conceived in the broadest of narrative implications, becomes Davis's ongoing focus.

As if anticipating the later stress on trivial or wayward annoyances, "The Mice" (1997) opens the collective quintet on a piquant note, with a first-person narrator wondering almost aggrievedly why it is that their own messy kitchen attracts no mice—"there is so much loose food in the kitchen I can only think the mice themselves are defeated by it" (*CS* 154)—while their tidy neighbors paradoxically, so it would seem, endure a pest problem. Perhaps the neighbors' mice consider it an engaging "challenge...to find enough food night after night," while their own vermin consider "the overwhelming sights and smells" as embarrassing, and therefore retreat into a silent, unanswered enigma. That nine-sentence foray introducing the series is followed by "The Outing" (1997), a single sentence made up of clauses lacking an agent, focusing on actions in a narrative defined as isolated moments: "An outburst of anger near the road, a refusal to speak on the path, a silence in the pine woods, a silence across the old railroad bridge, an attempt to be friendly in the water, a refusal to end the argument on the flat stones, a cry of anger on the steep bank of dirt, a weeping among the bushes" (*CS* 298). That sequence, beginning with "an outburst" and ending with "weeping," consists otherwise of taut silences that almost seem to extend from the previous narrative.

2. Because her stories are short, Davis has repeatedly published five of them at a time in journals, following this 1995 appearance with a different "Five Stories" in *The Partisan Review* 205 (Summer 2013): 119–32, and "Five Short Stories" in *Five Dials* 25.1 (2014): 7–8. It may also be worth noting that *Can't and Won't* divides into five major sections.

"Odd Behavior" (1997), third in the series, expresses a resolute desire for quiet in two brief sentences about a narrator plugging his ears to re-achieve "all the silence I needed" (*CS* 182). As he asserts, "You see how circumstances are to blame," though of course we are given no information that might confirm this judgment now that he no longer lives alone. "Fear" then depicts in four sentences the calming of a panicked woman, requiring at last "all our strength . . . too, to quiet us" (*CS* 258). Neighbors "know she is making it up; nothing has really happened to her. But we understand" because the same has happened to each of them. At last, "Lost Things" (1997) translates the subsidence of voice and sound into all the things we have otherwise lost, all in six sentences. As the narrator admits, the coat and dog and "valuable button" have mysteriously disappeared, though not vanished: "They are somewhere else, and they are there to someone else, it may be" (*CS* 275). That narrative reminds us of Williams's "The Country," where alternative possibilities are imagined in place of what we see before our eyes. Of course, any vestige elsewhere forms small consolation, since the fact that things may be "there, still, only not where I am" is hardly a comfort. The doubly punctuated clause, with commas before and after "still" (functioning nicely here as both adverb and adjective: as "even so" in another place; and as "soundless") captures the recalcitrant acceptance of the narrator.

If all five stories seem distinct, initially all but irreconcilable, they also form a provocative arc in the randomly placed moments of silence dispersed among them, with sound amplified and quieted efficiently in their diverse narrations. Silence as embarrassment or as enigma, as refusal to speak or unattainable condition, as panicked alternative or evidence of all that has somehow been lost: the lack of expression so variously celebrated here occurs in partial expressions themselves, in stories that share little more than an apparent predilection for tranquility and quiescence. That preference, moreover, finds compelling reinforcement in the very diversity of scenes coupled with the apparent triviality of circumstances. A certain eerie anticipation registers itself in this quintet of mixed feelings and trivial concerns, consternation and cost, pointing to strains that will emerge more fully and variously later on.

Perhaps the predominant gesture here occurs in the all but ceremonious defiance of narrative sequence that structures Davis's earlier collections of flash fiction, those brief lightning bolts of silence punctuated by negligible diversions. In that too, she offers a further late evolution to the pattern, veering notably toward contrasting extremes in her focus on both the nonfictional and the hallucinatory. Testing alternative borders—between the actual and the fictional; between the surreal and the hackneyed—Davis further extends the parameters in a coherent single collection of what a short story can be. Before turning to her interest in nonfiction, take first those chimerical entries in *Can't and Won't* identified each time as a "*dream*," which had appeared nowhere in *Collected Stories* but now occur (with two exceptions) always in clustered units of two or three. Davis has long been casually drawn to the logic of dreams in their defiance of expectation, of sequence, of anticipatory coherence itself. And her early stories occasionally ricochet off dream-like moments (one character from her first collection [1986] "begins dreaming that her heart is a police station" [*CS* 139]; another from her third [2001] "no longer dreamed of sexual intimacy" [*CS 316*]).

Yet here, in thirty fragmentary pieces admittedly culled from her actual night dreams "and the waking experience in life that is dreamlike," she foregrounds the hypnagogic condition itself as part of an increasingly late style (Davis, "Lydia Davis and"). "The Bodyguard," "The Child," and "The Churchyard" occur in sequence in *Can't and Won't*, moving from a young man who "never opens his eyes" (*C&W* 26) to a mother photographing her dead child, to a narrator unlocking a churchyard gate, worried about having "offended or disappointed two women" as she is "cradling Jesus (who is alive)" (*C&W* 28). Events emerge not from each other, in something like a recognizable narrative sequence, but instead erupt on the page all in the forcefully immediate present tense, disorienting the reader much as a dreamer is mystified, with nothing linking the three "dreams" here other than peculiarly affected relationships.

If that pattern was anticipated in her earlier "Five Stories," the effect has now become even more dissociated and estranged, challenging ever more radically our abiding desire for plot explanation—something that rarely takes place, at least to this degree, in Munro, Dubus or Williams. That disruptive impact builds steadily in later triadic dream sequences, including "The Husband-Seekers," "In the Gallery," and "The Low Sun," which pivot vertiginously from women seeking husbands among "a tribe of very beautiful young men" (*C&W* 69), to an artist failing to hang her work for a show, to a college girl wondering about an evening sun whose "light must be filling the caves by the sea" (*C&W* 71). Yet Davis's dreams are not as far removed from her other late stories as one might expect, since many of them also seem equally surreal. "The Magic of the Train" (2014) consists of two sentences in which a narrator watches stylish girls walking "down the train car," and then "after a little while" returning when, "under the magical effect of the train, they have aged twenty years" (*C&W* 39). The unforeseen consequence of Davis's late, self-proclaimed "dream" sequences seems to have been to release her into a more generally hallucinatory mode, pressing the borders even further of what we conventionally assume are reasonable assumptions required for a story. In this, she offers an intriguing parallel to Williams, whose paranormal, post-mortal episodes openly defy common sense.

A final instance of dream triads exemplifies how far Davis has evolved from "Five Stories" in achieving a late style that extends the implications of those early efforts. "In the Train Station" presents a straightforward account of giving directions to a Buddhist monk, with nothing strange or untoward; and "My Footsteps," of a narrator briefly wondering why he must pause while walking, represents a similar scene of normal curiosity. But the second dream, sandwiched between these two, again delights by disarming expectation. "The Moon" depicts the narrator's insomnia in two brief paragraphs of simple sentences that describe the "underwater sort of twilight" of a full moon "falling directly on the toilet seat, as if sent by a helpful God" (*C&W* 94). This may remind a reader of Davis's very early account of insomnia, the longer, more sober "Liminal: The Little Man" (1986), though the transformation in the late story to a first-person narrator confused by whether he is asleep or awake, speaking in broken English, offers a more intensely immediate feeling of being out of control. "Liminal" had striven for a different effect, more languorous and self-consciously certain, narrated from a third-person perspective as "she planned things and remembered things and sometimes just listened to sounds and looked at the light and the dark" (*CS* 12). Instead of being immersed in a brief sliver of subconsciousness, the story depicts a figure over the course of five pages who finds herself caught unawares, cherishing "a thought that becomes a dream . . . and the mind says, But wait, this isn't true" (*CS* 13). In this earlier scenario, we remain fully outside the dream, delighting in quietude and control rather than perturbed by a silence that unnervingly seems to speak.

Still, while the stark isolation of Davis's later "dream" story captures a curious dislocation (is the first-person narrator dreaming of her own insomnia? or is her insomnia only a border to her earlier contented dream state?), the much earlier "Liminal" already ventures a more fully elaborated experience as seen not from within but without. Each section is bordered by white space, cloistering off experience and consciousness, returning midway to her as "She slept...She is lying...She was thinking," each time hoping for soporific relief. Desiring peace, she wants simply to force it "into herself" (*CS* 16). At last, the small mockingbird who accompanies her sleeplessness appears: "the figure returns, to her surprise, standing above her right shoulder," offering promise and yet a warning of others "in a room somewhere down the hall, standing in a close line, or two lines, with proud, white, and angry faces" (*CS* 16). The long sentence itself has a hallucinatory rhythm, becoming so for the reader as well, as time seems suddenly stopped in frozen tableaux. Davis's early story elaborates its appalling, unavailing obsession with insomnia ("the finality of it terrifies her" [*CS* 15]), offering a youthful impatience with the condition. Her later take enters into the experience as a dream from which we may or may not wake up, though that more belated perspective is gained only with the loss of years.

Bizarre details occasionally glisten in the late dream narratives, though Davis's delight in the irrelevant, undramatic minutiae of life extends as well to other nonfictional moments that accentuate the simple importance of observation. Increasingly, her interest in actual reported incidents seems premised on the belief that factual accounts and historical dispatches, especially when seen from odd angles, can also inventively test imaginative sensibilities. Davis even invents a bored reader in "Not Interested" (2014) who admits to being "tired of novels and stories" and instead prefers "books that contain something real, or something the author at least believed to be real. I don't want to be bored by someone else's imagination" (*C&W* 240). The wryly postured preference for authentic situations seems slyly self-mocking, especially since she once informally admitted in an interview that "I seem to have lost interest in making things up!" (McCaffery 73).

Yet if Davis is capable of ventriloquizing a boorish version of herself, she also offers a testament to the guileless value of witnessing. Authenticity accrues to a scene simply by having been seen honestly, with as little prejudice as possible (not "making things up!"), and that quality of attention contributes to a strain of narrative that becomes more concentrated through her career. What began with "Cockroaches in Autumn" (1986) as a three-page compilation of sentences describing

all the possible aspects of cockroach activity with an entomologist's eye
has evolved three decades later into a series of shorter, more frequent
stories of actual human events and accounts. As one character states, in
terms that seem again self-consciously intended for Davis herself,
though less ironic and more clearly aligned with her own perspective:

> Then I had a thought that was odd, though not unpleasant: I realized I could
> just as easily not have witnessed this scene, if I had chosen to stay in the bus
> station. I could have been sitting across the parking lot in the waiting room
> while this scene was taking place. It would still have taken place. I had never
> before thought so clearly about all the scenes that took place when I wasn't
> there to witness them. And then, I had a stranger and less pleasant thought: not
> only was I not necessary to those scenes, and not necessary to those lives that
> continued to go on without me, but in fact, I was not necessary at all. I didn't
> have to exist.   ("Letter to the Foundation" 206)

The very activity of witnessing is, so it seems, an unerringly humanizing
endeavor. We may disappear in our testimony, erased in the very process
of articulating our vision, but we also confirm the links connecting us
to others and the scenes they engage. We too are thereby engaged as
part of the narrative contract that underwrites honest testimonial.

So, just as the cited "*dream*" is a decisively new generic form in *Can't
and Won't*, the self-consciously nonfiction entries are as well, if of a
different sort. Mostly, they appear as *objets trouvés* to remind us how
often wonder can emerge from the banal interstices of daily life, the
quiet commonplaces that lurk around us. The first of these occur as
grammatical manglings, beginning with the skewed expression in
"The Language of the Telephone Company" (2014), which as a story
consists entirely of "The trouble you reported recently is now working
properly" (*C&W* 77). That had been anticipated in a previous collection as "Example of the Continuing Past Tense in a Hotel Room" (2007),
which likewise consisted of nothing but a card left behind: "Your
housekeeper *has been* Shelly" (715 *CS*). The quotation is at once mundane
and skewed in its italicized tense, which as Ivan Callus observes,
"formalizes even as it personalizes a polite but still unmistakeable
request for a tip and which, in the process of reframing, has its subtle
importunateness subtly revealed" (Callus 123). Then again, the ability
to read that *billet* at various levels already suggests the richness of such
found objects. Sometimes, late stories themselves appear to be found
objects, as with "The Results of One Statistical Study" or with
"Grade Two Assignment," that begins "Color these fish. / Cut them
out" (*C&W* 86).

But the genuinely innovative debut in *Can't and Won't* that relies on actual history is the paratext category of a "*story from Flaubert*," which appeared in *The Paris Review* in 2010, a year after *Collected Stories*. Instead of pushing narrative into some surreal territory, these fourteen pieces raise a different question by unsettling the border between original and derivative, since these were all created from anecdotes in the novelist's letters.[3] An interviewer recently queried Davis, saying "More and more you seem to use found materials in your stories," and she responded:

Back in the early eighties, I realized that you could write a story that was really just a narration of something that had happened to you, and change it slightly, without having really to fictionalize it. In a way, that's found material. I think it's hard to draw the line and say that something isn't found material.... I'm not making it up. I find what happens in reality very interesting and I don't find a great need to make up things, but I do like retelling stories that are told to me. (Aguilar)

That distinction between "reality" and "mak[ing] things up" lies at the heart of Davis's more recent stories, indicating directions she has been taking for some time as she conceives of seeing others from a slant, rendering them verbally, "inventing" them.

Still, her forcefully evocative effort raises the question—as Jonathan Evans has asked—of how thoroughly these "found objects" can actually function as such:

Duchamp's readymades were everyday objects that almost anyone in his audience would recognise. The recognition is the source of the duality.... But Davis did not translate Flaubert's passages dealing with artistic creation, rather the stories from the letters. They are seldom the main part of the letter, but rather observations or anecdotes that fill it out. As such, it is unlikely that a reader of Davis' stories would know the source texts without going looking for them. (Evans 105–6)

Evans seems more perturbed by Davis's framing context than the content of these pieces, challenging her transposition of such moments

---

3. Davis acknowledges in a final note that these entries "were formed from material found in letters written by Gustave Flaubert, most of them to his friend and lover Louise Colet, during the period in which he was working on *Madame Bovary*. This material...was excerpted, translated from the French, and then slightly rewritten. My aim was to leave Flaubert's language and content as little changed as possible, only shaping the excerpt enough to create a balanced story, though I took whatever liberties I thought were necessary" (*CS* 289).

as well as their scattering throughout *Can't and Won't* rather than (as originally published) keeping the stories tied together. He also implies that they pointedly expose how often Davis relies on episodes from her own life thinly disguised as fiction. Still, one might respond that their dispersal throughout does nicely offer a provocative contrast of fictional and nonfictional texts. And whether not knowing the source of such material makes it any less compelling is a question Evans disregards, since attaching the name "Flaubert" to the entry indicates how citational recognition may be less the issue than a famous author's actual epistolary observations and experiences.

The "after Flaubert" entries would seem to demand a different kind of attention than do the other stories in her last volume, as if urging us to heed the implications of occasions lived, recounted, and set down historiographically. The very invocation of those moments serves to relive them, and to bring Flaubert somehow alive, a testament to the writer whose daily experiences created the art. In "The Visit to the Dentist" (2014), Davis steals Flaubert's musing about place, age, and guillotines, the idea of a dream shared with another, as if "thoughts are fluid, and flow downward, from one person to another, within the same house" (*C&W* 31). In "The Funeral" (2014), Flaubert acknowledges going "to Pouchet's wife's funeral yesterday. As I watched poor Pouchet, who stood there bending and swaying with grief like a stalk of grass in the wind" (*C&W* 68). People talk as she watches "poor Pouchet standing forlornly in front of us," and finally exclaims: "Oh, we writers may think we invent too much—but reality is worse every time!" In an earlier story from the same collection, "Pouchet's Wife," we have already been prepared for this account, evoking the loss: "He loved her very much and will be devastated" (*C&W* 47)—though interestingly, the second part of this sequence comes as an earlier story.

Life is unordered, leap-frogging in its absent sequences, and the very rhythm of Davis's unfolding stories confirms that truth. In short, the invention of "Flaubert's stories" seems little different from the "dream" stories with which we began in pressing the fluid boundaries of any concept of story itself. Involuntary imagining, news account: both are simply forms in which consciousness is at once revealed and celebrated. Davis has from the beginning found experiments with the form of the short story invigorating, though in these two late modes she seems to demand that we engage at once the facts of a case as well as the nearly hallucinated possibilities triggered by those facts themselves.

III. Grammar, Philosophy, Letters To

Davis clearly broadened her efforts in *Can't and Won't* to press the
boundaries of what a short story could do, ranging between deliberately
avoiding narrative itself (replaced by sometimes surreal description)
and alternatively transcribing actual historical facts (as simply as possible).
Her late style is an effort to reorient earlier gestures toward brevity and
wonder, but as well to organize such an effort in structurally quite
different modes. Other writers devoted to flash fiction have foregone
that effort, which makes her success all the more impressive. One way
to appreciate it is in terms of three separate modes: grammatical puzzlers;
philosophical enigmas; and letters of complaint. For more than her
contemporaries, Davis silently engages the closing premise of Atwood's
"Happy Endings," questioning the invisible "How and Why" rather
than troubling too much over the "what." The facts are there, or even
simply the hallucination, and readers are left to wonder at what holds
them together. If the liminal aspects she explores are not so different
from the other three writers, she reduces encounters to more garden-
variety incidents. Among an array of authors extending from Donald
Barthelme to Jhumpa Lahiri, she offers a more circumspect if no less
telling investigation. Her efforts reflect a self-consciousness about not
only stories but language more generally and its peculiar capacity to
represent phenomena while also transforming consciousness.

That interest extends from her early translations and culminates in
playful fictionalizations of linguistic dilemmas that have long intrigued
Davis. Delving into the intersection of language with psychology,
she delights in the ways they complicate each other, as reflected in
"A Double Negative" (2001): "At a certain point in her life, she realizes
it is not so much that she wants to have a child as that she does not
want not to have a child, or not to have had a child" (*CS* 373). In the
shift from the denial of simple affirmative to the denial of a denied
state, then of a denied past state, with a gradual slippage in tense from
present to seemingly past perfect, lies a complicated but perfectly understandable emotional quandary that Davis might have expanded into a
full-blown psychological narrative. Consider "The Sentence and the
Young Man" (2014), which focuses on an "ungrammatical sentence
'Who sing!?!'," tossed away in a trash can, watched by the narrator as a
young man walking by was "eyeing the sentence curiously. We will stay

where we are, for fear that, at any moment, he will reach in quickly and fix it" (*C&W* 175). The scene, at once ridiculous yet riveting, forces the reader to consider a grammatical symbol as somehow abstract yet phenomenal, at once a mere sequence of phonemes in figurative conformity yet somehow literally there in lived life.

Analogously, the opening of the "dream" story, "Two Characters in a Paragraph" (2014), seems to defy the narrator as she works on its conclusion, and realizes her male character is growing out of her control, drifting in defiance of her efforts slowly over the female one: "True, it is a dense paragraph, and they're in the very middle of it, and it's dark in there" (*C&W* 217). Language simply refuses to stay put, seeming to adopt an authority all its own, defying grammatical rules and narratorial expectations to plunk down in the midst of grubby life itself (reminding us of Munro and Dubus, who found their own characters equally intractable, not always to be controlled by them). Indeed, we may well end up feeling this "dream" has greater immediacy than the stories presented as supposedly factual. Even the collection's title story pokes fun at Davis's reputation for not following the rules: "they said, I was *lazy*. What they meant by *lazy* was that I used too many contractions" (*C&W* 46). Once again the conflation between real and fictional, between Davis and her imagined narrator (in a scenario that sounds much like her), makes us aware of the porous fabric that only partially segregates fictional inventions from actual lives.

In a more serious vein, Davis keeps returning to grammatical challenges and writerly quandaries with stories that turn on niceties of syntactical correctness and lexical practice. A few early instances, like "Grammar Questions" (2001) and "Honoring the Subjunctive" (2001), reveal in their titles themselves a desire to make grammar central, though these two center on a solecism and an uncertain attribution that seem non-starters. Pressing linguistic concerns more fully in *Can't and Won't*, "A Note from the Paperboy" (2014) presents a suburbanite complaining about terms of delivery. Finally, after a brief page of description, the narrator intervenes, pulling back from the scene to observe that the boy's syntax is faulty: "In fact, according to the grammatical construction used by the paperboy in his note, it is the animals themselves who are not only walking through the yard but also delivering the paper" (*C&W* 92). The stakes seem ludicrously small, the delivery situation easily manageable, transforming the drama over faulty phrasing in the exchange between paperboy and client from a charged situation into a wacky one. The vehement web of words we spin in response to petty encounters tends to dissolve like mist without quite being erased from memory.

Another story begins "Description: spayed female, calico" (*C&W* 176), then goes on for three pages of sentence fragments and facts about a stray who has in fact been found. Again, we marvel at the interest generated by such limited, disorienting details. "Flaubert and Point of View" consists of a two-page run-on sentence that likewise keeps shifting perspective in a series of circular turns as items are held up for consideration, one after another: "At the Blessing of the Hounds, on the opening day of fox-hunting season, a Saturday (large horses sleekly groomed, men and women in red riding costumes seated on them..." (*C&W* 267). In each of these stories, as here in their reconstruction, we feel arbitrarily, syntactically, swept from event to event. Consider a fourth, a sing-song account of someone planning to move from town, eager to sell her things, which ends with the valediction: "It is time to say goodbye to Nancy Brown. We have enjoyed her friendship. We have enjoyed her tennis lessons" (*C&W* 282).

Yet even in this simple flash fiction of ten simple sentences, Davis pays fierce attention to its narrative construction, as she revealed in a description longer than the story itself:

as I reread it later I saw that because of the character of the piece, which is somewhat absurd, I should reverse the "natural" order and end on a stranger note, and so now the ending reads: "*We will miss her friendship. We will miss her tennis lessons.*" Because of this new concluding order, it is almost as though we actually value her tennis lessons more than her friendship. It is a better order not only because it is more absurd, but because it is more surprising. In some subtle way, you always want to surprise a reader.   (Davis, "Endings" 379–80)

The casual closing aside corresponds to the tone of all these late stories, in registering once more an acquired, more distanced, less readily empathic perspective on sketches that had in earlier collections seemed to warrant fuller treatment. Other stories, early and late, have turned all but self-consciously to the question of manuscript revisions, with the late "Revise: 1" and "Revise: 2" coupled as imperative instructions written by what seems to be a copy-editor who becomes increasingly impatient, abrupt, finally self-contradictory: "Continue with Baby but remove Priorities. Make Priorities Priority" (*C&W* 211). Nearly two decades earlier, "The Center of the Story" (1997) seems to have anticipated directions she would later pursue, though extended for five pages to describe the "problem" of finding a story's center ("There may be no center" [*CS* 176]) as well as its end, and that lingers over a series of imagined enactments of editorial problems as fictional possibilities.

Davis cannot help but turn a skeptical eye to the process of making stories, and increasingly reveals less interest in narrative coherence or plausibility than in sheer factual uncertainty coupled with grammatical intrigue. Syntax tends increasingly to confuse rather than clarify issues, as "Circular Story" (2014) suggests, compounding the efforts of her earlier collections. A mere six sentences describe a garbage truck that "always wakes me up. I always wonder what it is" (*C&W* 5), with sentences confirmed not only by the circularity of "always" that repeats before and after, but in their inversion later, in irritating confirmation of the experience being described. This late, more restive self-consciousness about syntactical pliancy is confirmed in "Reversible Story" (2014), which inadvertently offers a compelling example of Alice Munro's random theory of reading. Imagining mirror versions of the Charray couple's tastes and their home improvements, the story's first half has one first leading to the other, and then the other leading to the one in paragraphs suitably labeled "Necessary Expenditure" and "Expenditure Necessary" (*C&W* 61).

Unlike Munro, however, Davis seems intrigued by the ordering of sentences rather than of entire sequences, with the second paragraph reversing the presentation in the first to achieve a slightly altered view based simply on a progression's inversion. That willingness to play with mirrored reversals extends to words themselves, known as semordnilaps (for example, "evil" and "live"), and though generally Davis seems more intrigued by syntax than diction, she has been beguiled by sound, by the effect of modulations and sonorities on our interpretive impulses. The aggressively opinionated character in "A Mown Lawn" (2001) admits "She hated a *mown lawn*. Maybe that was because *mow* was the reverse of *wom*, the beginning of the name of what she was—a *woman*. A *mown lawn* had a sad sound to it, like a *long moan*" (*CS* 314). The story then continues through a long and peculiarly (if divertingly) clotted paragraph that dramatizes the exasperation provoked by the familiar phrase.

Clearly central to Davis's late focus are structural conundrums (language, behavior), revealing a link between her stories about linguistic oddities and those about philosophically puzzling subjects. Certainly, she differs dramatically from other story practitioners, turning from individuals confronted by various degrees of trauma to something less idiosyncratic, more mundane and familiar—something akin to Munro's observation about the suasions of "dear life." As Davis herself admits of her turn from dramatic exposition, her interest increasingly lies in the generically human, not in specific imagined figures or local characterizations. That explains (with a possible passing nudge towards Munro herself in naming her random character "Alice"):

> why there are no names, so rarely names. It just doesn't interest me to invent a character whose name is going to be "Alice" and have something happen to Alice. It's always, from way back, seemed sort of redundant to me or irritatingly arbitrary and gratuitous. I guess that my higher value is on some sort of philosophical investigation. What is the point of any of this if we are not arriving at some world-view, or some view of reality that makes sense, and pursuing an investigation of reality?   (Knight 533–34; also 549; also McCaffery 72)

Davis simply remains indifferent to the sundry dimensions of character, which prompted Larry McCaffery to confront her with what he perceived as a problem: "Your interest in the abstract instance of a person who could be anyone seems paradoxical for someone whose stories usually originate very concretely from real people and real names." In response, Davis explained: "It has to do with keeping the focus on the question or problem and resisting allowing the illusion that this thing might have happened" (McCaffery 73). Unlikely as that logic may seem for a fiction writer, she does succeed in imaginatively transforming general puzzles into immediate, closely felt experiences. And in this, if rather loosely, she ironically represents something like a return to the short story's beginning in Poe, with his focus on single emotions, on figures notably lacking background or motivation.

Certainly, she succeeds in evoking our interest, leading us willy-nilly to ponder the experiences of stick-figured characters. Consider the structure of "How I Know What I Like (Six Versions)" (2014), which shifts on a single page from "She likes it" to "I like it" to "I think I like it" (*C&W* 63), prompting the reader to reconsider narrative possibilities based simply on what seems like a teenager's momentary shifting of voice and mood. After all, teenagers so often seem compelled by the immediate, the local, the one isolated emotion that grips them at the moment. Moreover, the conundrums that have increasingly come to intrigue Davis often involve mixed borders between fictional verbal ploys and workaday engagements, first introduced in her playful

"Letter to a Funeral Parlor" (2001). That single instance of a complaint she actually sent, provoked by an ill-advised use of the neologism "cremains," is multiplied half-a-dozen times in *Can't and Won't*—so often, in fact, that the letters might be seen as actually helping to structure the diverse collection. Postal complaints suddenly proliferate along with an array of translations "from Flaubert" and multiple "*dream*"s marking (as Jonathan Evans argues) "the first sequences to appear in Davis' work, which normally consists of independent stories (or sequences within stories). The three sequences, though each is non-linear and each is distributed slightly differently throughout the volume, give *Can't and Won't* a cohesion that is clearer than in Davis' earlier collections (where structure is at best implicit)" (Evans 74). That turn forms another characteristic of her late style, casting a net over a set of similar examples meant to link the fictional and nonfictional, if also teasing out latent strains within the collection.

The "letters of complaint" are, like the two other sequences, based not only on kernels of actual experience but also on a notion of the quotidian, on sheer description, and especially on otherwise trivial if focused feelings that have acquired a compelling urgency. Distinctively, the letters seem of all Davis's stories most unlike Dubus, Williams, and Munro in their functional purpose, meant to perform as discursive prose to effect a specific end, to get something actually done. As well, their cross-hatched combination of seriousness and light-hearted humor comes to seem particularly characteristic of Davis. Consider "Letter to a Frozen Peas Manufacturer" (2014), which complains that the store-bought bag is illustrated in "a most unattractive color" (*C&W* 32), with "deceptive" advertising working ironically *against* those otherwise inclined to purchase the peas.

A more complicated, more nuanced version of this special mode is "The Letter to the Foundation" (2014), with a grant recipient filing a long report that reveals her deep ambivalence about teaching coupled with writing. Its confessional mode and thirty-page length define the piece as an outlier, returning to earlier strategies in providing a more full-fledged personality than most of her later stories. Yet as elsewhere, the story turns out to have been thoroughly autobiographical, which Davis later admitted: "That story is mainly made up of complaints about teaching. I find teaching difficult and let that all come out in the story. That was the part I enjoyed writing the most, all those crazy problems of teaching, all the dread" (Aguilar). The fictional narrator slowly reveals her motives, which delineate a character hard to distinguish from what we presume is true of Davis herself:

I had been given something I did not have to earn, something other people considered important, but I did not feel very important myself. I had not felt very important before, and now this thing that I had been given had reduced me further. I was certainly much smaller and less important than what had been given to me. I was only a recipient, in this interaction. A recipient is not very active or important.   (*C&W* 201)

Yet a central premise of the story is the narrator's need once again to bear witness to life's idiosyncrasies.

Extending this judgment in a near-perfectly harmonized syntactic structure, "If at the Wedding (at the Zoo)" (2014) reveals that premise via little more than its nominal linking in a series of conditional anaphoras anticipated by the title itself: "If we hadn't…," then "we wouldn't have seen" (*C&W* 261). The prose itself enforces an agenda at the heart of Davis's writing though here sustained in rhythms more straightforward than ever. Simply persisting, watching and listening, informs her entire narrative craft, attending carefully to whatever transpires and being an adequate witness. Often it requires a third-person narrator instead of first-, since the preferred vantage is on the edges of things, where one can linger and observe. As she once revealingly admitted, she wants to avoid becoming a "center-stage writer":

Whereas I've always thought you miss something, if you are the center of everything, you miss watching. And then if you're a translator, you have to become the other person, the other writer if you are going to be any good. You have to speak in the voice of the other person. You can't speak in your own voice; you can't have one consistent voice that you stamp on everything you translate.   (Knight 538)

That resistance to artificially reinforcing her own voice, moreover—refusing to hew to an obvious personal perspective and instead pursuing an impulse to inhabit another's separate point of view—itself forms an important link between the roles she most enjoys as both translator and story writer.

IV. Stylistic Suasions

For all her grammatical and even philosophical ambition, Davis's literary reputation has always rested on an ability to convey through the shortest of fictions a series of burnished insights and provocations. These depend less on ideas or logical puzzles than on dramatic literary performances, on verbal displays about which Davis is thoroughly self-conscious. As she once said of her earlier stories: "I think each idea demands its own form and length. 'The Fish' required only a single image, a single paragraph. 'Liminal,' being a piece about insomnia, sleep, the night, needed a lot of space around brief dreamlike sections. 'Break It Down' needed to have no space all—one headlong flood of language" (McCaffery 71). That "flood of language" in the fourth story of her first collection already confirms a perfect ear, finely attuned to the long wave of unending desire that is its subject. And part of the breathless urgency of those eight pages, in which lust is kindled, consummated, postponed, and rekindled again, owes to the contrast with the narrator's dull opening and closing efforts to assess, however misguidedly, the economics of the affair, as if neutrally calculating an emotional whirlwind. Everything in between occurs as syntactical excess, run-on sentences that gratify by delaying the end, expressed (as Beverly Haviland observes) "by the absence of those signs of commencement and closure that we take so much for granted in writing and imagine in speech: the capital and the period" (152). Though Davis tightens her focus considerably by her later work, she never loses her ear for a style commensurate to her reduced subjects.

That attention extends to simple sonorities and larger resonances, revealed even in the abbreviation of names themselves. Despite her admitted resistance to identifying characters, signatures and sobriquets on occasion do captivate her, not as a specious means of becoming more personal or individual but for largely stylistic reasons; a name like Mitch she finds appealing for the simplest of sonic logics: "because it's an emphatic name with interesting rhymes: *itch, pitch, stitch,* and *bitch.*" (McCaffery 73). More generally, her interest lies (as for any writer) in lexical and syntactical pleasures. Another early story, "Safe Love" (1986), about a woman fond of her son's pediatrician, may have been admittedly "absurd" as a situation, though Davis claimed: "and yet obviously so common. There's no meaning to the crush, no meaning to the relationship. . . . It wasn't the situation that interested me but the language I could use to play with it." As she added: "My stories often seem to reflect this divorce—the brain trying to teach the feelings how to behave" (McCaffery 79). Or, she might well have said instead, of stories that regularly exhibit feelings undoing what the brain otherwise dictates.

Davis's skill in finding "the language I could use to play with" a situation would develop not only towards concision but towards whimsicality, with syntactical innovation becoming ever more impish in *Can't and Won't*. Take "Idea for a Sign" (2014), on the premise of boarding a train, surveying others, and wondering whom to sit next to: "It might help if we each wore a little sign saying in what ways we will and will not be likely to disturb other passengers, such as ... " (*C&W* 6). After two brief introductory paragraphs setting up the premise, a long final paragraph consisting once again of a run-on sentence gathers together intense descriptions of all the activities she will or will not do, beginning with: "Will not talk on cell phone at all, aside from perhaps a short communication to my husband ... " (*C&W* 6). Instead of the surging emotion that wells up in "Break It Down," however, cresting through linked moments, this two-page sentence shuttles back and forth among a motley series of nervously clustered, quickly modified behaviors the narrator resolves to avoid. In the process, the mosaic of predilections and exclusions establishes a rather nervous passenger few of us would like to accompany. The sign she begins by assuming she would wear quickly becomes inadequate to the meaning she wants to convey, perhaps as most signs do. Indeed, her listed activities and desires finally expose the irrelevance of signs at all, compounded by the detailed exceptions isolated off by hesitant qualifiers ("aside from," "more rarely," "most of," "sometimes," "actually," "almost always," "though," with then a repetition of "may"). That sentence forms a gem of syntactic revision, as it nicely embodies a consciousness alive to the world's resistance to rule, in the process making us self-conscious of the way adverbs and adjectives can so thoroughly alter expectation.

Increasingly in her later stories, Davis exults in exploring moments that unfold without narrative need, in the resolute absence of plot, as simply part of a wandering eye (and wandering words whose characteristic rhythms shape what the reader's eye in turn sees). In "Almost No Memory" (1997), the title story of her second collection, she depicts someone suffering from Alzheimer's in the very language of lost memory: "She remembered enough to get by from day to day. She remembered enough to work, and she worked hard. She did good work, and was paid for it, and earned enough to get by, but she did not remember her work, so ... " (*CS* 259). The repetition of "remembered," and then of "work" shifting from verb to noun, seems to capture the sliding grip from one handhold of memory to the next as grip's power itself diminishes. That opening paragraph is followed by a second, revealing self-evidently less nimble play in its sheer repetitions: "She remembered enough to get by, and to do her work, but she did not learn from what she did." Two more long paragraphs follow in turn, compounding the effect with clauses likewise repeated in a stylistic rendering of the problem depicted, as if the narrator's intonations evoked the woman's failed memory, encapsulating the iterative yet deeply uncertain aspect of consciousness—"she would want to make a note...She wanted to make a note of a note...Or she wanted to make a note..." (*CS* 260)—all as part of the circularity of her own flawed reasoning yet persistent desire.

By *Can't and Won't*, Davis has further altered this perspective on aging and forgetfulness, in part by simply becoming more succinct in her treatment to match the slightly addled subject of her story. "My Childhood Friend" (2014) focuses on the quizzical gaze of aged misrecognition: "Who is this old man walking along looking a little grim with a wool cap on his head? But when I call out to him and he turns around, he doesn't know me at first, either—this old woman smiling foolishly at him in her winter coat" (*C&W* 235). Instead of three pages of reiterated clauses tirelessly dangling down the page without ever converging, the story now consists of two mirroring sentences: old man facing old woman; wool cap versus winter coat; "a little grim" confronted by "smiling" (*C&W* 235); all in a moment of forgetfulness sliding too slowly into recollection. Davis's late style, in other words, has the effect of making even flash fiction seem shorter, more fleeting.

In "The Fish" (1986), nearly three decades earlier, Davis had moved more slowly through a longer paragraph, lingering over a similar befuddled consciousness focused only on self: "She stands over a fish, thinking about certain irrevocable mistakes she has made today. Now the fish has been cooked, and she is alone with it" (*CS* 33). Little more is revealed in the four sentences that follow, other than that the fish itself "has never been so completely alone as it is now" (*CS* 33). Yet as Larry McCaffery observes of the story's adroit compression, it already anticipates the increasingly Spartan, stripped-down effect perfected by her late style:

We are given no exposition at all—no details about setting, personal background, not even the woman's name...Nor does Davis provide any "analysis" of this hideous moment, nor any hint of self-awareness or understanding by the woman that might resolve her plight and lead to change. What we are given instead is only a single, mysterious, powerfully resonant *image* that somehow seems to imply or contain—but does not refer to or depict (in the sense of exposition)—an entire lifetime of failure, loneliness, and mistakes.   (McCaffery 62)

The dead, cooked fish "has never been so completely alone," offering an objective correlative for the woman now preparing it in a scene whose "weary eye" defines both the woman and the reader.

In what might be seen as a belated companion story from *Can't and Won't*, offering the echo of a title as "Old Woman, Old Fish," Davis offers an even more succinct, less charged, but no less evocative rendering of a similar scenario: "The fish that has been sitting in my stomach all afternoon was so old by the time I cooked and ate it, no wonder I am uncomfortable—an old woman digesting an old fish" (*C&W* 242). The story reveals an adroit ability to turn repetition to differing ends, but the reiteration here of "old," in describing both the fish and the woman, offers a wry yoking of the two in a moment meant to be merely passing. Jonathan Evans has observed the "characteristic re-evaluation of the quotidian that appears in many of her stories" (3), though often in *Can't and Won't*, a less fraught, less emotionally violent, more commonplace understanding of daily occurrences emerges than had been true of earlier stories.

Possibly, that contrast is best defined by its obverse, with a throwback story of anger meant to suggest the opposite. In "Dreadful Mucamas" (2014), the narrator's maids "are very rigid, stubborn women from Bolivia. They resist and sabotage whenever possible" (*C&W* 51). A series of separate complaints are each broken by white space between sentences and paragraphs that only enforces the anger underlying this rant, pulling apart, refusing to merge or move towards a more sympathetic posture. We lumber through days of employee resentment that taint a struggle endured to the end: "But they give us such dark, Indian looks!" (*C&W* 60). This concluding exclamation is hard to know how to read, in supposedly pulling various threads of a story that seems so disjointed at last together.

By contrast, the syntax of the late story, "Wrong Thank-You in the Theater" (2014), deftly configures another moment of misguided intentions, mistakenly understood, as the narrator stands up to let a woman past. Belatedly, she realizes that the woman's apology has been meant for the usher, not her, and then endures the additional embarrassment of having her own misunderstanding thrown back at her: "She just wanted to make that clear" (*C&W* 253). The stakes, again as always admittedly small, detract little from the emotional entanglements that remind us of similar slights endured, sometimes inflated inordinately against genuine offenses. Yet that characteristic attention to incidental bruises we suffer all but hourly is perhaps Davis's signature theme, granting the trifling injuries of life their due. "Negative Emotions" (2014) traces a similarly small-minded response to a well-intentioned gesture, after a teacher "sent all the other teachers in his school a message about negative emotions" (*C&W* 103), only to learn his message had inspired those self-same "negative emotions" among colleagues.

As if to confirm the more pedestrian impulses of her later collection, Davis reduces desire itself to trivial dislocations, including "How I Read as Quickly as Possible Through My Back Issues of the *TLS*" (2014). Consisting of lists that repeatedly begin "I do not want," the whole slowly shifts to "Interested in," punctuated by far more instances of "Not interested in," only to end in "Not interested in—or, well, yes, maybe interested in: the history of diplomacy, Laura Bush's autobiography" (*C&W* 100). Again, in very different form the whole attests to the lingering stress of mundane decisions, offering in the process a whimsical shifting of interest that comes close to matching the reader's own. For all the underlying similarity of theme, each story offers a different barb, a dissimilar response, a distinct emotional context that interconnects through Davis's persistent attention to the appropriately suggestive tone. And in each case, that tone needs to be achieved all but immediately in stories that do not allow much lingering.

That pressure on style may best be exemplified in "The Seals" (2013), and for two salient reasons: first, in part paradoxically (in ironic contrast to the late emphasis on greater concision), because it constitutes the longest story (at twenty-five pages) in *Can't and Won't*; and second, because it initially appeared in a more straightforward, condensed form (at less than eight pages) as "Everyone is Invited" (2005), a contrast that proves intriguing. The narratives consist of random reminiscences on an unexplained train ride west from New York, each opening with the strangely disorienting claim that "I know we're supposed to be happy on this day. How odd that is. When you're very young, you're usually happy, at least you're ready to be" (*C&W* 146). That ruminative first-person voice is a disarming one for late Davis, initiating a narrative unfolding as an inner monologue responding to the death of her middle-aged half-sister a year or more earlier.

In fact, happiness "this day" seems an improbable emotion, as the narrator mulls over her memories, with the reader left to contemplate what might be at all cheering on such an occasion. Is it simply taking the trip? Is it an annual visit, since the landscape is familiar? What else could explain? The fact that nothing does, however, may well be the point, as the narrator grapples with grief that overwhelms her even now, well after her sister has passed away. She ventures that "maybe you miss someone even more when you can't figure out what your relationship was. Or when it seemed unfinished" (*C&W* 147), and the rest of her narrative surveys all she can recall of their relationship—the visits, the gifts, the sister's abandonment of their family, her own fatherless children (replicating her experience), and among other unanswerables the narrator's cluelessness about her sister's actual feelings for her.

Davis often achieves through brevity a shimmering intensity of effect, though here the opposite seems the case, in the dramatic multiplication of memories and expressions of affection that heighten the narrator's desolation in exact proportion to their failure to explain or otherwise ease the pain. "When she was alive, her presence was endless, time with her was endless, time was endless" (*C&W* 156), the narrator realizes with anguish, though "Once she was gone, every memory was suddenly precious, even the bad ones, even the times I was irritated with her" (*C&W* 156). Time alters from a condition of plenitude to one of deprivation in the death of her sister, marking a breach between possibility and negation. The inability to weave her thoughts into a cogent temporal account, reflected in the occasionally repetitive and fragmented syntax, is reinforced once again by white space separating sections of the revised version from each other. Later, the narrator admits to something like a brain freeze, caught between desire and fact, unstable recollection and whatever it was she actually lived through— "I don't know if I'm remembering that or making it up" (*C&W* 169)—a confession that significantly does not appear in the earlier story.

That unfocused desperation is compounded, moreover, by the trip's interruptions, beginning with simply gazing at passing scenery— "Trenton Makes, the World Takes—out the window" (*C&W* 149); "Nearly to Philadelphia—rounding the bend, by the river, there are boathouses on the other side" (*C&W* 155); "We're moving pretty fast now. When you slide by it all so quickly, you think you won't ever have to get bogged down in it again—the traffic, the neighborhoods" (*C&W* 157); "It's beginning to rain, little drops driven sideways" (*C&W* 163). Occasionally, amid the grief, sly humor intercedes, as when she feels compelled to remonstrate silently with a cell phone user: "I don't do business on my cell phone on the train. They should know better" (*C&W* 157). Or she finally acknowledges the usefulness of her sister's random gift of ceramic Nordic seals to absorb grody refrigerator odors. The whole ends with the tipsy invitation from a woman leaving the café car where people are laughing: "Oh, a party. It's a party—in the café car, she tells me. Everyone's invited" (*C&W* 170).

The revelation to be gathered from such an anguished account of grief unabated is that it always exists in consort with contrary experiences and ungovernable emotions, none of which can be withstood. The story, in fact, might well be seen as embodying (in its later version) the rhythm of the entire collection of *Can't and Won't* itself, leaving us off balance in our grasp of events, achieving its emotional resonance precisely through its disjointedness and intoxicating mix of modes. If Davis reverts in this instance to an earlier style, less abbreviated and condensed, it is still to serve even more effectively the agenda of her late style, which lies in her knowing that she requires words to reveal what she also knows they cannot bring to light (or rather, in her own informal idiom, "can't and won't").

V. Conclusion, Verbal Concoctions

Regularly, Davis has been exalted as a master of intriguingly brief situations, attuned to fleeting verbal conundrums, pithy metaphysical puzzles, recherché cultural habits, quizzically terse moments—an architect of small moments and their apparently large contradictions. Accurate or not, that judgment is certainly confirmed in her own expressed enthusiasm in interviews. What tends to get lost in this characterization, however, is the animating quality of her writing itself, in the rhythms of prose that draw our eyes (and ears) to the humor, the irritation, the astonishment revealed in deft rendering of moments askew, grammar defied, emotions somehow unsettled in all the insignificant ways that nonetheless stamp our days. As well, she willingly explores the shift (both *in* her stories and *between* them) among various registers of emotion, from belly laughs to tear-stained grief. Violence is as random as beauty, or humor, or boredom, and her subjects never know what will come next. But as well (and too often), subjects of her stories are assumed to be somehow divorced from their composition, with seemingly unembellished prose deemed more often than not as simply transparent rather than carefully crafted. This is the basis of Josh Cohen's claim that "her writing voids any attempt by the critic to burrow down to the kernel of unconscious thought that would unlock its secret meanings. Davis' fiction repeatedly carries us across an elaborate, often labyrinthine logical and emotional pathway only to leave both narrator and reader in ignorance" (507).

The focus on her stories as investigations of external enigmas rather than self-contained verbal achievements is typical. And Jonathan Evans would seem to agree, even as he tightens Cohen's claim by adducing patterns supposedly common to her fiction and her translations. Moreover, he registers the way other inflections keep displacing a subject's own singular voice:

> Davis' writing challenges the possibility of the work as a closed system; it always opens out through its inclusion of other writers' work within it. Davis's work is therefore filled with voices and texts other than her own. Translation is just one among many ways in which her work can be seen to fracture, breaking down its own boundaries. This mirrors the constant movement towards the other in Davis's stories and the porosity of subjectivity that leads characters to use other people's words to express themselves...or rely on external supports for their memories. (146–7)

True as this sounds, however, it nonetheless tends again to slight the actual rhetorical achievement of her stories, in their crafted wording itself and the way awkward syntax and strained diction, straightforward narrative sequence and its lack, at once sway us and alter our vision. The result too often has been that Davis is simply dismissed (or touted) as experimental, without the effort made to understand where the experiment leads, and how.

The features that contribute to Davis's reputation as a radically innovative story practitioner are as thoroughly textual and stylistic as they are for each of the other authors celebrated here. Each seized the narrative form and remade it to his or her own vivid (and vividly different) ends. Yet in also grappling with violent moments, or slyly squeezing the emotional and social disruptions so often created via narrative agitation, Dubus, Munro, and Williams draw readers' attention to the verbal means by which imagined states are constructed, advanced, suspended. In this regard as in so many others Davis differs, increasingly more circumscribed in her materials, more fleeting in her concern with narrative sequence, more confident in the interest to be found in ephemeral events and minuscule dramas. Instead of reinventing the allure of violence or untoward reversals, which have been subjects of short fiction from the beginning, she has chosen to focus on the ever more minor destabilizations that recur in our lives, throwing us off balance, ever-present in consciousness—the ambient noise (and music) that bestirs us casually and haphazardly.

A fascination with benign neuroses and low-level troubles, with the passing fixations and silly obsessions from which we cannot quite wrench ourselves free, may help explain why readers accept her writing without looking close enough, as if relatively unimportant experiences are self-evident with their constructions likewise more or less obvious. Yet Davis's increasingly taut presentation of experiences that remain awkwardly niggling, seemingly habitual, requires more attention, simply to appreciate how she achieves an astonished response out of materials so otherwise conventional, seeming to lack much punch. Her gift is one of insight but as well (if rarely acknowledged) one of words themselves, in unerringly compelling formulations.

Davis inadvertently conceded as much when an interviewer confronted her with something of a conundrum about her own writing: "Isn't it a paradox for you to be suggesting that writing and language are finally of no real help in organizing the chaos of people's lives and emotional responses to things?" Her calm response was salutary: "That paradox is analogous to the cliché about translation being impossible: it's true theoretically, yet translations are done all the time. A writer has nothing but words to convey this ongoing struggle that everybody has—to make something of the interpretation of language, to be able to make language mean, to make language more trustworthy" (McCaffery 79). Her point, worth keeping in mind, is that the focus is not on philosophical puzzles or grammatical enigmas or simply humorous intersections, but on words themselves, and the ways in which their careful construction makes us realize how fully perceptions and emotional life are subject to the conventional (and perhaps even more importantly, the unconventional) verbal forms we choose to describe them.

Epilogue
Silence and Slow Time

The twinned argument of *More Time* has been that major writers diverge not only from each other in their conceptions of the short story but from their earlier selves as writers. If that has turned into an observation less striking than I initially hoped, it has helped nonetheless to sort out myriad differences both innate and unfolding, to reveal how shape-shifting the short story continues to be as a form. My initial suspicion that little actually holds that form together has only been confirmed by the disparate, often conflicting visions perfected by Munro, Dubus, Williams, and Davis. But it has also become increasingly clear that writers age into their ripeness in altogether diverse fashions—some becoming more efficient, more hard-nosed, more stylistically abrupt, while others grow less impatient, less demanding of the kind of dramatic developments they favored as younger practitioners.

That interest in seeing how writers mature, how their focus alters and tightens (or loosens), is part of the hidden "more" itself suggested by my title. In fact, the phrase "more time" becomes something of a pun, evoking not only Chekhov's mistaken desire for narrative amplitude but also expressing many writers' urge to keep on writing as they age, eager to explore possibilities yet untested while refining techniques and altering their vision.[1] Surprisingly, a review of careers reminds us

1. The famous letter to which Katherine Mansfield refers was written by Chekhov on October 27, 1888, in response to a writer who said he should "develop" a character: "I would willingly, with pleasure, with feeling, in a leisurely way, describe the *whole* of my hero, describe his state of mind while his wife was in labor, his trial, the unpleasant feeling he has after he is acquitted...It would give me nothing but pleasure, because I like to take pains and dawdle. But what am I to do? I begin a story on September 10th with the thought that I must finish it by October 5th at the latest; if I don't I shall fail

of how few short story practitioners attain an advanced age, with major figures often dying relatively young: Poe and Kafka at 40, Crane at 28, Chekhov at 44 and Mansfield a decade earlier. Others have simply turned away from the short form, devoting themselves instead to novels. Joyce died at 58, but his last stories appeared in *Dubliners* (1914) when he was only 32. Faulkner died at 65, but had written his final short story in 1939, when 42. And Hemingway succumbed at 62, but had stopped producing stories in 1938, when only 39 years old. Still others (notably John O'Hara and Flannery O'Connor) did not really alter their styles, early and late. One significant writer who did, though he stands well outside the limits of this study, was Henry James, whose career trajectory resembles that of the major figures represented here.[2]

Yet if "more time" (at least as evoking Chekhov's lament over limits to length, not writers' desire for third acts) seems a misguided but ever-present lure, the obverse of that recognition is how much accordingly remains silent, often unspoken, alluded to in fugitive gestures and ephemeral moods. After all, part of the delight of dipping into a short story has always been the knowledge that one can finish in a single sitting. Unlike novels, which lie heavy in the lap and invariably promise multiple interruptions (its own kind of pleasure, to be sure), stories declare their terminal moments in their very beginnings. That also means, of course, that they risk seeming to move too fast, leaving less time to linger, to pause and reflect, reminding the reader of a certain hit-and-run experience, with narrative temporality elided and characters often left mysterious, only partially disclosed. As Virgil observed,

the editor and be left without money. I let myself go at the beginning and write with an easy mind; but by the time I get to the middle I begin to grow timid and to fear that my story will be too long... This is why the beginning of my stories is always very promising and looks as though I were starting on a novel, the middle is huddled and timid, and the end is, as in a short sketch, like fireworks." (11).

2. Perhaps the most intriguing encouragement to continue earlier celebrated efforts occurred when Ingmar Bergman turned seventy in July 1988, a year after declaring in his memoir *The Magic Lantern*: "I probably do mourn the fact that I no longer make films." Akira Kurosawa sent him a birthday greeting questioning this abandonment: "In Japan, there was a great artist called Tessai Tomioka who lived in the Meiji Era (the late 19th century). This artist painted many excellent pictures while he was still young, and when he reached the age of eighty, he suddenly started painting pictures which were much superior to the previous ones, as if he were in magnificent bloom. Every time I see his paintings, I fully realize that a human is not really capable of creating really good works until he reaches eighty." Then Kurosawa added: "A human is born a baby, becomes a boy, goes through youth, the prime of life and finally returns to being a baby before he closes his life. This is, in my opinion, the most ideal way of life."

"fugit inreparabile tempus" ("it escapes, irretrievable time"), a phrase anticipating by two millennia the drive-by matrix of the short story (*Georgics*, Book 3, line 284). And that admission of time's ready dispatch, leaving writer and reader slightly breathless, intersects with the observation made by Kafka's dog of how we are all "bulwarks of silence." What seems like the very constraint on short fiction becomes in fact its freedom, as Valerie Shaw remarked, allowing an often indeterminate, even ineffable experience to unfold through ellipses and lulls.[3] Chekhov may have complained about the restrictions of time preventing him from fulfilling his secret narrative wishes for dilatory expansiveness, but in fact he was really far more hedgehog than fox, the opposite of Tolstoy in Isaiah Berlin's famous description. This is likewise true of each of the authors treated above, each devoted to the form *for* its silences, its half-known figures revealed through singular moments instead of interconnected dramas and multiple life trajectories.

Where does this leave us, then, discussing "more time" at a moment when stories are becoming ever more abbreviated, when flash fiction, the six-word story, "twitterature," "the dribble" (or minisaga) and "drabble" (or microfiction) have proliferated online and in published collections? None of this may prove a particularly new development, though there is certainly a considerable new audience for very short fiction. Even Joy Williams, as noted above, has most recently published *Ninety-Nine Stories of God* (2016), all brief one- or two-page versions of flash fiction that offer a significantly different turn from the stories in *The Visiting Privilege*.

Thus, having opened with Margaret Atwood's "Happy Endings," it seems appropriate to close in a similar paradoxical vein, if only to indicate how minimalist stories themselves can reveal some of the premises threading through them, of sudden shifts and equivocal possibilities, even of self-consciousness about the form itself. Robert Coover's contribution to a 1986 anthology on "sudden fiction," aptly entitled "A Sudden Story," displays traditional materials in a postmodern reduction that is as provocative in its way as Atwood's forking narrative.

---

3. Charles Baudelaire spoke of the "bénéfices éternels de la contrainte" when referring to the "nouvelle" (464). Perhaps the most dramatic instance of a writer caught between a desire for briefly focused narratives and the lure of expansive digression is Henry James, who repeatedly found his short story ideas gaining weight as he wrote, becoming novellas, even novels, despite initial intentions.

Moreover, Coover himself has kindly supplied a deadpan summary of his own work, claiming it is "about a hero and a dragon, a narrative situation that goes back several millennia, at least as far as the Epic of Gilgamesh and his battle with the monster of the forest Humbaba, and probably much further" ("Storying" 134). And here is the story in full:

Once upon a time, suddenly, while it still could, the story began. For the hero, setting forth, there was of course nothing sudden about it, neither about the setting forth, which he'd spent his entire lifetime anticipating, nor about any conceivable endings, which seemed, like the horizon, to be always somewhere else. For the dragon, however, who was stupid, everything was sudden. He was suddenly hungry and then he was suddenly eating something. Always, it was like the first time. Then, all of a sudden, he'd remember having eaten something like that before: a certain familiar sourness... And, just as suddenly, he'd forget. The hero, coming suddenly upon the dragon (he'd been trekking for years through enchanted forests, endless deserts, cities carbonized by dragon-breath, for him suddenly was not exactly the word), found himself envying, as he drew his sword (a possible ending had just loomed up before him, as though the horizon had, with the desperate illusion of suddenness, tipped), the dragon's tenseless freedom. Freedom? the dragon might have asked, had he not been so stupid, chewing over meanwhile the sudden familiar sourness (a memory...?) on his breath. From what? (Forgotten.)

(Coover, "A Sudden Story" 1986)

The witty survey here of a recognizable narrative structure revisited over millennia is made at once new and strange in this "sudden" fiction format.

As always with Coover, moreover, the narrative offers a self-conscious perspective on its own creative aspirations. Plot corresponds with theme in the "suddenly" that keeps reappearing, as if the play on the adverb itself constituted the story's primary focus, contrasting the experienced hero (for whom "there was of course nothing sudden") with the stupid dragon (for whom "everything was sudden"). It is as if the hero's long experience is not his alone but that of his avatars reaching far back in literary history, shared by readers equally versed in "any conceivable endings... always somewhere else." Questions of freedom and memory emerge as well for the reader, coupled with the forgotten nature of familiar narrative structures in reading once again the same old plot that nonetheless surprises anew. That is what stories achieve at their best, lending to us as to the hero a "desperate illusion of suddenness." The fear of some mere narrative repetition of an action-adventure plot disappears ("Forgotten") in this brilliant revision, even as the whole confirms a recognizable formal pattern that would have perfectly satisfied Vladimir Propp (imagine his smile!).

It may be worth noting, especially here, that the story was written in what could be termed Coover's middle period, when he was already fifty-four though anticipating further changes in the prolific years to follow. And though the tone of the story is tinged with considerable comic relief, the whole fulfills Edward Said's more sober observation about Constantine P. Cavafy's great poem, "Myris: Alexandria, A.D. 340": "This is the prerogative of late style: it has the power to render disenchantment and pleasure without resolving the contradiction between them. What holds them in tension, as equal forces straining in opposite directions, is the artist's mature subjectivity, stripped of hubris and pomposity, unashamed either of its fallibility or of the modest assurance it has gained as a result of age and exile" (Said 148). That invocation of "disenchantment" as twined with pleasure though thoroughly unreconciled is hardly (as Said would have it) true of all late styles; if nothing else, this book has argued that. But the invocation does aptly speak to Coover's story as well as to Cavafy's poem in its impassive revelation of the narrative mechanics never quite suspected in texts long loved.

The fact that the claim does not apply anywhere near as readily to Munro and Dubus, Williams or Davis, simply testifies to how broad the "prerogative of late style" can actually be, in defiance of Said's attempt to nail it down to the singular, to some transcultural, transhistorical development proving the same for each and every artist. The burden of the preceding chapters—begun inspired by Said's ideas, ending convinced by their limits—has been to reveal as diverse a plurality of late styles as of short story configurations themselves. That is the takeaway from a reading of this brilliant quartet of writers as they evolve from early efforts into their sardonically termed "declining years." Each offers a valediction that ironically restores the singularity of "late style" as a benefit of old age, whether in confirmation or repudiation of glistening earlier efforts, but always as invitation to reread and re-evaluate the trajectory that creates entire careers.

Bibliography

Aguilar, Andrea, and Johanne Fronth-Nygren. "Interview with Lydia Davis, Art of Fiction No. 227." *The Paris Review* 212 (Spring 2015). <https://www.theparisreview.org/interviews/6366/lydia-davis-art-of-fiction-no-227-lydia-davis>. Accessed September 27, 2018.

Altman, Rick. *The American Film Musical.* Bloomington: Indiana University Press, 1987.

Altman, Rick. *Film/Genre.* London: British Film Institute, 1999.

Atwood, Margaret. "Happy Endings." In *The Art of the Short Story*, edited by Dana Gioia and R. S. Gwynn. New York: Pearson Longman, 2006. 22–4.

Atwood, Margaret. "Introduction." *Alice Munro's Best: Selected Stories.* Toronto: McClelland & Stewart, 2008. vii–xviii.

Awano, Lisa Dickler. "An Interview with Alice Munro." *Virginia Quarterly Review* 89/2 (Spring 2013): 180–4.

Baker, Carlos. *Hemingway, The Writer as Artist.* Princeton: Princeton University Press, 1972.

Baudelaire, Charles. "Théophile Gautier." *L'Artiste* 4 (March 13, 1859). In *Oeuvres complètes*, edited by M. Ruff. Paris: Seuil, 1968.

Baxter, Charles. "Against Epiphanies." In *Burning Down the House: Essays on Fiction.* Saint Paul, MN: Graywolf, 2008. 53–77.

Bendixen, Alfred. "The Emergence and Development of the American Short Story." In *A Companion to the American Short Story*, edited by Alfred Bendixen and James Nagel. Chichester, UK: Wiley-Blackwell, 2010. 3–19.

Bhattacharji, Alex. "My Old Friends." *The New York Times Style Magazine* (April 23, 2017): 86. <https://www.nytimes.com/2017/04/12/t-magazine/entertainment/david-lynch-twin-peaks.html>. Accessed September 27, 2018.

Blaise, Clark. "On Ending Stories." In *Making It New: Contemporary Canadian Stories*, edited by John Metcalf. New York: Methuen, 1982. 32–5.

Blin, Lynn. "Negotiating Loss and the Voice of the Translator in Lydia Davis's *Can't and Won't*," *(Re)Construction(s), Etudes de Stylistique Anglaise, ESA* No. 11, Société de Stylistique Anglaise, Université Jean Moulin, Lyon III. Lyon, 2017. 37–56.

Boddy, Kasia. *The American Short Story Since 1950.* Edinburgh: Edinburgh University Press, 2010.

Bodwell, Joshua. "The Art of Reading Andre Dubus." *Poets & Writers.* 36.4 (July/August 2008): 21–5.

Brada-Williams, Noelle. "Reading Jhumpa Lahiri's 'Interpreter of Maladies' as a Short Story Cycle." *MELUS* 29.3–4 (Autumn-Winter 2004): 451–64.

Bradley, Jane. "Joy Williams." In *The Columbia Companion to the Twentieth-Century American Short Story*, edited by Blanche H. Gelfant and Lawrence Graver. New York: Columbia University Press, 2001. 573–9.

Callus, Ivan. "Exhausted Replenishment: Experimental Fiction and the Decomposition of Literature." *Word and Text* 4:1 (2014): 116–35.

Campbell, Ewing. *Raymond Carver: A Study of the Short Fiction*. New York: Twayne, 1992.

Carver, Raymond. *Raymond Carver: Collected Stories*. New York: Library of America, 2009.

Chekhov, Anton. *Letters on the Short Story, The Drama and Other Literary Topics* (1924), translated by Constance Garnett, edited by Louis S. Friedland. New York: Benjamin Blom, 1964.

Chiasson, Dan. "Horse Sense and Heartache: Review of *The Collected Stories of Lydia Davis*." *The New York Review of Books* (April 29, 2010). <https://www.nybooks.com/articles/2010/04/29/horse-sense-heartache/>. Accessed September 27, 2018.

Chudakov, A. P. *Chekhov's Poetics*, translated by Edwina Jannie Cruise and Donald Dragt. Ann Arbor, MI: Ardis, 1983.

Cohen, Josh. "Reflexive Incomprehension: On Lydia Davis." *Textual Practice* 24.3 (2010): 501–16.

Cooper, Rand Richards. "The Dark at the End of the Tunnel: Review of *Escapes*." *The New York Times* (January 21, 1990). <https://www.nytimes.com/1990/01/21/books/the-dark-at-the-end-of-the-tunnel.html>. Accessed September 27, 2018.

Coover, Robert. "A Sudden Story." In *Sudden Fiction: American Short-Short Stories*, edited by Robert Shapard and James Thomas. Salt Lake City: Gibbs M. Smith, Inc., 1986.

Coover, Robert. "Storying in Hyperspace: 'Linkages.'" In *The Tales We Tell: Perspectives on the Short Story*, edited by Barbara Lounsberry et al. Westport, CT: Greenwood Press, 1998. 133–8.

Cox, Ailsa. *Alice Munro*. Horndon, UK: Northcote House, 2004.

Crouse, David. "Resisting Reduction: Closure in Richard Ford's *Rock Springs* and Alice Munro's *Friend of My Youth*." *Canadian Literature* 146 (1995): 51–64.

Davis, Lydia. "Coolidge's 'Mine.'" *Poetics Journal* 3: Special Issue, *Poetry and Philosophy* (May 1983): 91–6.

Davis, Lydia. "Lydia Davis." In *Sudden Fiction: American Short-Short Stories*, edited by Robert Shapard and James Thomas. Salt Lake City: Peregrine Smith, 1986. 230.

Davis, Lydia. "Five Stories." *Conjunctions* 24 (Spring 1995): 116–17. <http://www.conjunctions.com/print/article/lydia-davis-c24>. Accessed September 27, 2018.

Davis, Lydia. *The Collected Stories of Lydia Davis*. New York: Farrar, Straus and Giroux, 2009.

Davis, Lydia. "Everyone Is Invited." *The New York Times* (December 24, 2009). <http://www.nytimes.com/2009/12/25/opinion/25davis.html>. Accessed September 27, 2018.

Davis, Lydia. "On Jane Bowles's *Emmy Moore's Journal.*" In *Object Lessons: The Paris Review Presents the Art of the Short Story*, edited by Lorin Stein and Sadie Stein. New York: Picador, 2012. 73–6.

Davis, Lydia. *Can't and Won't*. New York: Farrar, Straus and Giroux, 2014.

Davis, Lydia. "Lydia Davis's Very Short Stories." *The Atlantic* (July/August 2014). <https://www.theatlantic.com/magazine/archive/2014/07/lydia-davis-very-short-stories/372286/>. Accessed September 27, 2018.

Davis, Lydia. "Endings and Order, or Order and Endings." In *Because You Asked: A Book of Answers on the Art and Craft of the Writing Life*, edited by Katrina Roberts. Sandpoint, ID: Lost Horse Press, 2015. 377–81.

Davis, Lydia. "Form as a Response to Doubt." In *The Writer's Reader: Vocation, Preparation, Creation*, edited by Robert Cohen and Jay Parini. New York: Bloomsbury Academic, 2017. 323–5.

Davis, Lydia. "Lydia Davis and Al Filreis discuss Davis's 'In the Train Station.'" May 17, 2017. <https://www.youtube.com/watch?v=tFrdgxyFMvMhttps://www.youtube.com/watch?v=tFrdgxyFMvM>. Accessed September 27, 2018.

Dickstein, Morris. "Something to Remember Him By: Review of John O'Hara *Stories.*" *Times Literary Supplement* (May 12, 2017): 11–12.

Dubus, Andre. *Separate Flights*. Boston: David R. Godine, 1975.

Dubus, Andre. *Selected Stories*. Boston: David R. Godine, 1988.

Dubus, Andre. *Dancing After Hours*. New York: Alfred A. Knopf, 1996.

Dubus, Andre. *Conversations with Andre Dubus*, edited by Olivia Carr Edenfield. Jackson: University Press of Mississippi, 2013.

Duncan, Isla. *Alice Munro's Narrative Art*. New York: Palgrave Macmillan, 2011.

Edenfield, Olivia Carr. *Understanding Andre Dubus*. University of South Carolina Press, 2017.

Ellmann, Richard. *James Joyce*. New York: Oxford University Press, 1982.

Evans, Jonathan. *The Many Voices of Lydia Davis: Translation, Rewriting, Intertextuality*. Edinburgh: Edinburgh University Press, 2016.

Ferguson, Suzanne C. "Defining the Short Story: Impressionism and Form" (1982). In *The New Short Story Theories*, edited by Charles E. May. Athens: Ohio University Press, 1994. 218–30.

Ferguson, Suzanne C. "Sequences, Anti-Sequences, Cycles and Composite Novels: The Short Story in Genre Criticism." *Journal of the Short Story in English*, 41 (Autumn 2003): 103–17. <http://jsse.revues.org/312>. Accessed September 27, 2018.

Fiamengo, Janice, and Gerald Lynch. "Alice Munro's Miraculous Art." In *Alice Munro's Miraculous Art: Critical Essays*, edited by Janice Fiamengo and Gerald Lynch. Ottawa: University of Ottawa Press, 2017. 3–14.

Ford, Richard. "Great Falls." In *Rock Springs*. New York: Atlantic Monthly Press, 1987. 29–49.

Frank, Joseph. *The Widening Gyre: Crisis and Mastery in Modern Literature*. New Brunswick, NJ: Rutgers University Press, 1963.

Franzen, Jonathan. "What Makes You So Sure You're Not the Evil One Yourself?" (2006). In *Farther Away*. New York: Farrar, Straus and Giroux, 2012. 283–96.

Friedman, Norman. "Recent Short Story Theories: Problems in Definition." In *Short Story Theory at a Crossroads*, edited by Susan Lohafer and Jo Ellyn Clarey. Baton Rouge: Louisiana State University Press, 1989. 13–31.

Garner, Dwight. "Review: The Stories of Joy Williams: Short, but Seldom Sweet." *The New York Times* (September 16, 2015): C1.

Gessner, David, and Wendy Brenner. "The Ecotone Interview with Joy Williams." *Ecotone* 3.1 (Fall 2007): 78–87.

Glover, Douglas. "The Style of Alice Munro." In *The Cambridge Companion to Alice Munro*, edited by David Staines. New York: Cambridge University Press, 2016. 45–59.

Gorra, Michael. "The Late Mastery of Alice Munro." *Times Literary Supplement* (August 26, 2009). <http://www.the-tls.co.uk/articles/public/the-late-mastery-of-alice-munro/>. Accessed September 27, 2018.

Grainger, James. "Life and How to Live It: Review of *Dear Life*." *Quill & Quire* 78.9 (November 2012): 25.

Gzowski, Peter. "You're the Same Person at 39 That You Are at 60: Interview with Alice Munro." *The Globe and Mail* (September 29, 2001): F4–F5.

Halford, Macy. "Our Live Chat with Lydia Davis." *The New Yorker* (December 10, 2009). <http://www.newyorker.com/books/book-club/our-live-chat-with-lydia-davis>. Accessed September 27, 2018.

Hancock, Geoff. "Alice Munro" (1982). *Canadian Writers at Work: Interviews with Geoff Hancock*. Toronto: Oxford University Press, 1987. 187–224.

Haviland, Beverly. "Missed Connections." *Partisan Review* 56:1 (Winter 1989): 151–7.

Heble, Ajay. *The Tumble of Reason: Alice Munro's Discourse of Absence*. Toronto: University of Toronto Press, 1994.

Hemingway, Ernest. "For Sale." <https://en.wikipedia.org/wiki/For_sale:_baby_shoes,_never_worn>. Accessed September 27, 2018.

Herzinger, Kim A. "Introduction: On the New Fiction." *Mississippi Review* 40–41 (Winter 1985): 7–22.

Hofmann, Michael. "The Rear-View Mirror." *London Review of Books*. October 31, 1996: 6.

Howells, Coral Ann. *Alice Munro*. Manchester: Manchester University Press, 1998.

Hoy, Helen. "Alice Munro: Unforgettable, Indigestible Messages." *Journal of Canadian Studies* 26.1 (Spring 1991): 5–21.

Hutcheon, Linda, and Michael Hutcheon. "Late Style(s): The Ageism of the Singular." *Occasion: Interdisciplinary Studies in the Humanities* v. 4 (May 31, 2012): 1–11. <http://occasion.stanford.edu/node/93>. Accessed September 27, 2018.

James, Henry. *Theory of Fiction: Henry James*, edited by James E. Miller, Jr. Lincoln: University of Nebraska Press, 1972.

James, Henry. *The Portrait of a Lady* (1881/1906). New York: Oxford University Press, 2009.

James, William. *William and Henry James: Selected Letters*, edited by Ignas K. Skrupskelis and Elizabeth M. Berkeley. Charlottesville: University Press of Virginia, 1997.

Jameson, Fredric. *The Antinomies of Realism*. New York: Verso, 2013.

Kafka, Franz. "Investigations of a Dog," translated by Willa and Edwin Muir. In *The Complete Stories*. New York: Schocken Books, 1971. 310–46. <https://www.vanderbilt.edu/olli/class-materials/Franz_Kafka.pdf>. Accessed September 27, 2018.

Kakutani, Michiko. "Recalling Lives Altered, in Ways Vivid and Untidy." Review of *Dear Life*. *The New York Times* (December 10, 2012). <http://www.nytimes.com/2012/12/11/books/dear-life-stories-by-alice-munro.html>. Accessed September 27, 2018.

Knight, Christopher J. "An Interview with Lydia Davis." *Contemporary Literature* 40.4 (Winter 1999): 525–51.

Kois, Dan. "The Misanthropic Genius of Joy Williams." *The New York Times Magazine* (September 6, 2015): 24–7.

Lahiri, Jhumpa. *Interpreter of Maladies: Stories*. Boston: Houghton Mifflin, 1999.

Lamb, Robert Paul. *Art Matters: Hemingway, Craft, and the Creation of the Modern Short Story*. Baton Rouge: Louisiana State University Press, 2010.

Levene, Mark. " 'It Was About Vanishing': A Glimpse of Alice Munro's Stories." *University of Toronto Quarterly* 68.4 (Fall 1999): 841–60.

Levene, Mark. "Alice Munro's *The Progress of Love*: Free (and Radical)." In *Critical Insights: Alice Munro*, edited by Charles E. May. Ipswich, MA: Salem Press, 2013. 142–59.

Levin, Harry. *James Joyce: A Critical Introduction*. Norfolk, CT: New Directions, 1941.

Lohafer, Susan. *Coming to Terms with the Short Story*. Baton Rouge: Louisiana State University Press, 1983.

Lohafer, Susan. "Introduction to Part I." In *Short Story Theory at a Crossroads*, edited by Susan Lohafer and Jo Ellyn Clarey. Baton Rouge: Louisiana State University Press, 1989. 3–12.

Lohafer, Susan. *Reading for Storyness: Preclosure Theory, Empirical Poetics, and Culture in the Short Story*. Baltimore, MD: Johns Hopkins University Press, 2003.

Mansfield, Katherine. *The Letters and Journals of Katherine Mansfield: A Selection*, edited by C. K. Stead. London: Allen Lane, 1977.

Matthews, Brander. "The Philosophy of the Short-Story" (1901). In *The New Short Story Theories*, edited by Charles E. May. Athens: Ohio University Press, 1994. 73–80.

Max, D. T. "The Carver Chronicles." *The New York Times Magazine* (August 9, 1998). *Literature Resource Center*, <http://link.galegroup.com/apps/doc/A150156176/LitRC?u=prin77918&sid=LitRC&xid=31b490f1>. Accessed September 27, 2018.

May, Charles E. "The Nature of Knowledge in Short Fiction." *Studies in Short Fiction* 21.4 (Fall 1984): 327–38.

May, Charles E. "Chekhov and the Modern Short Story" (1985). In *The New Short Story Theories*, edited by Charles E. May. Athens: Ohio University Press, 1994. 199–217.

May, Charles E. "Introduction." In *The New Short Story Theories*, edited by Charles E. May. Athens: Ohio University Press, 1994. xv–xxvi.

May, Charles E. "Why Short Stories Are Essential and Why They Are Seldom Read." In *The Art of Brevity: Excursions in Short Fiction Theory and Analysis*, edited by Per Winther, Jakob Lothe, and Hans H. Skei. Columbia: University of South Carolina Press, 2004. 14–25.

May, Charles E. "Living in the Story: Fictional Reality in the Stories of Alice Munro." In *Alice Munro's Miraculous Art: Critical Essays*, edited by Janice Fiamengo and Gerald Lynch. Ottawa: University of Ottawa Press, 2017. 43–61.

McCaffery, Larry. "Deliberately, Terribly Neutral: An Interview with Lydia Davis." *Some Other Frequency: Interviews with Innovative American Authors*, edited by Larry McCaffery. Philadelphia: University of Pennsylvania Press, 1996. 59–79.

McGill, Robert. "Alice Munro and Personal Development." In *The Cambridge Companion to Alice Munro*, edited by David Staines. New York: Cambridge University Press, 2016. 136–53.

McGrath, Charles. "The Short Story Shakes Itself Out of Academe." *The New York Times Book Review* (August 25, 2004). <http://www.nytimes.com/2004/08/25/books/the-short-story-shakes-itself-out-of-academe.html>. Accessed September 27, 2018.

McGuire, Ian. *Richard Ford and the Ends of Realism*. Iowa City: University of Iowa Press, 2015.

McIntyre, Timothy. "Doing Her Duty and Writing Her Life: Alice Munro's Cultural and Historical Context." In *Critical Insights: Alice Munro*, edited by Charles E. May. Ipswich, MA: Salem Press, 2013. 52–67.

McMullan, Gordon. *Shakespeare and the Idea of Late Writing: Authorship in the Proximity of Death*. Cambridge: Cambridge University Press, 2007.

Metcalf, Stephen. "*Honored Guest*: The Small Chill." Review of Alice Williams, *The Honored Guest*. *The New York Times Book Review* (December 19, 2004): 14.

Miller, Judith Maclean. "Deconstructing Silence: The Mystery of Alice Munro." *Antigonish Review* 129 (Spring 2002): 41–51.

Mitchell, Lee Clark. " 'Well, What Will She Do?': Stepping Through the Frame of *The Portrait of a Lady*." *Raritan* 17.3 (Winter 1998): 90–109.

Mukherjee, Neel. Review of *The Visiting Privilege. The Guardian* (November 26, 2016). <https://www.theguardian.com/books/2016/nov/26/the-visiting-privilege-new-and-selected-stories-by-joy-williams-review>. Accessed September 27, 2018.

Munro, Alice. *Dance of the Happy Shades*. New York: McGraw-Hill, 1968.

Munro, Alice. *Something I've Been Meaning to Tell You*. New York: McGraw-Hill, 1974.

Munro, Alice. "What is Real?" In *Making it New: Contemporary Canadian Stories*, edited by John Metcalf. Toronto: Methuen, 1982. 223–6.

Munro, Alice. *The Moons of Jupiter*. New York: Alfred A. Knopf, 1983.

Munro, Alice. "Introduction." *Selected Stories*. New York: Vintage Books, 1997.

Munro, Alice. *Runaway*. New York: Alfred A. Knopf, 2004.

Munro, Alice. "Corrie." *The New Yorker* 86.31 (October 11, 2010): 94–101. <http://www.newyorker.com/magazine/2010/10/11/corrie>. Accessed September 27, 2018.

Munro, Alice. "Amundsen." *The New Yorker* 88.25 (August 27, 2012): 58–69. <http://www.newyorker.com/magazine/2012/08/27/amundsen>. Accessed September 27, 2018.

Munro, Alice. "Corrie." *The PEN/O. Henry Prize Stories*. New York: Anchor Books, 2012. 392–409.

Munro, Alice. *Dear Life*. Toronto: McClelland & Stewart, 2012.

Munro, Alice. "Dolly." *Tin Can* 13.4 (Summer 2012): 65–80.

Munro, Alice. "To Reach Japan." *Narrative* (Winter 2012). <http://www.narrativemagazine.com/issues/winter-2012/fiction/reach-japan-alice-munro>. Accessed September 27, 2018.

Munro, Alice. "Train." *Harper's Magazine* (April 2012). <http://archive.harpers.org/2012/04/pdf/HarpersMagazine-2012-04-0083859.pdf?AWSAccessKeyId=AKIAJXATU3VRJAAA66RA&Expires=1493397711&Signature=GQwzSgZ1tnpQYzPWKD13LyAoEB8%3D>. Accessed September 27, 2018.

Nabokov, Vladimir. *The Annotated Lolita: Revised and Updated* (1955), edited by Alfred Appel, Jr. New York: Random House, Inc., 1991.

New, W. H. "Re-reading *The Moons of Jupiter*." In *The Cambridge Companion to Alice Munro*, edited by David Staines. New York: Cambridge University Press, 2016. 116–35.

O'Connor, Flannery. "Writing Short Stories." In *Mystery and Manners*, edited by Sally and Robert Fitzgerald. New York: Farrar, Straus & Giroux, 1969. 87–106.

O'Connor, Flannery. *The Habit of Being: Letters of Flannery O'Connor*, edited by Sally Fitzgerald. New York: Farrar, Straus, Giroux, 1979.

O'Connor, Frank. *The Lonely Voice: A Study of the Short Story*. New York: World Publishing, 1963.

Pascal, Blaise. *Pensées: The Provincial Letters*. New York: Modern Library, 1941.

Paul, Steve. "Forget the Hemingway Comparisons: Richard Ford is an American, Yes, But He Has His Own Voice." In *Conversations with Richard Ford*, edited by Huey Guagliardo. Jackson: University Press of Mississippi, 2001. 85–8.

Peden, William. In *Sudden Fiction: American Short-Short Stories*, edited by Robert Shapard and James Thomas. Salt Lake City: Peregrine Smith, 1986. 233.

Perloff, Marjorie. "Fiction as Language Game: The Hermeneutic Parables of Lydia Davis and Maxine Chernoff." In *Breaking the Sequence: Women's Experimental Fiction*, edited by Ellen G. Friedman and Miriam Fuchs. Princeton: Princeton University Press, 1989. 199–214.

Poe, Edgar Allan. "Review of *Twice-Told Tales*, by Nathaniel Hawthorne" (1842). In *The Selected Writings of Edgar Allan Poe*, edited by G. R. Thompson. New York: W. W. Norton, 2004. 645–50.

Pratt, Mary Louise. "The Short Story: The Long and the Short of It." *Poetics* 10.2–3 (June 1981): 175–94.

Prose, Francine. "Interview with Lydia Davis." *Bomb* 60 (Summer 1997): 81–96.

Reid, Ian. *The Short Story*. London: Methuen, 1977.

Rimbaud, Arthur. *Rimbaud: Complete Works, Selected Letters*, translated by Wallace Fowlie. Chicago: University of Chicago Press, 1966.

Said, Edward W. *On Late Style: Music and Literature Against the Grain*. New York: Pantheon Books, 2006.

Schaub, Michael. "No Solace in *Visiting Privilege*, But Plenty of Truth." *NPR Book Reviews* (September 9, 2015). <http://www.npr.org/2015/09/09/437275238/no-solace-in-visiting-privilege-but-plenty-of-truth>. Accessed September 27, 2018.

Schutt, Christine. "On 'Brass' by Joy Williams." *The Center for Fiction*. (n.d.). <http://centerforfiction.org/forwriters/the-model-short-story/christine-schutt-on-brass-by-joy-williams/>. Accessed September 27, 2018.

Scofield, Martin. *The Cambridge Introduction to The American Short Story*. New York: Cambridge University Press, 2006.

Shapard, Robert. "Introduction." *Sudden Fiction: American Short-Short Stories*, edited by Robert Shapard and James Thomas. Salt Lake City: Peregrine Smith, 1986. xiii–xvi.

Shaw, Valerie. *The Short Story: A Critical Introduction*. London: Longman, 1983.

Silber, Joan. *The Art of Time: As Long as it Takes*. Saint Paul, MN: Graywolf Press, 2009.

Simpson, Mona. "The Art of Fiction LXXVI: Raymond Carver." *The Paris Review* 88 (Summer 1983): 192–221.

Sklenicka, Carol. *Raymond Carver: A Writer's Life*. New York: Scribner, 2009.

Smith, Stephen. "Layers of Life: No More 'Single Paths' for Alice Munro (Interview)." *Quill & Quire* 60.8 (August 1994): 1, 24.

Stein, Jean. "The Art of Fiction XII: William Faulkner." *The Paris Review* 12 (Spring 1956): 28.

Stone, Robert. "Introduction." *The Best American Short Stories 1992*. New York: Houghton Mifflin, 1992. xiii–xviii.

Struthers, J. R. "The Real Material: an Interview with Alice Munro." In *Probable Fictions: Alice Munro's Narrative Acts*, edited by Louis K. MacKendrick. Toronto: ECW Press, 1983. 5–36.

Taylor, Christopher. "Review of *The Collected Stories of Lydia Davis*." *The Guardian* (August 6, 2010). <https://www.theguardian.com/books/2010/aug/07/collected-stories-lydia-davis-review>. Accessed September 27, 2018.

Treisman, Deborah. "On *Dear Life*: An Interview with Alice Munro." *The New Yorker* (November 20, 2012). <http://www.newyorker.com/books/page-turner/on-dear-life-an-interview-with-alice-munro>. Accessed September 27, 2018.

Trussler, Michael. "Suspended Narratives: The Short Story and Temporality." *Studies in Short Fiction* 33.4 (Fall 1996): 557–77.

Tsvetaeva, Marina. *Art in the Light of Conscience*, translated by Angela Livingstone. London: Bristol Classical Press, 1992.

Ussery, Elizabeth. Blackboard post for ENG368, Princeton University (November 10, 2014).

Wachtel, Eleanor. "An Interview with Lydia Davis." *Brick* 81 (2008): 129–37.

Wachtel, Eleanor. "Interview with Alice Munro" (2004). *The Best of Writers & Company*. Windsor, Canada: Biblioasis, 2016. 205–22.

Walker, Elinor Ann. *Richard Ford*. New York: Twayne, 2000.

Williams, Joy. "Another Season." *Prairie Schooner* 40.2 (Summer 1966): 123–30.

Williams, Joy. *Taking Care*. New York: Random House, 1982.

Williams, Joy. "Craving." *Ploughshares* 17.2–3 (Fall 1991): 235–45.

Williams, Joy. *The Visiting Privilege: New and Collected Stories*. New York: Alfred A. Knopf, 2015.

Winner, Paul. "Interview: Joy Williams, The Art of Fiction No. 223." *The Paris Review* 209 (Summer 2014): 32–55. <https://www.theparisreview.org/interviews/6303/joy-williams-the-art-of-fiction-no-223-joy-williams>. Accessed September 27, 2018.

Woolf, Virginia. *The Common Reader*. First Series, edited by Andrew McNeillie. San Diego: Harcourt Brace Jovanovich, 1984.

Index